Penguin Handbooks
Grandmother's Secrets

Fourteen years ago Jean Palaiseul was the editor in
chief of a leading French weekly. Then, after thirty
years in Paris, he decided to start a new life in a
remote valley in the Auvergne. There he has
devoted himself to his garden and his books.
Grandmother's Secrets combines both these interests,
in which M. Palaiseul is expert.

Jean Palaiseul

Grandmother's Secrets

HER GREEN GUIDE TO HEALTH FROM PLANTS

Translated from the French by Pamela Swinglehurst

Penguin Books

Penguin Books Ltd,
Harmondsworth, Middlesex, England
Penguin Books, 625 Madison Avenue,
New York, New York 10022, U.S.A.
Penguin Books Australia Ltd,
Ringwood, Victoria, Australia
Penguin Books Canada Ltd, 2801 John Street,
Markham, Ontario, Canada L3R 1B4
Penguin Books (N.Z.) Ltd,
182–190 Wairau Road, Auckland 10, New Zealand

First published by Éditions Robert Laffont S.A., 1972
This translation first published by Barrie & Jenkins 1973
Published in Penguin Books 1976
Reprinted 1976, 1977

Made and printed in Great Britain by
Cox & Wyman Ltd, London, Reading and Fakenham
Set in Monotype Bembo

Contents

Translator's Note

In this book I have been obliged to employ the traditional language of the old herbals, particularly when describing diseases and disorders, and the therapeutic virtues of the various plants. The reader may find some of these expressions quaint or outmoded, but it must be remembered that the knowledge of herbal medicine evolved throughout the ages. There are often no modern equivalents for herbal terminology, since present medical concepts are so much more sophisticated and elaborate. Herbal remedies were largely empirical: no one understood how or why they worked – they had simply been handed down from generation to generation. Little was known about the mechanisms or causes of disease, and the tendency was to classify them by symptoms.

Thus we find references to a 'stitch' or 'pain in the side', to 'congestion of the liver', and to 'fluidity of the blood'. We now know that a pain in the side may be due to many different causes – indigestion, gall-bladder inflammation, or even pleurisy – and that congestion of the liver can arise through infectious hepatitis, cirrhosis, etc. Similarly, 'fluidity of the blood' is no longer a valid criterion of health.

This in no way invalidates the virtues of herbal treatments. They are frequently of proven efficacy, so much so that a whole branch of science – known as pharmacognosy – is devoted to investigating the active principles of plants used traditionally in folk medicine.

The author has quoted various passages from the ancient herbalists (Dioscorides, Pliny, etc.) as well as from the works of P. A. Mattioli (commonly, if incorrectly, called Matthiolus), a sixteenth-century commentator on Dioscorides. Where possible I have located these quotations in their original translations: Dioscorides, *De Materia Medica*, Englished by John Goodyer in 1655 (published OUP 1934); Plinius Secundus (Pliny the Elder), *Naturall Historie in Thirty-Seven Books*, translated by Philemon Holland and published in 1601. The work of Matthiolus has unfortunately never been translated into English, but, together with Dioscorides, Pliny, Galen, Avicenna, etc., he was extensively quoted by the English herbalist John Parkinson in his *Theatrum Botanicum: The Theater of Plantes*, published in 1640, from which I have accordingly included relevant passages.

For the reader's interest, I append this brief information concerning the herbalists and naturalists chiefly quoted in this book:

Dioscorides, Pedanius: Greek naturalist (c. 2nd century AD) was born in Cilicia and served in the armies of Nero. His *De Materia Medica* was the leading text on pharmacology for sixteen centuries, and deals with the properties of about 600 plants.

Galen (Claudius Galenus): next to Hippocrates, the most celebrated of ancient physicians. Born in AD 130, practised medicine in Rome, where he attended the Emperors M. Aurelius and L. Verus. Wrote a great number of works on medicinal and philosophical subjects.

Pliny the Elder (AD 23–79), Roman naturalist, dedicated his great work *Natural History* to the Emperor Titus. He died of fumes and exhaustion while investigating the eruption of Vesuvius. (His nephew, Pliny the Younger, is famed for his series of historical *Letters*.)

John Parkinson (1567–1650), apothecary and herbalist, was apothecary to James I.

I crave the author's indulgence for substituting, at the end of his introduction, lines from our own Rudyard Kipling in place of his own quotation from an unknown French poet.

Preface to English Edition

For nearly fifteen years now – and after a quarter of a century of the infernal tumult of life in Paris – I have been living in a mill house deep in a green valley in Auvergne where, apart from a few passing planes, the only sounds to be heard are the sounds invented by nature: the birdsong which varies with the seasons, the chirping of the crickets in summer, the rustling of the spring breeze and the roar of the winter wind in the alders and the poplar trees, the cool ripple of the river by the walls of the house or its angry boom when the waters are in full spate.

Here I have learned that the key to happiness lies in a return to those simple truths which were born with our distant ancestors and confirmed by centuries of experience. Wisdom and common sense are one and the same thing; we are wrong to forget the fact or to obscure it with pretentious intellectual edifices that are part of the great myth of progress at all costs. Technology, however advanced, cannot solve everything, and it is not by a routine investigation of the cosmos that man will achieve a sense of peace.

By having less ambitious aims, by turning once more to the age-old customs and traditions from which, willingly or unwillingly, he has allowed himself to depart, he would again be in touch with a world that fits him – a world of which the 'environment', on which so much ink and breath is being spent today, is part; he would return to his true nature, becoming free of most of those artificial problems that burden him on all sides; once this essential balance was restored, he could become aware of his rightful place in the universe and all that it had to offer; he would conform to the rules which order

9

his well-being and hence experience a genuine *joie de vivre*.

Since man first began to reflect on his nature and record his conclusions in writing, many have voiced the opinion that happiness – a goal to which all aspire – resides in a few simple rules. Essentially, all we have to do is to obey nature, the reflection of the wisdom of creation (and therefore of the Creator). Herein lies the key to health. Few have paid heed, myself included, probably because the experience of others cannot be passed on – we can only profit from what we have learned for ourselves.

And so, I must admit, I should certainly not have such confidence in plants to protect me from illness had I not proved to myself the beneficial virtues of dozens of medicinal herbs which, as I have learned during these last years, are commonly employed by country folk.

This book has been written with the wish to share this confidence with you, but without any intention of decrying orthodox medicine. The latter plays its part as well as it can; the advances made by medicine since the start of this century protect us from many illnesses and have undeniably saved the lives of millions of people. But there are a great many minor ills that can be treated perfectly well with the almost innocuous weapons nature has so discerningly put at our disposal, namely by the use of simple herbal infusions or a few compresses.

There was a time when grandmother used no other remedies for the ailments that can affect a family in the course of the year. When anyone suffered from indigestion, colds, headaches, rashes, etc., she would intervene like a good fairy, drawing on the precious secrets of her green guide to health.

Let us rediscover these secrets.

Moulin de Saint-Alyre, 1973

Introduction

To introduce you to the colourful, fragrant Plant Kingdom and its subjects, I am going to quote a passage from a book written two hundred years ago. Not only because it tells us, with pleasing simplicity, all we basically need to know about the life of plants, but also because it leads us to meditate on the relativity of all knowledge, thus serving as a timely caution against pride and over-confidence in what knowledge we now possess.

Indeed, how can we be sure that what our textbooks teach us today will not make our descendants smile in the year 2200, just as we now smile at what was written in 1773 by a certain M. Bucquet, with his imposing title of 'Docteur-Régent of the Faculty of Medicine of Paris'? It may be that new paths in other dimensions will lead to the discovery that plants have a language, a memory and a fragment of what we call 'soul' . . .

But let us keep away from 'plant-fiction' (there's already enough of that about!) and return to this passage from *Introduction to the study of natural bodies drawn from the plant kingdom*, which dates from an epoch when man still experienced a certain difficulty in drawing a demarcation line between the plant world and the animal world:

Plants are organic bodies attached to the surface of the earth, or slightly below that surface. They are composed of stalks inside which are contained fluids, the purpose of which is to provide nourishment and foster growth. Plants differ from Minerals inasmuch as they have a kind of life; they draw in through the mouths of their vessels the juices on which they feed . . . they convert the fluids contained in the sap and assimilate them into their own tissues. They experience all the vicissitudes of the different stages of life, and resemble animals in many respects, with the exception of movement and feeling which they are denied; for the contraction experienced by the Sensitive plant[1] when it is touched is far from the feeling of even the least sensitive animal, and the rate of progress of roots in the earth in no way compares with the movement of animals ... Nevertheless one has to acknowledge that the animal Kingdom and the vegetable Kingdom meet at an infinite number of points and there is perhaps nothing more difficult than establishing the barriers that divide them ...

In form, bearing, scent and taste, plants are so varied that with a little practice and some knowledge of botany, one cannot confuse even the most closely related species. Choice of soil is also particular to the different plants; some like dry sandy soils, others like damp and marshy ground. . . . Whilst most plants like a sunny position, and only do well in sunlight, nevertheless quite a large number of plants only grow in shady spots completely screened from the sun ...

So we are reminded: (1) that plants engage in a real alchemy, drawing from the soil vital nutritive substances which they store and convert, and that they are therefore a natural reservoir of precious elements of which it is up to us to make use; (2) that plants, like human beings, have their own particular preferences and characteristics, so we must know where to look for them and learn to recognize them, which is scarcely more difficult than recognizing the people we often see.

If I wanted to make myself out to be very learned – which I am not – I would provide each of the plants named in this book with the long litany of its chemical components, from sugars, fats, nitrogenous substances to essential oils (phenol, terpene, etc.), via the long list of mineral salts – phosphorus, potassium, calcium, sodium, etc. – not forgetting the vitamins, of course, which will end up more numerous than the letters of the alphabet.

1. i.e. *Mimosa pudica* and others, possessing a high degree of irritability, causing the leaflets to fold together at the slightest touch. (*Translator's note.*)

I shall not do so, on the one hand because I wouldn't for a moment presume to write a medical book and because our grandmothers, with their down-to-earth common sense, concerned themselves less with the active elements of a herbal tea than with learning which malady it would assuage or cure; and on the other hand because the findings of a French research worker, C. Louis Kervran,[1] have shown that chemical elements in the organism are not unchanging and that Lavoisier's law, 'matter can neither be created nor destroyed' should be revised, at least with regard to biology, where one witnesses undeniable transmutations from one element into another, the which considerably detract from the value of the minutely detailed balance sheets drawn up by chemists with the aid of many analyses since, for example, we may observe that it is not those plants that are richest in calcium that will bring about the best recalcification but those that are rich in silica, such as horsetail.

I shall, however, describe in some detail the lesser known 'medicinal herbs' – it is pointless, I think, to describe the nettle or the dandelion! – in order to help you to identify them. For fuller information you can turn to one of the many reference books available on the subject, which give clear and accurate descriptions accompanied by full colour plates.

I shall also give you a selection of the various names for each plant – the Latin name, which keen botanists will want to know (and thank goodness there still are people keen on botany); the usual common names, so that you can look them up in a dictionary or illustrated reference book for further details; some of the local names which reflect the appearance, history, legend or medicinal use of the plant, since you may find that in some country areas people only know these plants by their folklore names.

I shall not recommend you to grow in your own garden such plants as you can still happily find almost anywhere, providing

1. *Transmutations naturelles, Transmutations biologiques, Transmutations naturelles en agronomie*, Librairie Maloine, Paris.

you are prepared to tear yourself away from your car and walk about the countryside instead of contemplating it through the windscreen. This would only lay you open to the gentle irony of the true peasants, who know better than anyone that nature is the best gardener in the world and that, however talented a 'specialist' he might be, man will never attain to her unerring choice of the soil and exposure (shade or sun) best suited to each type of plant.

If you want poppy petals, flowers of broom or dog-rose, leaves of burdock or dandelion, they are at your disposal in the precious dispensary of nature which is open to anyone at any hour of the day. It is up to you to make the effort – or to give yourself the enjoyment that I admit it gives me – of picking them in the proper season and giving them the modest care they require in order to conserve their virtues intact.

I must, however, add one word of advice, of capital importance in view of the rampant chemical invasion of the world in which we live: never gather plants that grow on cultivated land or in orchards; they may well be poisoned – and in any case they are no longer as nature created them – for the soil that feeds them is saturated with chemical fertilizers, synthetic hormones intended to destroy what are called weeds, and they are repeatedly subjected to a fall-out of equally poisonous insecticides which are sprayed from 'atomizers' (a name significantly reminiscent of Hiroshima) from spring to harvest time.

You must gather your health-giving plants far away from the 'benefits' of civilization. There are still easily enough areas of as yet uncontaminated and waste land, valleys and mountains, to satisfy all who have a liking for herbal infusions.

It is obviously important that plants should be gathered at the right moment. As far back as the reign of Nero, Dioscorides, the 'prince of herbalists', wrote in the preface to his treatise: 'Before all else it is proper to use care both in the storing up and in the gathering of herbs each at its due season, for it is according to this that medicines either do their work, or become quite ineffectual.' Fifteen centuries later his annotator Matthiolus added that 'all inferior bodies being ruled and governed by superior bodies, the moon, which is the planet closest to earth and most rapid in its motion, must assuredly exert an influence upon plants and all other things of this low territory when she waxes and wanes every month'.

Our contemporary Doctor Leclerc is of the same opinion in his *Précis de phytothérapie*, basing his argument not on empirical observations but on data furnished by quantitative analysis. 'The active substances contained in plants', he notes, 'vary, in at times considerable proportions, according to the age of the plant, the time of picking, the nature of the soil and the climate.'

Hence the cardinal rules that must be respected and which I shall endeavour to summarize as simply as possible in order not to swamp you with a flood of complicated recommendations that moreover often differ from one region to another and according to local customs or superstitions.

Gathering

Plants should be gathered 'at the moment of their full maturity and their greatest vigour' – the moment that Van Helmont, the famous early seventeenth-century doctor and alchemist, called the 'balmy time' (balmy signifying 'possessing properties comparable to the healing virtue of balm, or balsam').

For a certain number of plants this time naturally falls in summer and, because the hours of the solstice have from time immemorial been considered by all peoples as particularly propitious, tradition has it that plants should be gathered on St John's Day, or Midsummer Day. This is why so many different herbs and plants have come to be called 'St John's wort' by country-dwellers in different areas.

In fact, even if the eternal rhythms of the cosmos have been shown to exercise an influence on the living things of our 'low territory', the date of St John's Day really only serves as a reminder, for it is more important to take into consideration the stage of development reached by the flowers – which should not be full-blown, whether the flowers alone or the flowering tips of the plant are being picked. Now, according to meteorological conditions, geographical situation, aspect and altitude, the ideal moment will vary from year to year, falling correspondingly earlier or later than the midsummer solstice. The determining factor should therefore be observation of the plant itself and not mere observance of tradition, however well founded.

It is best to gather plants on a dry and sunny day. You should not start to pick them too early in the day, nor continue too late, on account of the dew – damp flowers and leaves deteriorate rapidly and so almost completely lose their virtues. The roots and rhizomes, on the other hand, which must be taken out of the ground at the beginning of spring or the end of autumn, can be pulled up more easily after it has rained.

A certain amount of care should be taken when handling the plants; for example, you should not hold them for too long nor should you squeeze or crush the flowers and leaves you are gathering, for if they are allowed to become warm or bruised they will be less effective. You should also be careful not to remove too much from the same head: if it is stripped of too much bark or too many leaves or branches, either it will be incapable of bringing its seeds or fruit to maturity, thereby assuring the survival of the species, or else it will wilt and die, and you will not be able to draw upon it the following year. For the same reason it is to your own interest to be circumspect when collecting roots, by refraining from taking too many within a limited radius, and by collecting them only in an area where that particular species grows in abundance, the right technique being to decimate the plants in the correct sense of the word, namely by sacrificing one out of ten.

Choice of plants

The ancients were certainly not far wrong when they laid down the following rules which you might follow:

1. A wild plant must always surpass a cultivated plant, because nature herself had allotted it its rightful place and climate and it therefore contains the best active principles.
2. It is preferable to select plants that are growing some distance apart from each other: they will be better nourished, bigger, and will possess greater virtues, because they have not robbed each other of nourishment from the air and the soil.
3. Choose always those plants that have the most fragrance, taste and colour, if they are plants that should have these characteristics.

It is obvious that you should avoid collecting plants that are stunted or have blotchy yellowed leaves, showing that they have been attacked by pest or disease, on the one hand because such plants would be difficult to preserve, and on the other hand because their properties are weaker than those of healthy plants.

Drying

Your plants will be adversely affected if they are not dried correctly: the active principles contained in the plant will be impaired, for they are infinitely more fragile than their synthetic equivalents contained in laboratory remedies.

The rules to be followed are simple but imperative:
1. Dry your plants in a place that is easily ventilated, always – with few exceptions – in the shade (the heat of the sun destroys the volatile principles: the essential oils of aromatic herbs), and never in a bright light that would completely discolour the flowers, which already lose their brilliance.
2. Spread out your plants as soon as you return from collecting them. If you leave them in the bag or basket in which you have carried them, they will quickly rot and this will affect their drying.
3. Never wash the plants before putting them to dry: there is no need to do so, since you *must* in any case collect them only in

areas free of insecticide fall-out and dust from passing traffic.

4. Spread them out in a single layer; never put one plant on top of another for they might rot or mildew.
5. For the first few days keep turning them over so that drying is even and thorough.
6. When drying is completed, and only then, cut up your harvest of leaves, stems and flowering tips into small pieces, ready to be stored and used.

Roots require different treatment: they must be washed as soon as they are taken up. 'At this stage', a venerable pharmacopoeia explains, 'the water will not penetrate below the exterior and will therefore dissolve none of the desired extractive elements, for the roots are at their strongest and most resistant when freshly taken from the ground.' To accelerate the drying process, one can initially expose roots to a few hours of sunshine. Lastly, it is advisable to cut them into pieces before drying, since afterwards it is practically impossible to do so.

Storing

When flowers, leaves, stems and roots are perfectly dry (and you must make sure that they are, because the least trace of dampness will trigger off a chain-reaction of mildew that would ruin your entire harvest), they should be stored out of the air in a dry place, whether in paper bags or tins or glass jars stoppered with a cork or a scrap of linen.

If you opt, as I do, for the latter system, which has the advantage not only of affording the best protection from the damp but also of enabling you to check at a glance on how well the contents are keeping, you should store your jars in a dark place, such as a cupboard. Indeed, as you will presently see, it is light (as well as heat) that is used to extract the active principles from the plants and transfer them to oil, wine or alcohol, so that by exposing your jars to light or heat, their contents will inevitably be subject to the effects of this mysterious alchemy.

But above all – and I cannot sufficiently emphasize this point – never store your plants, whether fresh or dried, in plastic wrappings. These may be ideal and very practical for covering inert matter such as shirts or saucepans; but they are not so for living matter such as herbs. Scientific experiments have shown that plastic wrappings bring about certain alterations and that plants kept in this way no longer have the same efficacity.

With these practical instructions to guide you, all that remains is for you to take advantage of your holidays and week-ends to build up your own little family herbalist's. Your choice of plants will be dictated by the disorders to which you and your family are most commonly subject, and by the directions relating to each of the plants studied in our 'green guide'. (I have excluded from our repertoire toxic plants such as belladonna, buttercup, digitalis [foxglove], hellebore and aconite, which are too tricky for a layman to manage and should only be prescribed by qualified practitioners.)

You could alternatively – if you are not bucolically inclined or if it is not possible for you to indulge in gathering simples – procure the necessary raw materials for the preparation of the goodly infusions known to our grandmothers from a herbalist's shop – if any still exist in your neighbourhood.

This brings me to my last point, one which is often given too little consideration – namely, the ways of 'cooking' herbs. I use this culinary term quite deliberately, for whilst the art of cooking plants offers fewer subtleties than the art of cooking food, there are just as many basic rules that must be observed if your preparation is not to lose its flavour – which would be pity enough – and its efficacity – which is much more serious.

The *tisane* or herb tea is, to quote a recent definition, a 'drink containing a low proportion of a medicinal herbal substance obtained by the maceration, solution, infusion or decoction of plants', but it is no mere whim that dictates which of the listed means of extraction should be employed. It is essential to know the characteristics and desired action of the plant in question.

So 'one should be very careful to avoid boiling aromatic substances and substances that contain volatile principles, such as chervil, the antiscorbutic plants, etc., because the greatest virtue of these ingredients lies in their volatile principles.' One should also, except for a few rare exceptions, never boil flowers.

For the preparation of flowers and aromatic plants whose essential oils dissipate completely above a certain degree of heat, you must confine yourself to infusion or maceration. On the other hand, decoction is the method advocated for hard parts (roots, rhizomes, stems) and for plants – whose virtues are not dissipated by extreme heat – of which a higher concentration is required.

Here are the recipes for these different methods:

Infusion

Place the plants in a teapot, pour onto them the prescribed quantity of boiling water; cover and leave to infuse for the necessary length of time, which will depend on the type of plant or the effect desired; strain.

Decoction

Place the given amounts of plant and cold water in a saucepan, preferably enamelled or stainless steel (phytotherapists and qualified dieticians generally advise against aluminium); cover and bring slowly to the boil; simmer gently for the prescribed length of time; remove from the heat and leave to infuse, again as prescribed; strain.

Maceration

Put the prescribed amount of plant into the given quantity of liquid (water, oil, wine, vinegar, alcohol); leave to soak for the specified length of time (which may be anything from a few hours to several weeks); strain through a clean cloth, making sure you squeeze all the juice out of the plants. It is worth

20

noting that water is seldom used, for it has the disadvantage of fermenting very quickly (Doctor Besançon, who called it a 'culture medium for microbes', declared that water has killed more people than wine !). The wine you use will depend on the purpose of your preparation: red wine, being rich in tannin, has an astringent effect; white wine is diuretic.

I would add that maceration is used in homoeopathy to extract substances of plant origin (and even certain products of mineral origin), thus producing the 'mother tinctures' from which are prepared the prescribed low, medium or high-strength dilutions, either liquid (drops) or solid (granules). In our 'guide to health' I shall therefore give the name of the homoeopathic medicine corresponding to each plant, providing one exists – which it generally does, the majority of plants, whether foreign or indigenous, being included in the 1,500 medicines prescribed by the disciples of Doctor Hahnemann.

Three more small pieces of advice:

1. Prepare your herb tea with the purest possible water – tap water in most big towns hardly answers to this definition, considering the chemical treatment it has undergone to make it drinkable. Very mild mineral waters will also do very well (waters with a heavy limestone content harden the plants and prevent them from fully releasing their active principles).
2. Preferably use honey to sweeten your herb tea: itself derived from plants, it harmonizes well with them, heightening their flavour and quite possibly their effect.
3. Remember that an infusion or a decoction should not be prepared too long in advance for, as I have already emphasized, the elements contained in plants are living principles, and thus in constant evolution, so that by the end of twenty-four hours their intrinsic structure has changed. For the same reason it is also obviously inadvisable to reheat these preparations. (When they must not be drunk cold

they can at a pinch be warmed gently by the *bain-marie* method.)

Lastly, I think I should remind you to respect the prescribed amounts and not make too free a use of your plants on the assumption that, as one often hears, 'if it doesn't do any good, it can't do any harm'.

Certainly plants do not cause the same havoc as chemical drugs, which are frequently toxic, but they do stimulate or check the principle organic functions – in this lies the secret of their effectiveness – and to continue treatment longer than necessary is tantamount to needlessly tiring the kidneys, the stomach, the intestines, the liver, the heart, in other words going against nature. This, you must agree, would be paradoxical, when one is turning to nature to protect one's health. Whatever the critics of phytotherapy may say, herbal tea is not 'hot water contaminated with more or less active herbs'.

In conclusion, let me leave you with three quotations that need no further comment from myself.

The first was written by a medical practitioner, Doctor Paul Fruictier:

The spectacular advances made in therapeutics by industry during recent years tend to make us forget the medicinal value of plants. Their usefulness is far from negligible; their active principles are manifold and well-balanced. Judiciously employed, plants can provide a flexible and effective form of medical therapy, totally without dangerous side-effects, and adaptable to the needs of each individual patient. The doctor is thus able to prescribe a personal course of treatment that is much appreciated by the patient, who feels he is being treated as an individual and not like everyone else . . .

The second quotation is taken from one of the lesser known books of the Old Testament, *Ecclesiasticus*, which is a collection of maxims and precepts on the practice of virtues and the conduct of life, in short a book of common sense:

The Lord hath created medicines out of the earth; and he that is wise will not abhor them.

The third is from Kipling, who wrote:

> Anything green that grew out of the mould
> Was an excellent herb to our fathers of old.

Dictionary of Plants

A

AGRIMONY
Agrimonia eupatoria.   Eupator's Agrimony, European
Agrimony

Extolled by Pliny, who considered it a 'herb of sovereign
power' emphasizing that 'the seed of this herb drunke in wine,
is a singular remedie for the dysenterie or bloudie flix', agrimony for centuries held an important place in medicine.
Parkinson reported: 'Galen saith it openeth the obstructions
of the liver, and clenseth it; it helpeth the jaundice, and
strengtheneth the inward parts, and is very beneficiall to the
bowels.' It was used in many unguents, balms and vulneraries
by reason of its astringent action and its pleasant, slightly
aromatic scent (which it unfortunately loses when dried,
although this in no way detracts from its healing properties)
Then it was forgotten; only the peasants remained faithful to it,
for they knew its many uses.

In some regions, particularly in the North of France, a weak
infusion of fresh leaves (3 grammes per cup) is drunk instead of
tea. This drink, which Dalechamps found 'pleasing, being the
colour of claret wine', has a beneficial effect on chronic disorders of the liver, kidneys and bladder (incontinence of urine).
However it should be borne in mind that, being astringent,
whilst it is salutary in cases of diarrhoea and dysentery, it is
not to be recommended for anyone inclined to be constipated.

It is principally employed as follows:

Asthma, spitting or vomiting blood, diarrhoea, dysentery:
infusion or weak decoction of dried leaves (3 to 5 grammes to
100 grammes of water), three to five times a day, between or
immediately after meals.

Aphtha, stomatitis, gingivitis, inflammation of the throat,

tonsillitis, chronic pharyngeal quinsey affecting public speakers and singers: gargle four or five times a day with a decoction of 100 grammes of leaves to a litre of water, which should be boiled down until reduced by a third, with the optional addition of 5 grammes of rose honey and a few drops of vinegar.

Badly healing wounds, varicose ulcers, contusions, sprains: boil 200 grammes of dried leaves in a litre of red wine for five minutes, then leave to infuse for an hour; clean the wounds with this tepid decoction, then apply on compresses. This treatment is naturally also good for animals' wounds.

The distinctive features of Eupator's agrimony (so named from the Greek 'argemos', albugo or leucoma, because it was said to cure cataracts, and from Mithridates Eupator, King of Pontus, who introduced its use in medicine) are as follows: its leaves, which may be up to 20 centimetres long, are neatly serrated, very downy, green on top and whitish on the under-side, with very small leaflets in between; its yellow flowers, with five petals, are arranged in a long upright spike at the top of the stem; they bloom consecutively, from the bottom to the top, throughout the summer, leaving seed-urns in the form of burrs that stick to the clothing; it reaches a height of 40 to 60 centimetres, and grows in almost any kind of soil, along paths and hedges, on slopes and embankments, on the edges of woodland, in meadows and on waste ground.

ALKANET, COMMON
Anchusa officinalis.   Dyer's Bugloss, Spanish Bugloss, Anchusa, Orchanet

To botanists, the common alkanet or dyer's bugloss is not the same thing as viper's bugloss (*Echium vulgare*) or field bugloss (*Lycopsis arvensis*); but to our grandmothers the one was as useful as the other, and they made no distinction between them, knowing that their resemblance to borage extended to their action as well as their outward appearance.

You too can utilize alkanet in the same way and for the same conditions as borage. Its features are identical; same height, same hairs all over the plant, same blue colour for the flowers, but with two slight differences: their petals are rounded rather than pointed, and they are all arranged on the same side of the terminal spike.

It is interesting to note that its botanical name derives from the Greek *anchura*, to dye, for the sap from its root gives a red dye that was employed to colour paper and cloth, and was also used as a cosmetic, particularly in rouge for the cheeks.

ANGELICA

Angelica archangelica.   Officinal angelica, Garden angelica, European angelica, Holy Ghost

I learned to recognize angelica in my earliest childhood: like the emerald drops in medieval (or sham-medieval) jewellery, its candied stems decorated the de luxe gingerbread that held pride of place in the shop window. It was only much later that I discovered that it is not only a delicacy for gourmands, but also a medicinal plant so highly valued that it has been paid such tributes as: 'if this plant had the merit of being foreign, it would be as precious to us as ginseng is to the Chinese; it would be worth its weight in gold' (Bodart) and 'it grieves us that a plant so active and rich in properties should be so little used today, whilst various exotic remedies, whose sole merit lies in their novelty, their rarity and their high price, are taken up with enthusiasm' (Roques).

These comments which date from the last century are just as relevant today; were angelica not still used in confectionery and in the preparation of certain liqueurs, it would probably be known only to a few gardening enthusiasts who grow it for its decorative value.

It is indeed a handsome umbelliferous plant that grows to a height of about 2 metres. Its stem is hollow, with fine grooves and ridges, and the large leaves on the lower part of the stem are broad, pointed with serrated edges, and whitish on the underneath. In summer the top of the stem bears a large rounded compound umbell of white or slightly pinkish flowers which give oblong, plano-convex or egg-shaped fruits. All parts of the plant exhale a sweet musky aromatic fragrance that, according to some, gave the plant its name, while others maintain that it owes its name to its medicinal virtues.

It grows wild in Norway, Austria, Switzerland, Silesia, on the slopes of the Alps and the Pyrenees and along the rivers that flow near to these mountains, as well as in many southern counties of England. There also exists another species, the wood angelica (*Angelica sylvestris*), which is less tall and less aromatic and not so rich in active principles. It may be found in damp copses, on the margin of damp woods, in shady places and in the neighbourhood of streams throughout the country.

Renaissance doctors call its root the 'root of the Holy Ghost' by reason of its 'great and divine properties' against very serious illnesses, and Paracelsus relates that it was a 'marvellous medicine' during an epidemic of plague in Milan in 1510. It thus enters into the composition of most of the great remedies of olden days and is even thought to be, like ginseng, the elixir of long life.

What is certain is that angelica is a first-class stomachic (it is the principal ingredient in a kind of ratafia); an excellent general tonic prescribed for anaemia, loss of appetite, migraines, vertigo, faintness (the ancients said it could 'refresh the heart'); an antispasmodic that makes difficult menstruation easier and less painful; and lastly a highly effective liquefacient recommended in cases of nervous asthma, chronic bronchitis, and smokers' cough.

Angelica is prepared by infusion (20 grammes of finely-chopped dried root or 15 grammes of seeds to a litre of boiling water), one cupful to be taken after meals. Care should be taken not to exceed these amounts, for too strong a dosage of angelica can overstimulate the nervous system and, especially if taken in the evening, might cause insomnia.

You can also make an unusual and delicious punch by pouring a litre of boiling water on to 30 grammes of chopped root; add four centilitres of good brandy (or white rum) and serve with slices of lemon.

APPLE
Malus communis

For the same reason the apple has been identified with the 'forbidden fruit' that tempted Adam and Eve (the Bible speaks only of the 'fruit of the tree which is in the midst of the garden'), and was similarly given a place of honour in Greek mythology: golden apples grew on the tree guarded by the Hesperides, and a golden apple lay behind the famous judgement of Paris and the Trojan war ...

Over the centuries it has acquired a universal reputation as a health-giving food and remedy, both preventive and curative. Today we know that there is more than a grain of truth in such sayings as 'An apple a day keeps the doctor away', for it has been shown that the apple is a veritable reservoir of therapeutic principles, with its sugars, its pectin, its amino-acids, its significant amounts of various vitamins and its numerous mineral salts. It is prescribed for constipation, intestinal infections (colibacillus infections), rheumatism, gout, physical

and mental overstrain, anaemia, demineralization, bronchial diseases, hepatic insufficiency, excess cholesterol in the blood, myocardial infarct (two apples a day as a preventive measure, a kilo and more as a cure, as prescribed by various doctors for the latter conditions).

So as often as possible eat raw apple *with the skin* (particularly rich in active principles), and chew it well – people who complain that apples are indigestible are generally those who do not chew them properly. Be sure you choose apples that are as nature made them, maybe with blemishes and worms but not 'protected' by insecticides, the dangers of which we are at last beginning to appreciate. You can obtain chemically untreated fruit from health food stores.

Apples do most good if eaten first thing in the morning, before breakfast, or last thing at night (they encourage sleep), and before meals. At the Bircher-Benner Clinic in Zurich, where people come from all over the world to be 'renovated' by their special diet, the famous 'muesli' is served as a first course at breakfast and dinner.

Here is the recipe for this delicious, appetizing and well-balanced health food: soak a tablespoon of flaked whole cereal (wheat, oats, rye or barley) in three tablespoons of cold water for twelve hours; blend a tablespoon of lemon juice and a tablespoon of sweetened condensed milk (or three tablespoons of yoghurt and a teaspoon of honey) and add to the cereal; mix together. Just before serving – to avoid it going brown – add 200 grammes of grated raw apple to the mixture, and sprinkle with a tablespoon of grated hazel nuts or almonds if desired. Eat at once – muesli should never be prepared in advance.

Apple is to be recommended for the following:

For hoarseness, coughs, pulmonary, gastric and kidney conditions, and also as a refreshing drink in any illness: slice two or three large unpeeled apples into rounds and cover with a litre of cold water; add a few pieces of liquorice and boil for a quarter of an hour; strain. May be drunk, unsweetened, as often as desired. In cases of illness, the decoction should be drunk at room temperature.

For rheumatism, gout, urine retention: to each cup (100 cubic centimetres) of water allow one tablespoonful of powdered apple peel (dry the peel, then crush it) and boil for fifteen minutes, strain, four or five cupfuls per day.

For infantile diarrhoea: feed the patient only raw apple, finely grated and very ripe; one tablespoon every hour until the stools have returned to normal. To drink, give weak tea, unsweetened.

For severe coughing, hoarseness: at each attack eat a baked apple, mashed with a little butter and a tablespoon of honey.

For demineralization, fatigue, hypertension, microbial infections: each day drink a glass of apple juice, sweet cider (dietetic of course) or even cider vinegar, once or twice a day take two teaspoonfuls of cider vinegar in a glass of water with two teaspoons of honey.

Used externally, a poultice of grated raw apple will alleviate the pain caused by a blow on the eye; a poultice of the pulp of cooked apples (whether boiled or baked) is prescribed for aches and pains, badly healing wounds, inflammation of the eyelids (M. du Barry, husband of Louis XV's favourite, would have treated his tired and swollen eyelids in this way).

For falling hair and itching scalp, Doctor Jarvis recommends dipping a comb into a solution of one teaspoonful of cider vinegar in a glass of water and combing it through the hair, morning and evening, until the hair is soaked.

External application of the pulp or a compress of apple juice restores firmness to the tissues and so constitutes a beauty treatment. This was known to the women of ancient Rome, who used to macerate apples studded with cloves in the wool grease of sheep (or lanoline), and use the unguent to take care of their skin; hence the word 'pomade'.

ARNICA
Arnica montana.   Mountain tobacco

Arnica is to be found in the northern hemisphere, but not in England. It grows in the mountains, at an altitude of between 1,200 and 2,800 metres exactly, and shares many features in common with betony, marigold and plantain (flower colour and aromatic scent with the first two, rosette arrangement of leaves around the base of the stalk with the third). Its dried leaves are smoked as a kind of *ersatz* tobacco, and its flowers, if breathed when freshly crushed, cause sneezing, hence one of its French nicknames, Sneezewort. It is both stimulant and vulnerary, largely used as a local application to the bruises, swellings, etc., that usually result from a fall, as well as for fever or the minor indiscretions of good living.

'Arnica', Abbé Kneipp used to say, 'is known throughout the entire world as an excellent medicinal plant. What I cannot understand is why this is disputed by so many people who could and should know better.'

I find it no easier to understand half a century later. I try telling myself that its reputation may have been damaged by various mishaps due to failure to respect the prescribed dosages, and that our supercivilized society no longer believes in anything except the complicated chemical drugs produced in laboratories, but I still cannot really understand how arnica can have practically disappeared from the family medicine chest. It certainly deserves a place, in view of its many uses.

So take advantage of your summer holiday, which is its flowering season, to drive into the mountains and collect its flowers (otherwise sought only by goats) which look like yellow-orange daisies. The plant grows to a height of 40 to 60 centimetres, and on its hairy stem the leaves are arranged in opposite pairs, whereas on other composites with which it might be confused the leaves are arranged alternately. Collect the flower heads entire, detaching them from their green calyx, and dry them in the shade, for use either in infusion or tincture.

The infusion for external application (hot compresses) is prepared in the proportions of 10–15 grammes of dried flowers to a litre of boiling water – in Germany, beer is used instead of water. The infusion for internal use should not exceed the minute amount of 1 gramme (a small pinch) per cup, and you should take no more than one cupful per day, being careful to strain the liquid through a fine cloth to remove the minute pappus, downy barbed hairs that catch in the throat and make you feel sick.

The tincture is prepared as follows: macerate 100 grammes of dried flowers in half a litre of alcohol (60°) for ten days in a stoppered vessel, shaking it from time to time; strain by squeezing through a cloth and preserve in a well-stoppered, tinted glass bottle. (The homoeopathic parent tincture – *Arnica montana* – is prepared with the whole plant.)

Externally arnica is used as a compress soaked either in the strong infusion or in diluted tincture (one tablespoonful to a quarter of a litre of water – the tincture should never be used pure as it is highly active) for bruises, ecchymoses, sprains, dislocations, as well as for sore throats and irritations of the larynx.

Great care should be exercised when employing internally either the low-dosage infusion or the tincture (three or four drops in a glass of lukewarm water) to combat fever, to stimulate the heart, the circulation, the nervous system, the digestive tract and secretion of bile. Arnica as a homoeopathic treatment is recommended for cases of trauma, muscular fatigue, fever, heart conditions (feeling that the heart is gripped in a vice), vertigo, hoarseness (as a preventive treatment for singers and lecturers).

Lastly, it appears – although personally I have not tried it, being too fond of my pipe – that a small phial of arnica carried in the pocket will cure you of the habit of smoking . . .

ASH

Fraxinus excelsior.   Common ash, Lofty ash, European ash, Weeping ash

People lend only to the rich, as is well known, and certainly this tree, which is to be found everywhere in Europe, is so rich in genuine properties that people have willingly endowed it with others that are far more illusory.

The ancient Teutons attributed magical powers to the ash: convinced that the roof of the world was supported by one of its giant specimens, they had dedicated it to the god Thor, and it was in the shade of an ash tree that their priest-sorcerers carried out human sacrifices to appease their numerous divinities. They also used the wood of the ash to make the spears that were supposed to render them invincible (it is interesting to note that, according to Homer, the great spear of Achilles was also made of ash).

Elsewhere it was considered to be a snake-repellent. It was said that if you carried a leaf on your person or hung leaves from the beams in stables, no snake would bite you or attack the cattle. Pliny says of these trees that,

so forcible is their vertue, that a serpent dare not come neare the shaddow of that tree, either morning or evening, notwithstanding at those times it reacheth farthest; you may be sure then they will not approch the tree it selfe, by a great way. And this am I able to deliver by the experience which I have seene, that if a man doe make a round circle with the leaves thereof, and environ therewith a serpent and fire together within, the serpent will chuse rather to goe into the fire, than to flie from it to the leaves of the ash. A wonderfull goodnesse of dame Nature, that the Ash doth bloome and flourish alwaies before that serpents come abroad; and never sheddeth leaves, but continueth green, untill they be retired into their holes, and hidden within the ground.

This belief is certainly behind a popular remedy still much employed in certain areas against viper bite: drink an infusion of 250 grammes of ash leaves and apply their marc to the wound . . . It was also claimed, as Parkinson puts it, that 'the water distilled from the young and tender branches and leaves of the Ash is a singular good medicine to take every morning fasting a small quantity, for those that . . . be already grosse and fat, or tending thereunto, to abate their greatnesse, and cause them to be lancke and gaunt,' and, according to Dioscorides, that its seeds 'provoke lust' or 'render a man more spirited with the ladies'.

What is certain is that the ash is a medicinal boon to country-dwellers. The tree is easily recognizable by the ash grey colour of its bark; its black buds; its flowers that have no petals, only a bottle-shaped seed-vessel between two stamens with fat purple heads, and appear in thick bunches, before the leaves, on the tips of the twigs; its leaves comprising seven to thirteen oval leaflets with finely toothed edges, and its fruits in clusters, encased in a membranous sheath.

The bark, which is taken from the branches in springtime,

was commonly employed as a febrifuge for intermittent fevers prior to the discovery of quinquina. It is still a classic family remedy for intermittent fevers, either in a decoction (15 to 60 grammes to a litre of water; boil for five minutes; one cupful three times a day before meals), or in powder form (10 to 20 grammes in honey, three or four times a day, between meals, for several consecutive days).

Its leaves – which are more active dried than fresh and should be gathered when they are exuding a kind of sticky substance, that is to say in May, June or July, according to region – have earned the ash the name of 'anti-gout and anti-rheumatism tree', given to it by Professor Binet. In infusion or mild decoction (30 to 40 grammes to a litre of water, plus three or four leaves of mint to give aroma), they eliminate urates, and are therefore advocated in cases of gravel, renal colic, gout and rheumatism. One cupful every three hours during attacks is what is generally recommended, and to avoid attacks a fifteen-day course of treatment (one cupful in the morning on an empty stomach and the rest of the litre to be taken during the day), to be repeated regularly every two months. I might add that an infusion of ash leaves (25 grammes to half a litre of water) taken every morning features in count-less prescriptions for exceptional longevity; it seems that 'the man who revealed this secret lived to the age of 107' . . .

The seeds, which used to be said to 'greatly aid those who cannot urinate', are in fact a remarkable diuretic in cases of dropsy, either in a decoction complete with their sheath (10 to 30 grammes to a litre of water; boil for two to three minutes; to be drunk during the day), or in powder form (5 to 15 grammes per day, mixed with honey or stirred into a drink).

But this eulogy would be incomplete if I failed to mention the drink known as *frênette* or *frênée* which, in the days of my youth, was still a household drink in many homes. Although I never failed to watch it being made – threatening to deprive me of the spectacle was one of my grandmother's ways of keeping me on my best behaviour – I had forgotten the exact recipe.

But fortunately it has been preserved by my colleague Jean Mary,[1] and I give it to you in his words:

1 Make a decoction of 90 grammes of chicory (roasted) in boiling water; 2 Dissolve 3 kilogrammes of sugar and 45 grammes of tartaric acid in several litres of boiling water; 3 Moisten 60 grammes of ash leaves (picked in summer and dried in shade) with a sufficient quantity of boiling water; leave to infuse for two hours; strain.

Next pour these three preparations into a 60 litre cask; add more water, but not right up to the top. When the mixture is cold, add 60 grammes of yeast mixed with cold water. Fermentation should continue for at least eleven days, the bung of the cask being kept open.

When this time has elapsed, pour into bottles which should be tightly corked and wired (that was another performance I wouldn't have missed for a king's ransom!) – ready for drinking after the fifteenth day.

Mary very rightly stresses that the ingredients of *frênette* endow it with their medicinal properties: chicory is tonic, stomachic, diuretic and febrifuge; tartaric acid is refreshing and ash leaves are laxative, diuretic and sudorific. In short, it is a real health drink, and we would be well advised to restore it to popularity . . .

AVENS

Geum urbanum.   Wood avens, Colewort, Herb bennet or benet

It has been said that avens is a plant that is often undervalued. There is some truth in this, for it is a sure ally against intermittent fevers, colic, diarrhoea, dysentery, circulation and liver disorders, gastric debility following acute illness, states of weakness and exhaustion, and moreover has the advantage of

1. *L'Armoire aux herbes*, ed. Les Écrits de France.

being easily available since it grows wild everywhere in Great Britain and Europe.

It is commonly found in woodland, along hedges and ditches, in cool shadowy places, at the foot of walls, along streams. Its stems, reddish at the base and slightly downy, reach a height of 40 to 60 centimetres; the leaves on the flowering stem consist of a terminal leaflet which resembles a strawberry leaf, and lower leaflets which are small, oval, toothed. The flowers have five bright yellow petals, and when they wither they are succeeded by a brown ball of seeds covered with hairs or bristles. Its horizontal root – brown on the outside, white or reddish on the inside – thickens with age to form a sort of conical stump, covered with thin bark and hairy light-brown rootlets. Freshly crushed, it smells very like cloves. It should be collected in the autumn and dried in the shade, in gentle heat so that it will retain some of its aroma, although this disappears progressively in the course of a year (it is preferable, when possible, to use the roots fresh).

Paracelsus recommended the root of avens for catarrh of the stomach and intestine. His successors considered it 'good for strengthening the stomach and clearing the liver' as well as 'useful for swiftly reducing fever', in which function it was widely used by the doctors of the Rhine Army in the fourth and fifth years of the Republic, since, quinquina being rare, it was thanks to the root of avens that they cured a great number of soldiers struck down by intermittent fever.

It is administered: (a) in an infusion or mild decoction (30 to 40 grammes to a litre of water, 3 cupfuls per day); (b) as an aromatic wine (40 to 50 grammes of root macerated for eight days or boiled for ten minutes in a litre of good wine; press and strain; 2 or 3 wine-glassfuls per day). This wine is tonic, digestive, depurative: it is 'good for the heart and clears the eyes, nose, teeth, brain and heart of anything that should not be there', states one nineteenth-century writer.

I must also call attention to a usage still practised in certain regions: the root of avens, gathered before sunrise and placed in a linen bag worn around the neck like an amulet, will arrest all bleeding, particularly in haemorrhoids, cure ophthalmia (inflammation of the eye), strengthen the sight, and curb the tears and acrid fluids that flow from the eyes. The treatment, we are told, 'works just as well on humans as on horses'.

B

BALM
Melissa officinalis.   Sweet balm, Lemon balm, Honey plant, Cure-all. The old herbalists knew it as *bawm*

Balm shares many points in common with melilot: they both have flowers that particularly attract bees; they both derive their names from a Greek word (*melissa* means bee); they have both enjoyed great renown in the past; lastly they are both antispasmodic, digestive and sedative.

Originally from the lands around the eastern Mediterranean, it grows wild in hot regions but will do well as a garden plant almost everywhere. Its slightly hairy square stems, which grow to a height of 50 to 80 centimetres, bear leaves that are opposite, oval, coarsely serrate and slightly downy, smaller on the flowering stems; its flowers are small, from white to bluish, appearing in groups of three to six at the axil of the leaves.

We employ the flowering tips and the leaves, dried in the shade. They are picked at the moment of flowering, for later the pleasant lemon odour they exhale when crushed between the fingers takes on a rather nasty smell.

Arab doctors were the first to boast of the virtues of balm (Avicenna said that it 'maketh the heart merry, and strengtheneth the vitall spirits') and their colleagues followed in their footsteps, prescribing it for an impressive range of illnesses – including apoplexy, epilepsy, lethargy, melancholia, mania – especially in the form of a distilled water, whose reputation as an elixir of youth equalled that of the water of the Queen of Hungary.[1]

The infusion (20 to 30 grammes of leaves or flowering tips to a litre of boiling water; leave to infuse for ten minutes;

1.See *Rosemary*, page 273

four or five cupfuls per day) is recommended for poor or painful digestion, vertigo and buzzing in the ears, palpitations and nervous colic, insomnia, headaches and the various disorders common to nervous subjects. It is most particularly recommended (up to 6 cupfuls per day) for the cramps and uterine pains experienced by many women at the time of menstruation. In summer it will be found to make an excellent cool drink, both refreshing and invigorating.

Spirit of balm, taken in a little lukewarm water, has the same uses. A few drops on a lump of sugar constitute the classic remedy for fainting, aerophagia and indigestion.

It would be too complicated to prepare your own spirit of balm – its other ingredients include zest of lemon, cinnamon, coriander, cloves, nutmeg, angelica, and it has to be distilled after maceration. But you can easily make a cordial and stomachic that has the same virtues by macerating for fifteen days in a litre and a half of spirit or alcohol (45°), 15 grammes of leaves of the following plants: balm, basil, hyssop, mint, sage, wormwood, plus 15 grammes of angelica root; strain and store in tightly stoppered bottles.

BARBERRY

Berberis vulgaris. Barbery, Berberidis, Pipperidge-bush, Piperidge.

For homoeopaths this is a precious plant that provides them with *berberis*, valuable remedy for hepatorenal insufficiency. They prescribe it for cases of hepatic or renal calculus (especially to promote draining between attacks of renal colic), as well as for those suffering from rheumatism or gout and for lumbar pains.

For farmers it is a harmful plant, damaging to surrounding crops, since the wheat-rust fungus spends a period of its life on the common barberry. It should, therefore, not be planted near wheat fields, but allowed to grow only where it can do no damage – on the edges of woodland, in hedges adjoining pastures, or around the farmyard.

For keen gardeners and anyone interested in unusual plants, it is an ornamental shrub that takes on magnificent red hues in autumn and is characterized by a fairly rare feature among our plants: the stamens of its flowers contract at the slightest touch and spring upward against the central pistil 'where they remain for some time, as if to protect it from any outside interference'.[1]

As its name implies, the barberry bears sharp thorns or spines on its twigs. Its main shoots may attain a height of over two metres; its leaves are ovate, smooth, with toothed edges, and grow in clusters; its pendulous groups of pale yellow flowers appear at the axil of the leaves and give ovoid red berries with a black spot on the tip.

A yellow dye is extracted from the whole plant (stalk and root) which is used for dyeing wool, cotton, linen and for staining certain woods employed in marquetry work (in Poland the bark was used for polishing leather, to which it imparts a beautiful tawny sheen).

The inner rind of the stalk and the root is held to be a specific for the functions of the liver, the gall bladder, the spleen and the pancreas; it is employed as follows: macerate for a quarter of an hour 30 to 40 grammes in a litre of cold water; bring slowly to the boil; remove at once from the heat and leave to infuse for a further twenty minutes; one cupful (morning, midday and evening) after meals. This treatment is recommended for liver disorders (jaundice, calculus) and disorders of the digestion (dyspepsia), and also in the treatment of dropsy and rheumatism.

For metrorrhagia, most likely to occur during the period of menopause, Doctor Leclerc recommends a mild decoction of

1. This is part of the plant's remarkable mechanism to compel insects to do its bidding. The merest touch of the bee's tongue releases the anthers (or pollen boxes), and as the stamens spring upward a sudden shower of pollen flies out of the anthers and lands on the bee. (Translator's note.)

2 to 5 grammes of bark and the same quantity of cypress cones in 200 grammes of water, one tablespoonful to be taken every two hours.

The berries, dried and crushed (40 to 60 grammes to a litre of water; leave to soak for two hours; bring to the boil; boil for barely a minute and leave to infuse until tepid; 3 or 4 small (coffee) cupfuls during the day), make a refreshing slightly acid drink for feverish patients; it is also very useful in the treatment of diarrhoea and dysentry.

BASIL
Ocimum basilicum.   Sweet basil, Garden basil

There is no need for me to stress the gastronomic virtues of basil, for these are already sufficiently well known to all lovers of good food. Some dishes, such as the famous *soupe au pistou* of the Nice district and the *pesto* sauce of Genoa, depend entirely on fresh basil for their existence. As long ago as the sixteenth century Matthiolus observed: 'There are few gardens, indoor or out, that are not full of basil growing in wooden boxes or clay pots' and Chomel, in the time of Louis XV, declared: 'There are cooks who make such skilful use of basil, thyme, bay leaves, wild thyme, savory and our other aromatic herbs that the dishes they prepare with these seasonings are just as pleasing and tasty as if they had used spices from foreign lands' – a statement which is not less true today, incidentally, and which lovers of good cooking would do well to ponder . . .

Like the majority of the most fragrant aromatic herbs, basil has in its time been associated with religious or magic rites.

In its native country, India, according to the Brahmanic religion, it was imbued with the divine essence of the 'three brides'; every family possessed its sacred basil, their protective spirit, to which they made daily offerings of flowers and rice.

In medieval Europe it was said that 'if a sprig of pounded basil be left under a stone it will turn into a scorpion, and if pulped and exposed to the heat of the sun, it will turn into worms'. It was also credited with the power of relieving the pain of a woman in labour if she held a root and a swallow's feather in her hand, and was believed to be an antidote to the sting of a scorpion. It is probable that these beliefs stemmed from the confusion of its name (Latin *bascilicum*) with *basiliscus*, basilisk, fabulous reptile alleged to be hatched by a serpent from a cock's egg, its very look so fatal that it would kill itself if it saw its own reflection, or strike dead anyone who crossed its path.

Pliny recommends it as a cure for epilepsy. From the Renaissance to the French Revolution doctors advocate it for 'cheering the spirit and restoring the humours that compose the blood' and for 'clearing the brain, by causing the water humours to be discharged through the nose' for 'the qualities of basil are allies of the body'.

In fact basil has an undeniable sedative and antispasmodic action in addition to its digestive properties. It is therefore recommended for nervous predisposition, stomach disorders, insomnia of nervous origin, vertigo, migraines, angor – in short it serves as a natural and non-toxic kind of 'tranquillizer'.

It may be employed either as an infusion (3 to 5 grammes of leaves or flowering tips to 100 grammes of water, two or three times a day after meals) or in wine (macerate a handful of leaves in a litre of wine for three days, strain and sweeten or not, according to taste; one small wineglassful after meals). This wine, mixed with an equal quantity of olive oil (3 or 4 table-spoonfuls of the mixture to be taken during the day) will 'end the most persistent constipation and restore the stomach and intestines to good order'.

The sap of the fresh leaves acts beneficially on inflammations of the ear (a few drops in the ear) and the powdered dried leaves, taken like snuff, is, according to Doctor Cazin, 'a pleasant sternutatory employed with success to remedy loss of sense of smell caused by thickening of the nasal mucous membrane or concretion of nasal mucous, in chronic nasal catarrh'.

Lastly, it is interesting to note that basil (of which there exist more than 100 varieties) is also grown in Africa where it is utilized both as a seasoning and a medicine: it is given to children as a treatment for worms, to adults for persistent headaches, migraines and for certain rheumatic diseases. Among the Fang tribes, the 'speakers' chew basil leaves before playing their role in the 'palavers' (native ceremonies) to gain inspiration and assurance: for them too it is a 'tranquillizer'.

BILBERRY

Vaccinium myrtillus. Huckleberry, Whortleberry, Hurtleberry, Whin-berry, Wimberry, Black heart, Hurts

A few years ago the great town-dwelling public suddenly realized that bilberries are not merely useful for making jam and pies and brandy, but that they also possess therapeutic virtues: the discovery had just been made that the skin contained a substance that acts upon the retinal purpura and improves night vision, a discovery of the highest interest for the protection of all those who take their lives in their hands when they get behind a steering wheel.

This news made less impact on country-dwellers, who are less affected by the cult of the car and who have moreover long made use of this little shrub to cure various disorders.

Its small oval leaves with finely-toothed edges are employed in a decoction (20 to 30 grammes to a litre of water, boil for five to ten minutes; 2 or 3 cupfuls per day) to treat inflammation of the urino-genital tract (particularly cystitis), incontinence of urine (bed-wetting in children), skin diseases (pruritus, eczema). They lower the blood-sugar level and are therefore recommended in the treatment of diabetes, either alone or mixed with an equal quantity of strawberry leaves (30 grammes to a litre of water; boil for five to ten minutes; to be drunk during the day).

Its delicately scented black berries have been known for centuries for their astringent and disinfectant properties (recent work has shown that a decoction of bilberries will sterilize in the space of twenty-four hours cultures of colon bacillus and of Eberth's bacillus, which is the typhoid bacillus). They constitute the natural remedy for persistent diarrhoea, acute enteritis, dysentery, intestinal fermentation.

Dried in the shade, they will keep perfectly from one year to the next and are utilized either as they stand (a good pinch of dried berries, to be chewed at length and then swallowed), or as a decoction (60 grammes of berries to a litre of lukewarm water; soak for an hour, then bring slowly to the boil; boil for fifteen to twenty minutes and macerate until tepid; a small cupful every hour). This decoction is also prescribed as a mouthwash or gargle for stomatitis, aphtha, pharyngitis; as a lotion for skin conditions (eczema, pruritus); as compresses for haemorrhoids and haemorrhoidal flux.

With the fresh berries you can make a tincture of bilberry that the Abbé Kneipp called 'the first and most indispensable of all the tinctures in our family medicine chest'. To 2 or 3 handfuls (100 to 150 grammes of fresh berries add a few cloves and some cinnamon; make up to one litre with alcohol (45°) or spirit. The tincture will be ready in fifteen days, but the longer you leave the berries to macerate (even for years), the stronger and more effective the tincture will become.

Its medicinal uses are, of course, the same as for the decoction. It is taken either on a lump of sugar (10 to 30 drops, according to the degree of the condition), or in hot water or wine (one coffeespoonful to 125 cubic centimetres of liquid, to be repeated eight to ten hours later; a third dose is rarely necessary).

BINDWEED, GREAT

Convolvulus sepium. Hedge bindweed, Convolvulus, Bell-bind, Lady's nightcap, Wild morning-glory, Rutland beauty

It is amusing to compare what two doctors have said about this plant over a span of several centuries: for Matthiolus 'it seems that it might have been nature's trial shot when she was practising to make the lily'; for Georges Duhamel it is 'a dreadful, unscrupulous creature; it crawls and climbs and smothers everything round which it entwines itself . . .'

Like its close relative the small bindweed (*convolvulus arvensis*, also known as field bindweed, devil's guts and corubine) it is damaging to surrounding plants, for it takes possession of much soil, but both are endowed with powerful purgative properties, mentioned long ago by Dioscorides. You will never see a peasant chewing on the flower of the bindweed: he knows too well what would be in store for him!

This in no way means that one cannot use the plant; on the contrary, both to obtain a gentle laxative action on the bowel and to promote the secretion of bile, infuse 3 to 6 grammes of leaves (fresh or dried) in a cup (100 cubic centimetres) of boiling water for five minutes, and drink this infusion a quarter of an hour before breakfast.

As a purgative – and one that causes no colic and does not irritate the bowel – employ either a simple infusion (10 to 12 grammes of leaves in 250 cubic centimetres of water; infuse for five minutes; to be drunk first thing in the morning on an empty stomach), or a compound infusion (6 to 12 grammes of leaves, 5 or 6 grammes of linseed to 250 cubic centimetres of water; leave to infuse for five minutes; strain; add one tablespoonful of honey; to be drunk first thing in the morning on an empty stomach), or a dose of 1 gramme of powdered dried leaves, to be taken in honey or jam first thing in the morning on an empty stomach.

Employed externally, six or eight fresh leaves of hedge bindweed crushed between the fingers and applied as a poultice will cause a boil to break within twenty-four hours.

BIRCH, EUROPEAN
Betula alba.   White birch, Silver birch, Paper birch

No other tree has been as useful to man in so many ways, especially in Nordic countries where its graceful silhouette, with its white trunk marked with dark bands and its drooping branches covered with glossy toothed leaves, is part and parcel of the landscape.

Its wood has been used for making wheel felloes, hoops for casks, clogs, brooms and rods for schoolmasters. In Sweden and Lapland its sap has replaced sugar and been used to make wine; its bark has been used as roofing for huts, to make baskets, cord, woven shoes, nets, bottles, plates, torches; oil extracted from the bark is used in tanning leather and lends Russian leather its particular fragrance and superior quality; beer has been made from it, and also a kind of pasta that certain Russian peoples used to mix with their caviare; lastly the very thin but extremely tough and durable skin taken from the bark was long used as parchment or paper.

Although it is no longer put to many of these uses – progress cannot be halted, as we all know – the birch is still employed medicinally today, even though its therapeutic uses are as old as the others mentioned above.

Already in 1565 the Siennese physician Matthiolus claims 'The water that commeth out of the tree of its owne accord, being bored with an auger, or destilled afterwards, being drunke for some time together is helde availeable to breake the stone in the kidnies or bladder, and is also good to wash sore mouths' (Parkinson). And three centuries later, Baron Pierre-François Percy, army surgeon and inspector-general of the medical service of Napoleon's armies, declares:

Throughout the whole of northern Europe, from our departments of the Rhine to the northernmost borders of Russia, birch water is the hope, the blessing and the panacea of rich and poor, master and peasant alike . . . It almost unfailingly cures skin conditions such as pimples, scurf, acne, etc., it is an invaluable remedy for rheumatic diseases, the after-effects of gout, bladder obstructions, and countless chronic ills against which medical science is so prone to fail . . .

The many virtues of this water, sometimes called 'birch blood', have been proved over and over again by country people, who never fail to lay in a supply of it in the spring. Before the tree is in leaf, they bore a small hole in the trunk and insert a straw through the hole. The rising sap trickles through the straw into a container covered with a cloth to protect it against dust and insects. In order not to exhaust the tree, they continue extracting the sap for only two or three days, after which they stop up the hole with a wooden plug. They preserve the liquid either by sterilizing, or by adding four to six cloves and a little cinnamon to each bottle. This birch water is taken medicinally in doses of 4 to 6 tablespoonfuls per day. It is also used, when there is enough of it, to make a sweet fizzy wine not unlike champagne: the sap is put into a small cask, together with honey, raisins and a few aromatic herbs and spices (sage, thyme, cinnamon, for example); the cask is sealed and the contents left to ferment for one month; the wine is then drawn off and poured into stoppered or screw-top bottles.

If you live in a city, so that these alternatives are not open to you, do not despair: you can obtain the same benefits from a decoction of birch leaves, gathered in the spring and dried in the shade: allow 30 to 60 grammes of leaves to a litre of water, and simmer gently for two or three minutes, remove from the heat and, when it has cooled to approximately 40°C, add a pinch of bicarbonate of soda, which helps the active principles to dissolve; leave to infuse for several hours. This tea (which increases fourfold or fivefold the output of urine), taken in the amount of 4 or 5 cupfuls per day between meals, is prescribed for skin diseases, albuminuria, dropsy, obesity due to fluid retention, gout, rheumatism, stones in the kidneys and bladder, cardial and renal oedema. As a disinfectant lotion or compress, it is applied directly to the skin in the treatment of skin disorders such as herpes, eczema, spots, etc., and facial blemishes.

The bark, in decoction (30 to 60 grammes in a litre of white wine or water; boil for five minutes and leave to infuse for at least as long again; one small glassful morning and evening), is recommended for intermittent fevers.

Lastly, here are two real old country remedies that have evidently proved their worth, since I found them quoted in several herbals.

The skin of birch, worn inside the shoes, promotes a perspiration that can prove salutary in various chronic conditions.

Peasants affected by rheumatic or arthritic pains, or suffering from serous oedematous, or congestive conditions, lie in a well-warmed bed filled with birch leaves which, together with a covering of blankets or a good eiderdown, induce a heavy sweat that will bring the patient relief.

BISTORT

Polygonum bistorta. Snakeweed, Adderwort, Dragonwort, English serpentary, Osterick, Passions

Its name and several of its most common synonyms derive from the shape of its red-brown root, about as long as a finger, generally twice (sometimes three times) bent back upon itself in a serpentine S-shape.

The root is the only part of the plant that is used, for it is rich in tannin (20 per cent), and therefore a very powerful astringent. However, in order to locate the root, you must know how to recognize the plant, which grows in shaded places in woods in the north of England, and is also a garden plant. (Elsewhere in Europe it is widespread in mountainous areas, growing in damp meadows where the soil is silicious.) Its stem (40 to 50 centimetres in height) is gnarled, erect and cylindrical; its leaves are alternate, lanceolate, with slightly wavy edges, dark green on the upper surface, bluish-green underneath: the upper leaves have no stalk and ensheathe the main stem; its flowers, from bright pink to pale pink, are very small, bristling with stamens, and grouped in a terminal spike of about 5 centimetres.

For grazing stock – except horses – the plant is a great delicacy. Human beings are only interested in the root, which they collect in autumn, no longer to treat smallpox, severe fevers and 'to sweat out plague poison' as in the sixteenth and seventeenth centuries, but in order to have at hand one of the most powerful indigenous tonic astringents whose action is comparable to that of the famous rhatany root imported from South America.

Used internally, it is prepared either by a decoction (40 to 50 grammes of chopped root to a litre of cold water; bring slowly to the boil; leave to infuse for a quarter of an hour; 4 or 5 cupfuls per day between meals) or by maceration (60 grammes to a litre of cold or tepid water; macerate for six to ten hours; 4 or 5 cupfuls per day, always between meals) as a remedy for dysentery, diarrhoea, colic, spontaneous haemorrhages (nose-bleeds, metrorrhagia), venous conditions (varicose veins, haemorrhoids, phlebitis).

Bistort can also be prepared as a wine (macerate 125 grammes of chopped root in 250 grammes of alcohol (45°) for twenty-four hours; add a litre of good red wine – preferably bordeaux – and macerate for a further four days, stirring frequently; strain) which is recommended for persons subject to stomach trouble, diarrhoea and enteritis (one sherry-glass to be taken before lunch and before dinner). Doctor Leclerc prescribed a daily dose of 50 to 150 grammes for tubercular patients and 'candidates for tuberculosis' by reason of its 'manifest tonic action'.

Used externally, prepared either by decoction or maceration, as a mouthwash or a gargle, bistort strengthens the gums, clears up aphtha, stomatitis, gingivitis, inflammation of the mouth and throat; administered by douche, it is prescribed for leucorrhoea, metritis and uterine haemorrhages. Lastly it can be applied as a compress to purulent wounds to decongest the tissues and promote cicatrization.

BITTERSWEET

Solanum dulcamara. Woody nightshade, Woodbine, Felonwort, Felonwood, Violet bloom, Scarlet berry, Dulcamara, Mortal

Member of the large family of *solanaceae* – which includes belladonna, henbane, thorn apple and the common potato, plants that all contain in their stems, or tubers, and leaves a poisonous alkaloidal glucoside, solanine, that dangerously affects the nervous system to a varying extent – bittersweet has in its time been both over-praised and under-valued.

It has been credited with cures that were purely accidental, and blamed for damaging effects that were equally so; its action on syphilis or pleurisy is as unsubstantial as the belief that thirty of its berries will kill a dog in the space of a few hours (average-sized dogs have evinced no symptoms after being given as many as 150). So we should not ask of bittersweet more than it can give – it is no panacea – and remember always to take certain precautions when handling it.

It is a climbing plant that grows in hedges and damp ditches and on the edge of streams. Its trailing stems can reach a height of 2 metres; they bear alternate leaves, the lower leaves oval, almost heart-shaped, the upper leaves lobed (one large leaf with a small one each side); the flowers appear in small groups of six to eight, on the tip of the stem, between June and September; the corolla has five purple lobes surrounding a golden-yellow cone formed by the stamens around the ovary; the berries which succeed in autumn are small and egg-shaped and go through a series of colour changes from green through yellow and orange to a bright red, forming highly decorative clusters.

The year-old greenish-brown shoots, gathered in May or June or towards the end of the summer, are the part used, being first dried in the shade. (Country children sometimes chew them, because their initially bitter taste becomes sweet, like the root of liquorice.)

It is mainly employed, because of its depurative properties, in the treatment of cutaneous eruptions (pityriasis, eczema, herpes), as well as of rheumatism and gout. The most usual method of preparation is to boil 20 to 30 grammes of dried shoots in a litre of water until reduced by a third, to be drunk between meals in the course of two or three days.

Employed externally, applications of bittersweet leaves boiled in wine are used in some regions to relieve sprains; compresses soaked in the decoction bring about an immediate improvement in non-bleeding haemorrhoids. Lastly, the fresh juice will remove facial blemishes.

BLACKBERRY
Rubus fruticosus.   Bramble

The blackberry is yet another example of nature's wisdom and the harmony of creation: its fresh leaves, crushed between the fingers and rubbed on the skin, will at once check bleeding from the scratches that might be inflicted by its thorns. It grows freely in woodland, and foresters have nicknamed it 'the mother of the oak', for the oak 'will only do really well in its infancy under the cover and shelter it provides'.

Above all the blackberry is the benefactress of our mucous membranes, both by virtue of its leaves with their three or five leaflets – armed, like the long supple stems, with hooked prickles – and its tempting black fruits so popular with children. Pliny praised its effects on inflammations of the mouth and the bowel, remarking that nature did not 'create it solely to harm mankind', and Saint Hildegard recommended it for 'haemorrhages of the buttocks'. As for modern scientists, they have discovered that the blackberry can be grown in a test tube (a minute fragment weighing 80 milligrams, placed on nutritive gelose, will in the course of seven or eight months reach 5 to 6 centimetres in length and weigh about 10 grammes!) and that blackberry juice is capable of stimulating the growth of other vegetable tissues. This extraordinary vitalizing property, only recently demonstrated, doubtless plays a part in its triple action – astringent, tonic and restorative – on the mucous membranes.

The blackberry can be prepared either as a decoction, or as a jam, syrup or tincture. The decoction is made with dried leaves (which are more aromatic than fresh ones): 40 to 50 grammes to 1 litre of water; boil for five minutes and leave to infuse for ten minutes. It is taken in the amounts of 3 or 4 cupfuls per day, between meals, for inflammation of the mouth, throat and mucous membranes of the digestive tract (gastritis, enteritis, chronic diarrhoea, dysentery); it is also recommended in the treatment of haemorrhoids, urino-genital disorders (chiefly cystitis) and congestive conditions of the female reproductive organs. It is further employed as a gargle and mouthwash (the addition of honey increases its soothing power) for sore throats, angina, affections of the mucous membranes of the mouth (aphtha, ulcers, swollen gums); as lukewarm injections for leucorrhoea or 'whites', vaginitis, metritis.

Let me mention, incidentally, that an infusion of the dried leaves, either alone or preferably mixed with woodruff leaves, make an excellent tea that can be drunk as a substitute for China tea.

Blackberry jam (the same recipe as for strawberry jam) can be enjoyed by everyone, but it is also a particularly agreeable treatment for sore throats of all kinds, hoarseness and irritation of the vocal chords and the upper respiratory tract, diarrhoea and enteritis: one tablespoonful, sucked and swallowed slowly, several times a day.

Blackberry syrup (cook to a syrupy consistency equal weights of juice – obtained by pressing the berries which should be picked before they have fully ripened, which gives them the slightly acid taste that should characterize the syrup – and sugar) is prescribed, in the dosage of 2 or 3 tablespoonfuls per day, for bronchial catarrh and sore throats; one tablespoonful in a glass of water makes a refreshing drink for sick persons and convalescents.

Tincture of blackberry (one good handful of berries to 1 litre of alcohol (15°); macerate in the sun or near a hot stove for three weeks, stirring occasionally; filter and add honey to taste) is used as a gastric tonic; one liqueur glassful each day.

BLACKCURRANT
Ribes nigrum

Rarely has any plant given such good results with such a large number of disorders: retention of urine, gout, rheumatism, gravel, inflammation of the urinary tract (cystitis, nephritis), renal colic, dropsy, eruptive fevers, chronic diarrhoea, general fatigue, albuminuria, oedema, arthritic pains, inflammations of the stomach and the bowel.

All who have had recourse to it are loud in their praises, from Doctor Durville who states that the infusion of leaves (one glass morning and evening or in wine with meals) 'soothes acidity and is a superior substitute for magnesia and bicarbonate of soda' to Doctor Cazin who states that the cold infusion of blackcurrant leaves 'is of all drinks the most suitable and least costly for quenching the thirst during the heat of summer and the heavy work of harvesting'.

You can utilize it in whichever way you prefer.

Infusion: 40 to 50 grammes of fresh or dried leaves (in the latter case, soak for an hour in cold water that will then be used for the infusion) to a litre of water; bring gently to the boil; remove from the heat; leave to infuse for ten minutes; 3 or 4 cupfuls per day, before, after or between meals. If you wish to increase still more its anti-rheumatic action, prepare the following mixture: 100 grammes of dry blackcurrant leaves, 50 grammes of dry ash leaves, 50 grammes of dried flowerheads of meadow-sweet; one good tablespoonful of this mixture in a cup of boiling water, to be taken each evening.

Wine: about twenty fresh leaves in a litre of good white wine: macerate for ten to fifteen days; strain and add sugar if required – personally I do not do so, preferring to add a drop of blackcurrant liqueur; one wineglassful to be taken before meals.

As a refreshing and diuretic drink: 30 grammes of fresh or dry leaves (the latter must always first be soaked) and 30 grammes of liquorice to a litre of water; bring to the boil; leave to infuse for ten minutes; strain; drink at will.

The blackcurrant is also credited with another far from negligible virtue: for centuries it has been thought to favour longevity and oppose the onset of old age. 'It is', we read in a text dated 1753, 'an excellent elixir of life, that maintains good health and makes elderly persons look younger than they are.'

BORAGE
Borrago officinalis.   Burrage, Cool-tankard

Some say its name is of Arabic origin, given to it by the Moors in Spain who knew its sudorific virtues and called it *abou-*

rach: father of sweat. Others say it stems from Latin, *borrago*, being a deformation of the words *cor ago*: I stimulate the heart, for the ancients believed that borage, like its cousin bugloss, dispelled melancholy and induced such euphoria, that 'if your wife and children, your father and mother, your brother and sister and all your friends were to die under your very eyes, you would find it impossible to be sad or to shed a single tear over them . . .'

It is not for this imaginary virtue that I would advise you to gather borage, but for its other very real properties, as a plant that is demulcent, emollient, refrigerant, depurative, sudorific and diuretic.

You will recognize it by its hollow, hairy cylindrical stalks that grow to a height of between 30 to 70 centimetres; by its broad alternate leaves with stiff hairs on both sides; by its slightly drooping flowers that appear at the tip of the stems, their five petals shaped like a five pointed star, from red to dark blue in colour, and generally much frequented by the bees on account of their wealth of sweet fluid or nectar.

It has been found that borage is more emollient when in the stage of young growth (this is when it is picked for use in salads and soups or as a vegetable like spinach in certain regions); more depurative and sudorific when it is in flower; lastly more diuretic when its fruits – four brownish-black nutlets containing black seeds – are ripening. These subtleties are less important than the fact that *the whole plant* must be collected and dried for, contrary to widespread opinion, it is not the flower that is most rich in active principles, but the stem, and then the leaves.

It can be utilized as a decoction (20 to 25 grammes of dried plant to a litre of water; bring slowly to the boil; continue boiling for two to three minutes, then leave to infuse for a quarter of an hour; 4 or 5 cupfuls per day) for all fevers due to chills, influenza and other contagious diseases (measles, scarlet fever, chicken-pox), as a depurative and diuretic in the treatment of skin conditions, rheumatism and certain disorders of the urinary tract.

A stronger decoction (80 to 100 grammes of plant to a litre of water) is recommended as a vapour treatment for remedying bronchial complaints.

You can also subscribe to tradition by preparing in spring the 'depurative herb juice' (fresh leaves crushed together with the leaves of watercress and dandelion) formerly sold by apothecaries and herbalists.

BOX
Buxus sempervirens

In Germany in the eighteenth century there was a charlatan (in the original sense of the word, namely a man who – with a good line in patter – pulled teeth and sold drugs in public places) who sold a particular 'wonder drug' for the treatment of fevers. Emperor Joseph II bought his secret from him for 1,500 florins and made it public knowledge, so that everyone would benefit: it was alcoholic tincture of box. The writer who recorded the story adds: 'Whereupon, being thus stripped of its prestige, this medicine was consigned to oblivion.'

Notwithstanding, box is an excellent febrifuge, especially recommended for patients who do not respond well to cinchona (quinine). The decoction is prepared as follows: 30 grammes of grated root (or wood) to a litre of water; boil until reduced by half; sweeten with honey; drink in three doses during the day.

It also has a strong sudorific and diuretic action, as well as being an incontestable cholagogue. It is therefore recommended to be taken at the onset of all types of influenza, for sluggishness of the liver, for functional disorders of the urinary tract, for rheumatism, gout, oedema and skin diseases. 'All who suffer from liver or ague,' one treatise advises, 'should try taking it for several days,' and Parkinson writes: 'I remember that Doctor Smith, that was one of Queene Elizabeths Physitions, appointed the decoction of an ounce of the leaves of Box for a purging medicine, to be boyled in whey, and a dramme of the pouther in broth.'

If you are unable to obtain fresh root, you can employ the leaves and the tips of the stems, dried and crushed into small pieces, to make a decoction: 40 to 50 grammes to a litre of water; boil for five to ten minutes; leave to infuse for a further half-hour; sweeten; 4 or 5 cupfuls per day, between meals. This also has a purgative action.

It is odd that the box – originally from Persia – did not much attract the attention of the ancients. They certainly recognized its virtues as a sudorific and depurative (Saint Hildegard recommended it for smallpox, then it was prescribed for rheumatism and the pox), but they were chiefly preoccupied with its less propitious aspects, noting: 'It is highly dangerous to the brain to sleep beneath this tree, inasmuch as its very odour is hostile to nature; it is said that a wounded snake is at once cured if it can eat the root of box.'

However, they praised its usefulness for dyeing the hair and encouraging hair growth. Matthiolus declares that 'used when washing the hair it will make the hair red' and Bosinus Centilius informs us that box not only enabled a peasant woman to regain a thick head of hair but that she also found her face and neck, over which she had also spread the lotion, covered with hair 'so that she looked exactly like a monkey'.

Without wishing for such results, it is certain that box has a beneficial effect on the scalp by means of a daily friction with the following lotion: macerate 50 grammes of finely-chopped fresh leaves in half a litre of alcohol (45°), or marc-brandy or rum, for ten to fifteen days; filter, if wished, perfume with a little natural essence (lavender, rosemary). Jos. Triponez, who gives this formula, says: 'I believe there can hardly be a better remedy for dandruff.'

BROOM

Sarothamnus scoparius or **Spartium scoparium.**
Common broom, He-broom (no flowers), She-broom (with flowers)

There is a legend that at the time of the flight into Egypt all the plants spread wide their branches to make a path for the Virgin and the Infant Jesus, and then closed them up behind her to conceal her track from the soldiers of Herod; only one plant, broom, remained stiff and unbending, and that is why it was condemned to remain hard and dry to the end of its days . . .

It is because of this quality that broom came to be used for making broomsticks – including the broomsticks medieval witches rode! – for building huts, for heating potters' and bakers' ovens, whilst its bark was utilized for making very hard-wearing rope and yarn. The legendary curse also meant that broom long had a bad reputation, the more so as it was known to be an ingredient in numerous magic philtres, and was reputed to keep witches away.

Eventually its remarkable therapeutic properties were discovered, firstly as an exceptionally powerful diuretic (modern research has shown that it triples renal elimination), then as a heart tonic, and lastly, recently, as an antivenom (research in this field stemmed from the observation made by shepherds in the Auvergne that sheep which had grazed on broom were proof against viper bites; it was in fact discovered that sparteine, an alkaloid obtained from the common broom, renders harmless the poison of the viper and even of the cobra).

As a diuretic employed in the treatment of dropsy, oedema, albuminuria, renal insufficiency, nephritis, uremia, disorders of the urinary tract, intestinal congestion, malfunction of the liver and the gall bladder, urinary calculi, rheumatism, gout, the parts of the plant used are either the ashes of the whole flowering plant (burn the whole plant and collect the ashes), or the flower alone, either fresh or dried.

The use of the ashes is that most commonly employed by

country healers – it is one of the 'secret remedies'! – following a very old tradition: the remedy of Mlle. Fouquet, a famous seventeenth-century cure for dropsy, was simply ashes of broom macerated in white wine, and the identical treatment was given a century later to the Maréchal de Saxe to cure him of a dropsy for which 'the most famous physicians of the army and the Faculty of Paris had prescribed without success'.

The shock treatment applied in those days was as follows: 500 grammes of ashes and two handfuls of wormwood leaves macerated in 2 litres of Rhenish wine; drink 125 grammes of this wine first thing every morning on an empty stomach. Today we use a less brutal but equally effective prescription: 60 grammes of ashes of broom infused for forty-eight hours in a litre of cold white wine; filter; 60 to 90 grammes of this wine two or three times per day, before meals.

However, the flowers – which Chateaubriand, in his description of springtime in Brittany (*Mémoires d'outretombe*), said 'one might take for golden butterflies' – are more easily employed and give equally excellent results. Picked before they are fully in bloom and dried in the shade, they are prepared by decoction (25 to 30 grammes to a litre of water; boil for one minute), 3 or 4 cupfuls per day to be taken in the treatment of the above-mentioned conditions. As a cardiac tonic, dosage is 1 or 2 cupfuls.

You can also prepare an excellent tea that is diuretic, stomachic, digestive, tonic and hepatic – and a jealously guarded secret by some! – in the following way: into 750 grammes of water, put 15 grammes of broom flowers, 15 grammes of dandelion root, 15 grammes of juniper berries; boil until reduced by a third; drink 2 or 3 cupfuls during the day.

BRYONY, WHITE

Bryonia alba. English mandrake, Bryonia, Mandragora, Wild vine, Lady's seal, Devil's turnips

Those of you who trust homeopathic medicine to alleviate

your ills know it well; this is the plant that gives us *Bryonia*, one of the most important medicines of the medical doctrine founded by Hahnemann since it is a kind of specific for serous inflammatory conditions, whence it is prescribed for broncho-pneumonia, pleurisy, acute articular rheumatism, intestinal colic, constipation.

It could be said that bryony is an 'irritating' plant in every sense of the word. It throws up long climbing stems, with curling tendrils, which invade hedges and twine themselves round trees like tropical liana, draping them with a mantle of rough leaves, rather like vine leaves, with here and there, according to the season, groups of greenish-white star-shaped flowers with five petals, or clusters of berries about the size of a pea, at first green developing into bright red. Its root – yellowish grey on the outside, white inside – resembles a huge turnip (sometimes growing to the thickness of a thigh), and it contains active principles that can, if taken in too large a dose, cause all the symptoms of irritant poisoning (vomiting, gastric and intestinal pains, syncope).

However, it is the root which is the part employed – with great care and in minimal amounts – either fresh (like the carrot, it will keep very well in sand) or dry (it is gathered in autumn or winter, cut into small rings and dried over a stove, on riddles or threaded on to strings).

It possesses strong purgative properties, but is also diuretic and cholagogue, which is why it has been utilized since earliest antiquity (the Egyptians included it in several preparations) both to 'relax the bowels' as well as in the treatment of jaundice, dropsy, rheumatism and acute or chronic catarrh.

To help the liver and the bowel, use a simple decoction (10 grammes of dried root to a litre of water; bring to the boil; leave to infuse for ten minutes; one small (coffee) cupful two or three times a day).

As an expectorant for chronic chest complaints, follow this prescription of Doctor Cazin's: 45 grammes of crushed dried root, 500 grammes of honey, 750 grammes of vinegar; boil all ingredients together for twenty minutes; one coffeespoonful to be taken every two hours.

As a slow-but-sure purgative I suggest the method generally used in country areas; you make a hole in the root and fill it with caster sugar; after twelve hours it will give a syrup that should be taken in the dose of 2 tablespoonfuls per day.

To treat dropsy French peasants also rely on bryony wine: macerate 50 to 60 grammes of dried root in a litre of white wine for four to five days; strain; 2 tablespoonfuls per day before meals (this diuretic wine is also laxative).

Lastly, the fresh root, cut in half and rubbed directly on parts affected by articular rheumatism, will swiftly bring relief, whilst the fresh pulp, applied as a poultice, is recommended for contusions, ecchymosis and attacks of gout.

BUCKTHORN, Alder
Rhamnus frangula.   Black alder, Berry-bearing alder

Its action, today so well known, was first reported in the Middle Ages by Pierre de Crescences who speaks of a small tree whose 'middle bark, taken in meat or drink, marvellously loosens the body'.

It is in fact one of the best remedies for constipation, whether spasmodic or due to biliary insufficiency, which according to Doctor Leclerc can equally well be prescribed, being non irritant and well tolerated, for children or pregnant women or patients recovering from an abdominal operation.

The alder buckthorn is a deciduous shrub or small tree up to 2 or 3 metres high that is common in hedges and scrub and wet, peaty habitats, and is also grown as an ornamental shrub. Its blackish bark has a scattering of lighter, almost white, transverse marks; its ovate leaves are deeply veined and resemble the leaves of the alder; its greenish-white flowers – borne in the axils of the leaves in clusters of two to eight – are succeeded by blue-black berries a little smaller than bilberries.

Its straight flexible stems are used to make wickerwork furniture; from the juice of its berries, mixed with limewater and gum-arabic, is obtained the pigment known as sap-green (also called bladder-green) used for water colours, whilst its wood yields a charcoal used for fine sporting gunpowder.

But we are only interested in the second bark, removed when the shrub is in flower, and dried for at least a year.

To obtain a mild laxative – and at the same time a biliary and renal stimulant – you can either prepare a decoction (boil 2 to 5 grammes of dry bark in 200 grammes of water for a quarter of an hour; remove from heat and leave to macerate for four to six hours; decant and flavour if wished with mint or the zest of an orange; to be drunk at night before retiring or else in three doses during the day, taken before meals); or you can prepare an alder buckthorn wine (100 grammes of dry bark in a litre of red wine; boil for ten minutes; leave to infuse for several hours; one sherryglassful before the two main meals of the day). If you desire a purgative effect, double the amount of bark – using at least 10 grammes – in the decoction.

Used externally, a decoction (100 grammes to a litre of water, afterwards left to macerate as usual) is employed as a lotion or on compresses for persistent skin conditions.

I must stress that *the bark must never be used fresh*: it contains a ferment that induces nausea, vomiting and colic. This ferment only disappears through oxidation for a year in dry air, or else after being kept at a temperature of 100°C for an hour. The bark sold by herbalists is always several years old, for its properties are longlasting.

BURDOCK

Arctium lappa. Lappa, Lappa minor, Thorny burr, Beggar's buttons

This plant is always popular with children, who bombard one another or decorate their clothes with its fruits, covered with little hooks, that they call 'begger's buttons'. It is equally popular with adults, once they know how useful it can be.

Burdock is common in almost every climate (Virgil advised that meadows should be cleared of it, for it is a bad fodder) and adapts to all kinds of soil. It is distinguished by its height (up to 2 metres), its purple flowers and its huge leaves which have a whitish underside. Its stout root (it can be up to 5 or 6 centimetres in diameter) extends vertically into the ground to a depth of one metre.

The leaves and the root are the parts used medicinally – or gastronomically: in fact, in the Mediterranean areas of France, in Italy, in the Scandinavian countries and in Japan the young leaves are used as a salad and the root is eaten boiled and buttered like salsify, although Robert Landry's comment that 'gastronomically its rating is very modest' is admittedly not very encouraging.

Medicinally, on the other hand, it has rated high ever since King Henry III was cured, thanks to burdock, of what some say was syphilis, others a skin disease, by his physician Pena. It is known for a fact that burdock was used by Doctor Cazin to achieve an effective cure of a case of tertiary syphilis, and that it is one of the best remedies for cutaneous conditions. Its uses do not end there, however, as the following list will show.

For gout, rheumatism, arthritic conditions in general: pour three quarters of a litre of boiling water on to 40 or 50 grammes of fresh root cut into slices; leave to go cold; strain; add 4 or 5 spoonfuls of honey and half a litre of milk. This preparation should be drunk half in the morning, the rest in the evening. At the same time apply to the affected joints poultices of fresh leaves cooked in very little water or else fresh leaves macerated for twelve hours in salted water or salt vinegar, 8 to 1,000. Remove the poultice after two or three hours at most.

For furunculosis, acne, impetigo, scabbing and cutaneous eruptions: depurative decoction of root (40 to 60 grammes to a litre of water), 4 or 5 small cupfuls during the day at regular intervals. It is equally advisable to make local applications or lavages either of this same decoction or of another made with fresh leaves (3 spoonfuls of finely-chopped leaves to half a litre of water; boil for ten minutes). The pulp of fresh root, crushed with a little water, is employed in the same manner.

For persistent colds, chronic conditions of the bronchial tubes, diseases of the respiratory tract: fresh leaves, applied between the shoulders with their downy side next to the skin, will soothe any irritation.

For diabetes: a decoction of 60 grammes of fresh root, boiled for ten minutes in a litre of water, will lower the blood-sugar level; 3 cupfuls per day – unsweetened, of course.

For measles: boil 25 to 30 grammes of fresh root in half a litre of water; strain; add some honey and administer the preparation in dessertspoonfuls every five minutes. Within a few hours, eruption is completed and, keeping the young patient warm, he will recover in three or four days.

For blows, bruises, contusions: apply poultices of fresh leaves boiled for five minutes in lightly salted water.

For falling hair: (1) either repeated application of lotion or compresses made with a decoction of fresh leaves (15 to 20 grammes to a litre of water); (2) or daily massage of the scalp with a hair lotion obtained by macerating 100 grammes of fresh burdock root and 50 grammes of fresh nettle root (both chopped into small pieces) for eight days in 500 grammes of rum; strain through a cloth; (3) or rub the scalp morning and evening with a friction composed of equal quantities of decoction (roots or leaves) and wine vinegar.

C

CABBAGE
Brassica oleracea

The cabbage has been called 'the doctor of the poor, the medicine that is the gift of Heaven', and with considerable justification. The following list will give some idea of the many virtues of this, the most common of the cruciferae.

For varicose ulcers, eczema, gangrene, burns, wounds or contusions, carbuncles of phlegmon, bronchitis, pleurisy, rheumatic pains, neuralgia, migraines, sprains or wrenches, sciatica or lumbago, apply cabbage leaves to the affected area, renewing the application morning and evening, using Savoy cabbage when possible and selecting 'the greenest, freshest and most well-nourished', which are the most active. The procedure is as follows: wash the leaves well (especially in these days of chemical agriculture), remove the raised central rib, pound the secondary side ribs with a bottle or some other suitable object; warm the leaves (on a stove or radiator); apply them in several layers to the affected area and keep them in place with a bandage.

For hoarseness, bronchial affections, persistent cough, whooping-cough: drink as much as you wish of a concentrated decoction (five to six leaves to a litre of water; boil for at least half an hour; sweeten with honey); or else 1 or 2 glassfuls per day of cabbage juice with the addition of as much honey as it will absorb; or else three or four times a day, in your own choice of infusion to relieve the chest, take a tablespoonful of red cabbage syrup, which was advocated in the eighteenth century, under the name of 'Boerhaave syrup', as a secret remedy for consumption; this syrup is easy to prepare: pound the leaves of a red cabbage and then squeeze in a cloth, to extract the juice;

weigh the juice, add half its weight in honey and cook over a gentle heat, skimming as necessary, until it acquires the consistency of syrup. For persons with a weak chest, one tablespoonful of this syrup first thing every morning also constitutes an excellent preventive medicine.

For worms in children: first thing in the morning, for three successive days, give 20 to 30 grammes of freshly extracted cabbage juice.

To heal blisters, cook cabbage leaves in milk, leave until cold and then apply to the affected skin.

For lumbago and sharp pains or stitches, boil cabbage leaves in milk until a jelly is obtained; spread the jelly on a piece of cloth or flannel and apply while still very hot; remove after ten hours, by which time the pain has generally disappeared.

You might also – even in this age when new 'miracle' cleaning products appear almost daily – find it useful to know that the heart of a cabbage, cut in half and used like a brush, was one of the household tips known to our grandmothers for renovating and cleaning carpets.

CARLINE
Carlina acaulis

Carline is a European thistle found in the southern half of France, on the sunny slopes of the mountains of Auvergne, the Jura and the Alps, in the poor grasslands of Languedoc and Provence. Peasants use its leaves to curdle milk and in certain regions eat its receptacles which are as fleshy as artichoke heart. They also use it as a barometer: if its flower closes, rain is not far away. The plant is sought after only by goats ... and by those people who know that, once dried, it can be used for decorative floral arrangements that will keep all winter long, like everlasting flowers.

Carline has a thick brownish root, with tap roots, that reaches down to a depth of 20 to 25 centimetres, an almost non-existent stem rarely more than 20 centimetres long, spiky leaves arranged in a tight rosette; its flowers – or rather its flowering capitulum – has a kind of yellowish heart (the fruit-bearing florets will give feathery tufts) surrounded by silvery-white radiating bracts that resemble daisy petals in form; they can measure up to 10 to 15 centimetres in diameter, and when they are shining in the sunlight they look like constellations of stars fallen among the grass.

In olden times carline root was medicinally classed among the alexiterics or alexipharmics, that is to say as an antidote or counter-poison, and for this reason it featured in most of the preparations intended to counteract poisons or snakebite. Belief in its virtue in this respect – a virtue unsubstantiated by experience, incidentally – stemmed from the legend that in a divine revelation 'an angel revealed to Charlemagne that this herb would drive the plague out of his camp', hence the name carline, which evokes the name of the emperor Carolus Magnus.

On the other hand it is known for certain that carline root, gathered in autumn, dried and chopped in pieces, is aperient, tonic, sudorific, digestive and highly depurative. It is prepared by decoction (30 to 40 grammes to a litre of water, boil gently for five minutes, leave to infuse for ten minutes; 3 or 4 small cupfuls a day between meals).

You can also prepare an aperitif and depurative wine (for the treatment of skin conditions such as scabbing, eczema, pruritus) by macerating 10 to 30 grammes of root in a litre of red or white wine for eight days; one port-wine glassful before eating.

CARROT
Daucus carota

When I read, in Professor Binet's words,[1] that the carrot 'gives blood to the body', I seemed again to hear the good Burgundian accent of one of my great-aunts who, each time she gave us a huge plate of carrots (nearly always *à la crême*, to give me a treat), never failed to say, 'Eat plenty, little one: they'll give you nice rosy thighs and a good complexion!' If I followed her advice, it wasn't so much for these happy results, I must admit, nor because I enjoyed the taste. However, it is now

1. *Leçons de biologie dans un parc*, edited by Magnard.

scientifically known that the carrot increases the number of red blood corpuscles and that it is the best food-remedy for the liver . . .

By serving carrots often at your table – whether as a drink (raw carrot juice), as an hors d'œuvre (grated raw carrot salad), as soup or as a vegetable – you are insuring against many troubles (anaemia, liver and bowel disorders, skin diseases, demineralization, etc.), especially if they are organically grown, that is to say without toxic chemical fertilizers. But you can also employ them in the treatment of the following:

For disturbances of growth, infectious diseases, hepatobiliary insufficiencies, cutaneous disorders (notably vitiligo): each day, preferably first thing in the morning, take the juice of three or four medium sized carrots. 'Those who have adopted this habit', notes Doctor Pierre Oudinot,[1] 'have developed an interesting immunity to upper respiratory infections. Those who would not previously get through a winter without getting influenza, colds or bronchitis are no longer subject to these troubles. Chilblain sufferers are also equally favourably affected.'

For constipation: a soup made with a kilo of carrots boiled for two hours in a litre of water and blended in a liquidizer or rubbed through a sieve.

For infantile diarrhoea: 'Carrot soup is a very old, highly respected remedy,' says Léonce Carlier.[2] Here is his recipe: scrape and cut up 500 grammes of good red carrots; boil in a litre of water until soft; blend in liquidizer or rub through a sieve; add sufficient boiling water to bring up to 1 litre and season with 3 grammes of salt; keep in a cool place and use it up within twenty-four hours; stir the soup before filling the feeding bottle; give the semi-solids that remain in the bottle on a spoon. The child should be fed solely on this soup until its

1. *La Conquête de la santé*, ed. Dangles.
2. *Les légumes et les fruits qui guérissent*, ed. La Diffusion Nouvelle du Livre.

first bowel movement which generally occurs on the second or third day of the diet. Then start progressively adding milk to the feeds, diminishing the proportion of soup accordingly, until normal feeding is resumed, at the end of five or six days (during this period of readaptation the soup should be made less and less rich, going from 400 to 100 grammes of carrots to the litre of water).

For loss of voice, persistent cough, asthma: cook 3 carrots in water for a quarter of an hour; grate and then squeeze the pulp in a cloth to extract the juice; add two thirds water and drink hot, half a glassful five or six times a day.

To treat stomach ulcer, drink clear carrot soup at mealtimes (half pound, cut in rings, to 1.5 litre of water; cook for half an hour, season with salt in the usual way), to be drunk hot.

For intestinal worms: for three or four consecutive days eat raw carrots before taking a more powerful vermifuge; the effect of the latter will be more certain and more complete.

To relieve pain from burns and prevent the formation of blisters, to soothe itching in skin diseases (dartre, pruritus, eczema), to lessen the stabbing pains of varicose ulcers, abcesses, whitlows and boils: apply poultices of the pulp of freshly-grated carrots.

To clear the complexion, get rid of blotches and small spots, combat wrinkles: make a beauty mash with raw carrots, including the skin, grated and moistened with lemon juice; leave on for half an hour.

I would lastly like to make two culinary recommendations: (1) carrots should be scraped or brushed, never peeled (the outer part is the most rich in active principles); (2) carrots make an excellent natural colouring for sauces and clear soup: dry some small carrots in the oven, until they have turned dark brown, and store in a dry place until required.

CELANDINE, GREATER

Chelidonium majus. Garden celandine, Swallow-wort,
Felonwort, Tetterwort

Nowadays the only people who still maintain that swallows
pick a sprig of celandine and rub it on the eyes of a fledgling in
danger of blindness are a few peasants who, in the nicest
possible way, want to take a rise out of visiting town-dwellers
and romantically inclined holidaymakers.

There is no more evidence to support this ancient legend than
the belief that a sprig of basil placed under a stone will turn into
a scorpion. Nobody has seriously believed such tales since the
Middle Ages. True, Parkinson quotes Dioscorides and Pliny
as saying, 'It tooke that name from Swallowes that cured their
young ones eyes, that were hurt, with bringing this herb, and
putting it to them.' However, in Pliny we also read: 'Both
Celandines doe flower in the Spring, about the time that the
Swallowes come abroad and shew themselves unto us, and
those flowers begin to fade again upon the departure of that

bird from us', and in 1565, Matthiolus explained that whilst the name 'celandine' derives from the Greek word *Khélidon*: swallow, this is only because the plant 'first shows when the swallows arrive and withers when they leave'.

A far more serious matter is that, by heedlessly presenting the celandine as a kind of panacea, we run the risk of causing disastrous accidents. In fact, it contains violent poisons: 80 grammes of its juice is enough to kill a big dog and 'the watery extract prepared with the fresh plant', Doctor Cazin tells us, 'is equally poisonous; it causes acute inflammation of the digestive organs and, secondarily, irritation of the nervous system.'

Misled by what they had read or heard about its virtues, some people came to buy some from a herbalist friend of mine – at the same time asking for buttercup, which is also toxic – all ready to make miraculous infusions for themselves. Fortunately for them my friend dissuaded them (which incidentally shows what a monumental error – one might even say what a crime – we are committing if we allow this profession to disappear) and thus saved them from serious trouble.

Celandine is certainly still employed in internal use, but it requires such careful handling, and a simple error in dosage involves such risk that it is better left to doctors to prescribe. It was formerly advocated for plague, blindness (Pliny also says: 'A most holesome hearbe for the eyesight, the Swallows taught us how to use. For with it they helpe their young ones, when their eies be sore, and put them to griefe') and dropsy, and not so very long ago for cancer, whilst it has been variously credited with such magic powers as 'worn in their shoes that have the Yellow Jaundice so as their bare feet tread thereon it will help them of it',[1] and 'he who carries it upon his person together with the heart of a mole will vanquish his enemies and win his lawsuits', and 'it sings when a sick man is going to die and weeps when he is going to recover'.

Today celandine is used in the treatment of dropsy, gravel,

1. John Parkinson (1640) quoting Matthiolus.

abdominal congestion, liver disorders. For the latter, under its botanical name *Chelidonium majus*, it is the favoured homoeopathic remedy: Doctor André Thibault[1] says it is to be recommended for every type of liver trouble 'from simple and temporary congestion to the most serious cirrhosis, especially when pain is felt in the region of the lower corner of the right shoulder blade and the stools are golden yellow'. So if you wish to avail yourself of the therapeutic properties of the celandine, I would advise you to use only the homoeopathic preparation which, because of the infinitesimal amounts involved, can be taken without fear of any danger.

Used externally, however, the fresh plant is irreplaceable: the orange-yellow juice that oozes from the stem when it is cut amply justifies its names of felonwort and tetterwort for, applied daily – and strictly to the affected area only, otherwise it attacks the healthy skin – it will generally cause ugly cutaneous excrescences to vanish within the space of eight days.

You will not have to look far for your raw material for this treatment: the celandine grows everywhere, in hedgerows and on waste land, among rubble and in the cracks of old walls. It can be recognized by its downy stems, its equally downy, much-divided leaves, and its golden yellow flowers with four petals.

CELANDINE, LESSER
Ranunculus ficaria.   Figwort crowfoot, Figwort, Pilewort

The lesser celandine belongs to the large – 150 different species – buttercup family, the Ranunculaceae, a name which derives from *rana*, frog, because they prefer moist and marshy places.

Like its more famous brother, the buttercup or crowfoot, and its sisters, the bulbous buttercup or crowfoot, and the celery-leaved crowfoot, it is distinguished by its brilliant yellow flowers, and also contains in its fresh leaves and stems (although

1. *Initiation pratique à l'homéopathie*, ed. Farnèse.

in a lesser amount, it is true) a highly irritant substance, formerly used by peasants to poison rats, and by beggars to produce highly successful and convincing fake sores, designed to curry sympathy.

The plant is easily identified: it flowers in the early spring, well before the buttercup; its leaves are thick and glossy, ivy- or heart-shaped, with slightly toothed margins, and cover the ground closely like a carpet, for the lesser celandine nearly always lives in colonies; its flowers, with their pointed petals

perched on the tip of the stems which rarely reach more than 10 to 15 centimetres in height, look like gold stars; lastly, its roots consist of small whitish bulbs that look like haemorrhoids, the very affection for which the plant is a successful remedy.

Parkinson says 'the decoction of the leaves and rootes doth wonderfully helpe the piles or hemorrhoides, and also Kernels by the eares and throate, called the King's Evill, or any other hard wennes or tumors', and Thomas Burnet recorded the value of this treatment in 1672, after observing the successful cures obtained by a charlatan who treated his patients by giving them beer in which he had secretly macerated the leaves and roots of lesser celandine, and by recommending external applications of the same plant.

Although commonly prescribed by doctors in olden times, this treatment has since been abandoned in favour of other 'scientific' remedies. But medical opinions leave no doubt as to its results: 'Under its influence (the infusion made with roots),' one reads, 'stools become normal, are passed without pain and accompanied by plenty of mucous; if treatment is continued for a certain length of time, the haemorrhoidal affection loses intensity, and its characteristic signs and symptoms finally disappear.'

The above-mentioned infusion is in fact a decoction: 15 to 20 grammes of root to half a litre of water; boil for one minute; leave to stand for five minutes; to be taken in three doses during the day.

It is generally associated with an external treatment consisting of: either compresses soaked in a more concentrated decoction (30 to 40 grammes of root to half a litre of water) and applied very hot to the haemorrhoids; or applications, morning and evening, of a mild ointment prepared as follows: crush up the fresh roots, gathered in spring or autumn, with three times their own weight of fresh butter or lard; leave this mixture in a stoneware pot or a glass dish for four or five days; then heat gently to melt the fat; strain and press through a cloth, and store in a well-sealed pot.

CENTAURY, LESSER
Erythraea centaurium.   Century, Centory, Feverwort

'A universal purifier' – such it was called – rather exaggeratedly – by the author of an old herbal, who saw in it a specific for contagious diseases, a pre-eminent febrifuge, a vulnerary, detergent, aperient, adding that 'it will also remove obstructions from the viscera, cause the bile to flow, cure jaundice, relieve the liver, strengthen the stomach and kill worms.'

According to legend, the centaur Chairon – who taught surgery to Aesculapius, the god of medicine – was the first to use it to heal a wound Hercules had accidentally inflicted on him with a poisoned arrow. This led to the belief that the plant had magic powers: the Romans used to burn it to drive off snakes, and the Gauls employed it as an antidote.

It grows both on lowland and in mountainous areas (up to 1,400 metres), in clearings, sunny pastures, at roadsides, on sandy soils. Its stems are square, from 25 to 50 centimetres in height, branching only in the upper part, bearing small ovate and opposite leaves; its little rosy-pink flowers, tubular at the base and splaying out into a five-pointed star, form pretty clusters at the top of the stem.

The tops of the flowering stems are gathered and dried when they are in full flower (July to September) to prepare an infusion that is prescribed for the following: for fever (it has replaced quinine at times when cinchona has been in short supply), loss of appetite and poor digestion (as an aperitif, taken before meals, and as a digestive, after meals), hepatic insufficiency and constipation, infection of the bile ducts, anaemia, dropsy, threadworms and ascaris (it is not enough to destroy them, but reinforces the action of real vermifuges), dermatosis.

The usual infusion is prepared with 30 grammes of flowering tips to a litre of water (leave to infuse for five to ten minutes), 3 cupfuls per day, preferably before meals; as the taste is rather bitter, you may add some mint or angelica.

As a tonic and aperient, use centaury wine: 60 grammes of plant in a litre of good white wine, a few juniper berries; macerate for eight days; strain; sweeten (preferably with honey); one wineglassful before meals.

For external use, the decoction (60 grammes to a litre; boil for a few minutes) is prescribed for use as a lotion and on compresses in the treatment of varicose ulcers and torpid wounds; used as a lotion, it is thought to check falling hair.

CHAMOMILE, GERMAN
Matricaria chamomilla.   Single chamomile, Wild chamomile, Pin heads, Scented mayweed

As there are two Germanies, so there are two chamomiles: one, German chamomile, generally grows wild; the other, Roman chamomile, is nearly always cultivated.

Their properties are fairly identical, but opinion is divided as to which is the more efficacious, some holding Roman chamomile to be the stronger, while others give the prize to German chamomile. In fact, experience has shown that they share the honours equally, and I have personally opted for German chamomile because it is pleasant to drink, whereas Roman chamomile appeals less to sensitive palates (I discovered this difference in Switzerland and Germany, where chamomile tea is a popular drink both in restaurants and at home).

So I shall leave the big-headed Roman chamomile to those who like to suffer when they drink their herbal tea, and concentrate on German chamomile, which is anyway the one so praised by the ancients: the Egyptians dedicated it to the sun because of its effectiveness against fevers; Dioscorides and Galen also prescribed it for fevers, as well as for agues and female disorders (whence its botanical name *Matricaria chamomilla*).

It grows on all types of soil, even on rubble. It is an annual plant – whereas Roman chamomile is a perennial – classified as a weed by agriculture manuals. It grows to a height of up to 60 centimetres; its stems are erect and branching; its leaves are small, release an odour when crushed, and doubly pinnate ('bipinnatified' botanists call it), their denticulations calling to mind certain ferns and seaweeds; its flowers are like small-scale daisies, with a markedly convex yellow centre, shaped like a sugar-loaf, and a circle of white petals bent backwards around it like a ballet dancer's tutu; flowering time is from June to September; the flowers are the part of the plant that is used, gathered just before they are in full bloom and dried in the shade below 35°C (it is said that their odour prevents bees from stinging anyone collecting honey).

In olden times physicians considered chamomile a sovereign remedy, prescribing it frequently, but in much more concentrated amounts than those so often used today, which result in a tea that is 'totally actionless' according to Doctor Leclerc, who defines it as 'an anaemic mixture obtained by parsimoniously scattering a few flowers on the surface of an ocean of hot water'.

This is how to make sensible use of chamomile:

For sluggish digestion, flatulence, digestive difficulties, insomnia: an infusion (5 to 10 grammes of dried flowers to 100 grammes of water (one cupful); leave to infuse for ten to fifteen minutes) to be drunk preferably *before eating*.

For fever, trigeminal neuralgia, influenzal aches and pains, premenstrual migraines, painful menstruation: a concentrated infusion (one tablespoonful to 100 grammes of boiling water; leave to infuse for an hour; strain and press through a cloth) –

'the pains are relieved in less than an hour', says Doctor Leclerc. You may add a few drops of lemon juice which lightens the colour of the tea and apparently also reinforces its action.

For cramps, rheumatic pains and gout pains: prepare chamomile oil by putting 50 to 60 grammes of flowers into a glass jar with half a litre of olive oil; cork or stopper the jar; expose to the sun for two or three days, then macerate for two hours in a *bain-marie*, covered, stirring from time to time; strain and press. To be used very hot as a friction, on the affected areas. The same oil, applied hot on compresses around the throat, is prescribed for loss of voice.

As tonic and aperient: in a litre of good wine (red or white) macerate for ten days 50 grammes of flowers, 10 grammes of orange or lemon peel (from fruits guaranteed untreated with diphenyl, a highly toxic substance currently in use to prevent fruit going rotten in storage), 10 to 15 lumps of sugar (preferably brown sugar); strain; one port-wine-glassful before meals.

To combat inflammation of the eyelids, conjunctivitis, skin infections (scabbing, eczema): bathe, or apply on compresses, with a decoction of 50 to 60 grammes of flowers to a litre of water, bring to the boil and leave to infuse for about twenty minutes. Added to the bath water, this decoction relaxes the body and soothes away tiredness; it also soothes haemorrhoids, pruritus and rheumatic pains.

Lastly, blondes can take advantage of a beauty secret known to the women of central Europe: shampooing with a litre of water in which a sachet containing 100 grammes of flowers has been boiled for twenty minutes will impart magnificent golden lights to the hair.

CHERRY
Prunus cerasus

I always have a stock of this remarkable diuretic 'which succeeds where the chemical drugs prescribed by doctors have failed'.

I keep the 'earring' cherries – chemically untreated, otherwise there would be a risk of making an infusion of insecticide – the only problem being to dry them properly, so that they do not rot and become unusable.

We have the Roman general and gastronome Lucullus to thank for bringing the cherry tree back from the kingdom of Pontus and introducing it into Europe. Cherries are not only delicious to eat but also extremely good for you, because they are rich in vitamins. Crushed and applied to the skin, they also tone up tired tissues, and applied to the forehead they can cure migraine. Their peduncles – to use the correct word – are invaluable in the treatment of inflammation of the urinary tract (renal colic, cystitis), influenza, jaundice, arthritis, rheumatism, gout, dropsy.

The best way to prepare the decoction is as follows: macerate 30 to 50 grammes of cherry stalks to a litre of cold water for twelve hours; boil for a few minutes; pour directly, while boiling, on to half a pound of whole cherries or else apples cut into rings (according to the season); leave to macerate for a further twenty minutes; strain through a cloth, squeezing gently; 4 or 5 small cupfuls a day.

CHERVIL
Anthriscus cerefolium or **Choerophyllum sativum**

In the Middle Ages, chervil was prescribed for 'clearing the liver and the kidneys, encouraging the elimination of urine and gravel, facilitating the movement of fluids, stimulating circulation and purifying the blood', in the treatment of jaundice, green-sickness and puffiness, and in fomentation on the stomach in the treatment of colic. Women in labour were bathed with it, as were areas of incipient erysipelas or inflammation; it was administered after falls and violent blows to dissolve blood-clots.

Of all these virtues, those which experience has substantiated and which are still medicinally utilized are its qualities and action as stimulant, diuretic and resolvent. It is therefore prescribed for internal use in the treatment of circulation disorders, liver complaints, jaundice, chronic catarrh, lymphatic congestion, urinary disturbances, visceral obstructions; for external use in the treatment of skin conditions, inflammation of the eyes, haemorrhoids.

It is always employed fresh, for drying almost completely takes away its active principles – just as cooking takes away its aromatic taste, which is why it should never be cooked when used in the kitchen.

The infusion (30 to 40 grammes to a litre of boiling water; cover; leave to infuse for ten minutes) is taken in the amount of 3 cupfuls per day, preferably between meals.

Used externally, the decoction (40 to 60 grammes to a litre of water; bring to the boil and leave to infuse for half an hour) is used as an eyewash or compress (three times a day) for ophthalmia and inflammation of the eyelids. It is also utilized as a facial beauty treatment (lotion or compresses) for it keeps the skin supple and delays the appearance of wrinkles.

Chervil – cooked for ten minutes in milk or crushed fresh – applied on a poultice will soothe painful haemorrhoids.

But above all include as much of it as you can, as often as you can, in your food. It can be sprinkled, finely chopped, on hors d'œuvres, salads, vegetables; or added to soups, as in this delicious recipe which is one of my own favourites: peel some potatoes and boil with a suggestion of garlic; blend or rub through a sieve and return to the water in which they were cooked, adding 1 or 2 spoonfuls of fresh cream, return briefly to the heat and, just before serving, add a good handful of finely chopped chervil.

CHICORY, WILD
Cichorium intybus.   Succory

The much vaunted use of chicory as a substitute for coffee is already public knowledge, so I do not need to stress the tonic, restorative, depurative and digestive virtues of this beverage, which is prepared with the dried and roasted root of the plant. It is certainly an excellent alternative for those who find coffee does not agree with them.

Nevertheless I fully concur with Doctor Leclerc's opinion that: 'It is claimed that this substance, mixed with real coffee, will take away its harmful effects; what is much more certain is that it transforms the most delicious mocha into a bitter pharmaceutic potion that makes a gourmet's taste buds stand on end.'

That said, it must be admitted that chicory is still a valuable friend – 'the friend of the liver' Galen called it – and we would be wrong to neglect it in its wild form whilst appreciating the garden variety of wild chicory, namely the endive.

Chicory is not a plant over-endowed by nature. It has a skeletal look about it, with its stiff angular stalks that can grow up to a metre in height and that seem desiccated even before they are picked, their stumpy leaves attached to the angles of the stems with all the industrial grace of a Calder 'mobile'. The basal leaves, arranged in a rosette, are bigger so it is easier to distinguish their lobes, which are similar to those of the thistle leaf. Its brownish root carries tap-roots and is very brittle (which is why it is better to gather the roots after it has rained – preferably in September – particularly as chicory tends to grow in dry stony soils: embankments, road-sides, waste places). Its flowers are the only part of the plant with any charm: they are composed of some fifteen petals with toothed edges like a minuscule fringe which, from July to September, according to when they reach full bloom, form small bright blue bells or rosettes.

All parts of the plant are utilized, including the root, fresh or dried in the shade, gathered when the plant is in flower. It is prepared as a decoction (15 to 30 grammes to a litre of water; boil for five minutes, then leave to infuse for ten to fifteen minutes) and taken in the amount of 3 cupfuls per day, to be drunk before meals.

It sharpens the appetite, combats anaemia, stimulates the stomach and the bowel, purifies the blood, the liver, the spleen and the kidneys; in short it gives our body a good clean-out and has a generally invigorating action.

It is therefore recommended to persons troubled with digestive disturbances (discomfort and pain after meals, chronic constipation, etc.); to those who are overworked or who have overtaxed their strength; to anyone suffering from urinary infections; to diabetics (it lowers the blood-sugar level); for dropsy, gout, arthritis; for dermatosis (spots, eczema, etc.) due to poor elimination of waste products from the cells; lastly, and especially to all who have any of the conditions due to liver disorders (congestion, calculus, jaundice or simple biliary insufficiency), for its action in this field has been scientifically established: it is known that an intravenous injection of a solution of chicory will double and even quadruple the amount of bile excreted in half an hour.

Lastly, here are some of the ways in which our grandmothers employed it.

As an ideal depurative for infants and children: 'chicory syrup', prepared by gently simmering, until it acquires a syrupy consistency, 500 grammes of juice extracted by crushing fresh roots and then strained, with 500 grammes of sugar; store in a tightly stoppered bottle; one coffeespoonful from one to three times a day, according to age.

As a mealtime drink for persons suffering from skin diseases: an infusion of dried leaves (10 to 15 grammes to a litre of water; bring to the boil, leave to infuse for ten minutes), as much as wished.

For jaundice, boil 30 to 40 grammes of plant (leaves, stem and root) to a litre of water for five minutes; press and strain through a cloth; 3 port-wine glassfuls per day, and with each glassful eat a leaf of sage; to be repeated for three consecutive days.

To tone up paralysed limbs and 'arrest shrivelling and wasting': rub the affected limb once or twice a day with alcohol in which fresh chicory root cut into rings (one large handful per litre) has been macerated for one month (stirring from time to time).

COLTSFOOT
Tussilago farfara. Coughwort, Horsehoof, Foal's foot, Bull's foot, Hoofs

A much vaunted remedy in ancient times, and in popular use for centuries, with the advent of chemical drugs coltsfoot was consigned to oblivion. 'But', as one of its advocates wrote a hundred years ago, 'there are weighty reasons why we should bring it back into use.'

This has yet to come about, but nevertheless those who have continued to use it throughout the fluctuations in therapeutic fashion – which is as changeable as that other fashion! – are now more faithful to it than ever; I am speaking of country folk who every spring regularly lay in a stock of coltsfoot against the coming winter, and homoeopaths for whom *Tussilago* is a decongestant and expectorant of the thoracic cavity. Follow their example: you will not regret it.

Coltsfoot is easily found. It is common everywhere, on sandy and especially on clay soils; it can be seen by streams and rivers, in ditches, on the edges of woodland, on embankments, in waste places and even in the mountains, on scree and stony ground up to a height of over 2,000 metres. It often covers large patches of ground, for its thick perennial rootstock has many burrowing off-shoots.

Its golden yellow flowers, which resemble the flowers of the dandelion, appear with the first fine weather, borne singly at the top of a stem 15 to 20 centimetres in height and covered with long pinkish woolly scales. The leaves appear later, when the flowers have faded and become heads of soft down. Because of this unusual characteristic, in the Middle Ages coltsfoot was aptly named *filius ante patrem*, which means 'the son before the father'. These late-developing leaves are very distinctive: large and hoof-shaped, glossy green on the upper surface and coated with cottony down beneath, as if they had been floured (which is the meaning of *farfara*), with angular teeth on the margins.

The flowers and the leaves contain the same active principles (mucilage, tannin, resin, mineral salts); it therefore makes no difference whether you gather the former in March (dry in the shade) or the latter from May to July, since they are used in an identical way: 30 to 40 grammes of dried flowers or leaves to a litre of cold water; leave to soak for five minutes; bring to the boil; leave to infuse for ten minutes; strain through a cloth or some cotton wool to eliminate the down which would be irritant; 3 to 5 small cupfuls per day, sweetened preferably with honey.

This decoction is pectoral, demulcent, expectorant and has a restorative action on inflamed and ulcerated mucous membranes. It is therefore prescribed for all complaints of the respiratory tract: tracheitis, laryngitis, bronchitis, colds, side-effects of influenza, acute or chronic catarrh, smokers' cough. Because of its action on the mucous membranes it can also be very helpful in the treatment of conditions such as gastritis and enteritis.

Employed externally, the dried leaves, smoked as a cigarette, give relief to asthmatics (formerly the leaves were burnt on hot embers so that the smoke could be breathed by 'those who cannot get their breath without holding their neck straight'); mixed with woodruff [1] it makes an excellent tobacco used for smoking in pulmonary complaints, and believed to fortify the chest and lungs.

Used fresh, crushed into a little honey to form a poultice, they are good for badly-healing wounds, ulcers, erysipelas; for a long time they were applied to the neck to cure scrofula of 'king's evil', the glandular swellings that the king used to cure by touching them on the day of his coronation ... the donkey's hoof replacing the king's hand, one might say ...

COMFREY

Symphytum officinale.   Blackwort, Nipbone, Knitbone, Consolida, Bone set

Helping tissues to knit together is, obviously, the principal virtue of comfrey. Pliny affirmed that if comfrey root were boiled together with minced meat, the meat would at once knit together into a single piece, and ancient medical treatises held it to be 'good for closing up wounds'. For thousands of years it has been employed to promote healing of wounds and ulcers as well as to help fractured bones to knit together; it is for the latter purpose that it is retained in homoeopathy, which defines

1. See page 315.

Symphytum officinale as 'an important remedy in cases of bone injury'.

Comfrey grows to a height of up to 80 centimetres and is found chiefly in moist meadows and damp shady places, by streams and ditches. Its stiff, angular and hollow stalks are

covered with rough hairs as are the under surfaces of the long, pointed alternate leaves; its flowers, which may be pink, mauve, white or cream, have a five lobed corolla tube, and form tight little clusters that droop from the top of the stem, which is also very downy. Its thick root, black on the outside, white and sticky inside, is the only part used, fresh or dried.

In a maceration prepared cold or at a temperature of no higher than 30°C (100 to 150 grammes of root chopped in pieces to a litre of water, leave to macerate for about three hours, 3 or 4 cupfuls per day), it is prescribed for its emollient, cooling and astringent qualities as a remedy for haemoptysis, diarrhoea, enteritis, dysentery, and also for stomach ulcers, as it 'favours the development and growth of new tissues' on the inside as well as the outside of the body.

Hence it is employed, in external use, on compresses (made either with fresh grated root or dried powdered root mixed with water) for taking the sting out of burns and scalds, knitting wounds, hastening the healing of twists and sprains, soothing inflamed joints (gout), resorbing haematoma resulting from a blow or a fall, and lastly in the treatment of phlebitis.

This story from the Middle Ages testifies to its astringent virtues. A servant girl, on the eve of her wedding, prepared herself a bath containing a strong decoction of comfrey in order to recover her long-lost virginity; having omitted to inform her mistress of the purpose of this operation, the lady plunged into the same bath – water was scarce in those days! – and the results were such that her husband 'was not a little surprised to discover that his wife was a virgin once more . . .'

CORNFLOWER

Centaurea cyanus.   Blue knapweed, Bluebottle, Bachelor's button, Blue bonnet, Hurt sickle

For the Russians, the cornflower perpetuates the memory of a handsome young man beguiled by a nymph, who led him off into the golden fields of ripening corn, where she jealously changed him into a plant so that he would never charm another. The unhappy victim was named Vassili or Basil, which is why the Russian name for the cornflower is *basilek.*

For the Greeks, it was a child poet named Cyanos, who sang of the earth and its riches, whom the goddess Flora changed into a cornflower after his death, so that mankind would forever remember the poet who had so beautifully sung the praises of nature.

However, whilst the legends that surround the origins of the cornflower vary from one end of Europe to the other, its medicinal usage is the same everywhere; it not only pleases the eye but is known to protect the eyesight.

As a mild decoction (2 to 3 grammes of dried flowers in 100 grammes of cold water; bring slowly to the boil; leave to stand for ten minutes) it is employed tepid as an eyewash or on compresses in the treatment of conjunctivitis, irritation of the eyelids and weakness of the sight (the ancients claimed – there is no proof of it – that it 'little by little consumes the white specks on the eye').

Tradition has it that the cornflower should be prescribed especially for blue eyes whilst the plantain – which has brown seeds – should be prescribed for black eyes. The best solution, if the colour of your eyes is indeterminate, is to follow this prescription given by Professor Binet: pour 150 grammes of boiling water on to 10 grammes of plantain leaves, 5 grammes of cornflower flowers, and 5 grammes of melilot flowers; leave to infuse for quarter of an hour; strain through a cloth, squeezing gently.

The decoction of cornflower flowers is also prescribed as a mouthwash for inflammation of buccal mucosa (gingivitis, ulcerous stomatitis, aphtha), and constitutes an excellent lotion for the face, refreshing, toning and restoring firmness to the skin 'as well as any skin lotion with a famous name and learned formula', in the words of the Swiss herbalist Jos. Triponez.[1]

The cornflower is also employed internally; an infusion of dried flowers (20 to 30 grammes to a litre of water, one cupful three times a day before or between meals) is recommended for inflammation of the kidneys, gout, rheumatism (in the north a special antirheumatic beer is made by macerating 25 grammes of dried flowers or powdered whole plant in a litre of beer for several days – one glassful before meals); its seeds (2 grammes in a little honey, to be taken first thing in the morning) are purgative and also prescribed for jaundice (4 grammes in honey, four consecutive days).

1. *Trésors au bord du chemin*, Editions edit. Cherix et Filanosa S.A., Nyon.

COUCHGRASS

Triticum repens.   Twitchgrass, Quickgrass, Twitch, Squitch

Couchgrass is both a curse and a blessing – certainly the most difficult weed to extirpate, but also an invaluable aid to health.

Peasants and Sunday gardeners are all familiar with its extensive and vigorously creeping rhizome – erroneously called 'roots' – that looks like yellowish-white string. They know that if they leave the tiniest scrap of it in the soil it will soon send up a pretty, bright-green slender leaf, fast followed by several others, then a stem will develop that later gives a flattened ear of separate grains whilst other offshoots from the rhizome are repeating the same phenomenon all around.

The young stems and leaves (which dogs and cats instinctively eat as a purgative, since it induces vomiting) according to Fourcroy, the celebrated physician-chemist of the time of the Revolution, 'actively yet gently prevent the formation of gall-stones'. In fact it has been observed that whilst butchers frequently find gall-stones in the gall-bladder of beef cattle during the winter, they never find any once spring has come and the cattle are grazing plenty of couchgrass in the pastures. It is also known, as Doctor Cazin has noted, that 'in olden times, when people were overheated by the dissipated life they led in winter, suffering from gout, gall-stones, haemorrhoids, scabby skin conditions, acne, etc., in the spring they would take herb juices, lead a sober life, and feel all the better for it'.

These 'juices' were generally composed of the leaves and young stems of couchgrass, dandelion leaves and plantain leaves, in equal quantities, pounded together to extract their sap, which was swallowed several days running, preferably on an empty stomach, in doses varying from 100 to 500 grammes. Why not revive this tradition?

You can also take couchgrass sap by itself (30 to 100 grammes in the course of a week), or else incorporate a good handful of fresh leaves, chopped like fine herbs, in your salad each day.

These two prescriptions are particularly advocated for the treatment of biliary insufficiency, calculus and gravel.

As for the rhizome (gathered in spring or in autumn, the times of the year when its active principles are at their maximum, washed, thoroughly dried in the sun – or in the oven – and cut up into pieces), it can be used throughout the year to make an infusion which for centuries was the classic drink given to patients in hospitals.

Prescribed by Dioscorides for difficulty in urinating, praised by Pliny as a specific for urinary calculus and ulcers of the bladder, considered in the eighteenth century to be one of the most powerful dissolvents used in the treatment of cholelithiasis, couchgrass is recommended for gout and rheumatism, for disorders of the kidneys and the bladder (renal colic and cystitis in particular), for congestion of the liver, jaundice and bladder stones, inflammation of the stomach and the bowel, inflammatory fevers, cutaneous eruptions, chronic catarrh of the respiratory tract.

It would obviously be an exaggeration to say that all these troubles vanish as if by magic, but what is certain is that couchgrass treatment always – and within a fairly short lapse of time – brings real relief, and if continued will often lead to the complete disappearance of the symptoms.

The average dose is from 3 to 5 cupfuls a day of a decoction prepared as follows: soak 30 grammes of rhizome for several hours, then boil for one minute; discard the first water, which is very bitter; lightly crush the rhizomes before returning them to 1.25 litres of hot water; boil until reduced to a litre and leave to stand until cool. To counteract the bitter taste one can add, towards the end of boiling, 10 grammes of liquorice (previously soaked at the same time as the couchgrass) and, just before taking, add a slice of lemon or orange to lend fragrance to the infusion.

CRANE'S BILL
Geranium robertanium.   Herb Robert, Nightingale

There are geraniums and geraniums, or in other words, true geraniums and false. And, by a curious paradox that complicates matters even more, it is the false that are generally called geraniums while the true geraniums are known by other names . . .

The false are the 400 or so species that are cultivated, either for their ornamental value which assures them of pride of place on balconies and in gardens, or for their aromatic properties which are utilized in perfumery; these florist's 'geraniums' are in reality species of *Pelargonium*. The true geraniums are those of which some hundred species grow wild, on old walls and rocks, on the edges of woodland, in the hedges and shady meadows of temperate countries, commonly known by the names of herb Robert, crane's bill, heron's bill or stork's bill.

All these species actually belong to the geranium family; they all have an identically-shaped fruit that resembles the long tapering bill of the crane or stork, and their very names, derived from the Greek, point up this similarity, geranium deriving from *geranos*, crane and *peragos*, stork.

The ancients were familiar with the wild geranium, which is the one that interests us (the cultivated geranium – the pelargonium – was only imported into Europe from the Cape in 1690). They called it *ruberta* (from *ruber* – red) because its hairy stems, 30 to 50 centimetres high, are reddish, because its slightly hairy, deeply-cut leaves, like those of the chervil or the anemone, are often tinged with red, and because its flowers, with their five petals, which appear in groups of 2 or 4 at the top of the stem, are reddish-pink. They used it as a remedy for ophthalmia, milk retention in the breasts, quinsy (inflammation of the tonsils and angina), and held it to be a vulnerary capable of mending fractures and making cancers disappear.

In fact the whole plant, picked while in flower (from May to July) and dried in the shade, is prescribed for gastric ulcers, diarrhoea, internal haemorrhages, metrorrhagia, haemoptysis, gastro-enteritis, diabetes (it lowers the blood-sugar level), prepared in a decoction as follows: 40 to 50 grammes of dried plant to a litre of water; leave cold to soak for a few minutes, then bring gently to the boil; leave to infuse for fifteen minutes; 3 or 4 cupfuls per day, before or between meals.

Used externally, a more concentrated decoction (100 grammes to a litre of water) is recommended as a gargle and mouthwash for inflammations of the throat and mouth (angina, stomatitis, gingivitis, glossitis, aphtha), and as a lotion or compress for eye inflammation, skin irritations, facial neuralgia, ulcers and torpid wounds.

Peasants crush the fresh leaves – which give off an unpleasant odour comparable to the smell of a he-goat or the urine of someone who has eaten asparagus – to make healing compresses when they hurt themselves while working in the fields, and they also crush them between their fingers to keep off mosquitoes.

CYPRESS

Cupressus sempervirens.   Evergreen cypress

The cypress has a bad name, being associated as it is with cemeteries, and this is why Doctor Leclerc, praising its therapeutic effects, recommends other members of his profession to prescribe it under its Latin name, so as not to put any gloomy thoughts into the patient's mind.

Its reddish-yellow wood, hard, scented and rot-proof, was used by the Egyptians for making sarcophagi and by the Greeks for sculpting statues of the gods. The Assyrians used its leaves and its fruits to soothe painful haemorrhoids, for which it was also prescribed by Hippocrates who added uterine conditions, and Galen, who added diarrhoea. Later it was known as a febrifuge particularly advocated for quartan agues.

Its present uses are much the same, although nowadays we

employ only the fruits or cones, picked while they are still green.

Used internally, for its astringent and above all its vaso-constrictive properties, it is prepared by decoction (20 to 30 grammes of finely crushed cones to a litre of water; boil for five minutes; leave to infuse for ten minutes; one cupful, a quarter of an hour before meals, midday and evening) and prescribed for menopausal disorders, conditions of the venous system (varicose veins, haemorrhoids), metrorrhagia, incontinence of urine.

Used externally, the decoction (prepared in the same way, but with 50 grammes of cones) is applied as hot compresses on painful haemorrhoids, to be kept on for a few minutes; used as a footbath (ten to fifteen minutes) it combats offensive perspiration.

D

DAISY
Bellis perennis.   Herb margaret

The daisy bears witness to the wisdom that assures the balance of nature, for agronomists have discovered that it manufactures lime in the soil where it grows, and grows precisely in those soils that are lacking in lime.

Formerly the daisy was held in high repute. Not only were its fresh leaves eaten as salad, together with dandelion leaves, offsetting the bitter taste of the latter, or else cooked as a vegetable to be served with meats (thus pleasing the palate and loosening the bowels at the same time), but it was also widely used in medicine as vulnerary, emollient, depurative and diuretic. Today it no longer has a place in materia medica, except for homoeopaths and country folk who still consider it a salutary treat in springtime (it 'cleans the blood' at the end of winter) as well as a well-tried medication.

For complaints of the respiratory tract, rheumatic pains, skin diseases (eczema, scabbing), painful or over-heavy menstruation, use a mild decoction (30 to 40 grammes of fresh leaves and flowers to a litre of water, bring gently to the boil; boil for one or two minutes; leave to infuse for ten minutes; 3 cupfuls per day, between meals). This same decoction, which the patient should drink very hot while remaining in bed under as many blankets as possible, is also believed to stave off incipient pleurisy.

Another well-known prescription for relieving head pains resulting from a fall, a blow or concussion of the brain consists of macerating 2 handfuls of fresh plant (leaves and flowers) in a litre of white wine for twenty-four hours and drinking a glassful each morning. This treatment is also prescribed for dropsy, rheumatic pains, contusions, sprains, ecchymosis.

It is interesting to note that *Bellis perennis* – which together with *Arnica* and *Calendula* forms the trio of vulnerary plants in homoeopathy – is prescribed in fact for stiff neck, lumbago, contusions and painful aches and general stiffness.

Lastly, chewing fresh leaves will cure aphtha and mouth ulcers, and the infusion of dried flowers (15 grammes to a litre of boiling water; leave to infuse for ten minutes) is recommended in the amount of 2 cupfuls per day to help combat arterial hypertension.

DANDELION

Taraxacum officinale or **Taraxacum dens leonis.** Blow-ball, Milk gowan, Priest's crown

Legend has it that the dandelion was born of the dust raised by the chariot of the sun, whence the form and shape and behaviour of its flowers which open at dawn and close at the approach of dusk.

The dandelion is a botanist's delight, for it belongs to that rare group of plants that are parthenogenetic, which means capable of producing viable seed without outside fertilization. Since long before the fashion for horoscopes it has been used by unmarried maidens to tell their fortune: the number of times they have to blow in order to disperse its down is the number of years they will have to wait for a husband.

Its milky sap has been held to be a specific for disorders of the eyesight (its scientific name derives from two Greek words: *taraxis*, eye disorders, and *akeomai*, to cure), but the plant is now used only for its remarkable diuretic properties as well as its depurative action and beneficial effect on the functions of the liver.[1] It was its latter function that Matthiolus singled out

1. Parkinson says it is also called Pisse a bed; and 'very effectuall for the obstructions of the liver, gall and spleene, and the diseases that arise from them, as the jaundise and the hypochondriacal passion, it wonderfully openeth the uritorie parts, causing abundance of urine ...' (*Translator's note.*)

in the sixteenth century: 'The decoction of the whole plant', he wrote, 'is beneficial to sufferers from jaundice. Magicians say that if a person rub himself all over with it, he will everywhere be welcome and obtain what he wishes . . .

Whilst its magical properties remain unsubstantiated, the same is not the case with its medicinal virtues, for modern scientific investigation has established that dandelion extract doubles and even quadruples the volume of bile excreted in the space of half an hour. The more credit is therefore due to homoeopathy, which did not wait for such proof before prescribing *Taraxacum* to promote drainage in cases of congestion of the liver or hepato-biliary insufficiency.

Peasant good sense, founded on results, has seen to it that country people have remained faithful to the dandelion, which is all the more creditable in view of the dismissive attitude of learned doctors. You too can follow their example – as I do myself – and trust this valuable plant to protect your health.

A course of dandelion treatment in the spring will tone up your whole body, cleansing it of the waste matter deposited by the heavy clogging food eaten during the winter. Eat it raw as a salad (even more delicious if served with a sprinkling of little bits of fried bacon – providing one has a good digestion) or cooked, chopped and tossed in butter or meat juice, which makes a tastier vegetable than spinach. Include it all the year round in your soup along with a few potatoes, leeks, cabbage leaves, nettle and plantain: you will find these 'green soups' as delicious as they are good for your health. (However, do not fall into the error of choosing only blanched heads like endives, for though they may well be more tender, they are less tasty and less rich in the active principles – especially manganese – associated with the presence of chlorophyll.)

Remember too that infusions of its leaves and root (fresh or dried) are tonic, depurative, cholagogue, stomachic and mildly laxative. They stimulate the bladder, drain the liver and kidneys, eliminate cholesterol, urea and uric acid, and are therefore prescribed for hepatic congestion, waning jaundice, skin conditions, sluggish digestion, rheumatism, gout, constipation, diabetes, arteriosclerosis, disturbances of circulation, cellulite.

The decoction of dried plant (the leaves being picked in spring or summer, the root in early autumn) is prepared by soaking 20 to 30 grammes of leaves and the same amount of chopped root for two hours in a litre of cold water; then bring slowly to the boil; boil for only a few seconds, then leave to infuse for fifteen to twenty minutes; 3 cupfuls per day, a quarter of an hour before meals.

The flowers, picked at the moment when they are coming into bloom, are also used as a beauty treatment: one good handful, boiled for half an hour in a litre of water, then strained through a fine cloth, gives a toilet water with which the face is washed morning and evening to remove freckles.

DEADNETTLE, WHITE
Lamium album.   Archangel

As long as it is not in flower, the white deadnettle could easily be mistaken for the true nettle, and is in fact frequently found growing alongside it, since both plants like the same habitat. However, it can readily be identified by touching its leaves, which, unlike those of its neighbour, do not sting, and which are eaten cooked like spinach. From spring to early winter it is easily recognizable by its white flowers that are produced in dense whorls at the axil of the leaves towards the top of the stems.

Generally only the flowers are utilized, for they make an infusion that is pleasanter to the palate. But when it is a matter of treatment, considerations of taste should take second place to results, and this is why I advise you rather to use the flowering tips, dried in the shade, for although they are more bitter they are also more richly endowed with active principles.

The white deadnettle is prescribed for all kinds of catarrh (respiratory tract, urinary passages), hepatic insufficiency (it stimulates the function of the liver), diarrhoea, but it is also a sort of specific for female disorders thanks to its influence on the uterine circulation: painful or scanty menstruation (it helps girls in their early menstrual cycles), metritis, metrorrhagia, leucorrhoea or 'whites' (many are of the opinion that it is irreplaceable in this domain).

It is prepared as a mild decoction: 20 to 30 grammes of flowering tips to a litre of water; boil for one or two minutes; leave to infuse for five minutes; one cupful three times a day before meals. For leucorrhoea, treatment should be continued for at least three weeks.

DOCK

Rumex patienta. Patience dock
Rumex crispus. Curled dock or yellow dock

The two most widespread species – patience dock and yellow or curled dock – grow in woods, meadows, moist places, ditches, along roadsides and hedgerows. They have a tap-root, reddish-brown on the outside, yellowish on the inside, which extends deep into the ground (as much as 50 centimetres); the stem varies from 1.50 metres and 60 centimetres in height; their leaves are alternate, oval, pointed, large and smooth on the former, smaller and somewhat curled on the latter; the greenish flowers, which form a kind of terminal spike, are succeeded by triangular achenes.

The root has a high iron content – it fixes iron present in the soil and converts it into organic iron – and is therefore prescribed for anaemia, chlorosis, general debility, convalescence; in addition, because of its depurative and diuretic properties, it is recommended for chronic skin complaints (scabbing, eczema, etc.), rheumatism, atonic disorders of the digestive tract.

It can be gathered at any time of the year, but if it is to be dried, it is preferable to uproot it towards the end of summer (it should be dried in the sun or in a drying-cabinet, first either cutting it into rings or splitting it lengthwise).

It is prepared as a mild decoction (40 to 50 grammes to a litre of water; boil for five to ten minutes; leave to macerate for the same length of time; one cupful morning and evening. *Rumex crispus* is a homoeopathic remedy principally prescribed for inflammation of the trachea and the larynx, as well as for persistent dry coughs that are provoked by cold air or deep breathing.

Instead of the infusion you can, if you prefer, use dock wine which is made as follows: 180 grammes of root, 6 grammes of liquorice, 3 grammes of juniper, 120 grammes of sugar, 2 litres of good red wine; macerate all ingredients together in a covered receptacle – not made of metal; boil gently in a *bain-marie* until reduced by a third; strain and store in tightly-stoppered bottles. Drink 90 grammes each morning on an empty stomach, for fifteen consecutive days.

Externally the decoction, as a lotion or on compresses, or else poultices of pulped cooked root, are employed as a remedy for scabbing and infected ulcers.

DOG-ROSE
Rosa canina.   Wild briar, Wild rose, Hip tree

The leaves of this countryside version of the queen of flowers are similar to the leaves of the rose; its pink or white flowers with 5 petals are charming; but neither leaves nor flowers are medicinally of much interest. On the other hand the various parts of the hips (commonly called the fruits, although botanists tell us that the real fruits are the hairy achenes contained inside the hip) possess numerous properties.

The down, which surrounds the achenes, and which causes a disagreeable itching when in contact with the skin, is an ideal vermifuge for the treatment of lumbricoid ascaris, parasites that live in the small intestine of humans and pigs: administered on an empty stomach in the dose of 15 centigrams coated with honey, it acts immediately and mechanically on the worms, killing them without causing the least irritation of the intestinal mucosa and without any danger to the affected person. In certain regions, notably Catalonia, mothers make a jam of the hips, including the down, which they give to their children with worms.

The seeds or achenes, dried in the sun and reduced to a powder, are an old remedy for gravel, kidney stones and renal colic: 3 grammes of powder in a small glass of white wine; leave to infuse for seven or eight hours; to be taken half an hour before retiring, stirring well beforehand, on alternate days, preferably when the moon is on the wane.

The fleshy receptacles are gathered in autumn; they are split open to remove the hairy seeds and left to dry in a well-ventilated place below 45°C. They are depurative and therefore recommended to be taken in the spring, to cleanse the blood of the toxins accumulated during the winter. They are tonic and increase the body's resistance to infectious diseases, particularly influenza, by virtue of their high vitamin C content: 100 grammes of hips contain as much as a kilo of lemons. They exert an undeniable action on bleeding gums and also on the intestinal mucosa, and are therefore used in the treatment of diarrhoea. The prescribed dosage for all these complaints is the same: one cupful, after meals, midday and evening, of 3 to 5 grammes of hip rind cut into small pieces to 100 grammes of water, boiled for at least five minutes and left to infuse for the same length of time.

A stronger decoction (75 grammes to half a litre of water, boil for a good half-hour) to which honey is added is recommended for oedema and kidney complaints (calculi, renal colic).

Lastly, here is the recipe for rose-hip jam, of which the peasant women of eastern France, Germany and Switzerland never fail to make a few pots every autumn (it is delicious and constitutes one of the best treatments for looseness of the bowels – diarrhoea, dysentery – for it is mildly astringent): gather the berries when they have already been exposed to a few morning frosts; cut off the two extremities; split in two, remove seeds and hairs; leave in a cool place for forty-eight hours; cook as for ordinary jam in the following proportions: a pound and a half of sugar to a pound of fruit.

E

ELDER
Sambucus nigra.   Black elder, European elder

'In the good old days the elder stood close to every dwelling.
Nowadays this shrubby tree is rooted out almost everywhere,
yet it deserves to and should remain the closest neighbour of
every house, because every part of it can be used: leaves, flowers,
bark and roots.'

It is nearly a hundred years since the Abbé Kneipp wrote
those lines, but, contrary to his desire to see the elder restored
to its place of honour as the 'faithful friend of the family', the
massacre has continued unabated, worse than ever in fact, for
with the fashion for rare and costly conifers, nobody wants to
look out on to such an unfashionable and commonplace shrub.

I do not delude myself: I shall be no more successful than the
Abbé Kneipp in halting the slaughter. (If only the elder were
exotic, expensive and delicate – but it is truly 'at home' here,
common and sturdy.) However, there is no regulation against
hoping that a few will be spared once people realize just how
useful they can be.

Leaves Diuretic and depurative. Here are the Abbé Kneipp's
recommendations: 'When spring comes, do you want to
purify the body-fluids and the blood? Take six or eight elder
leaves, cut them up small like tobacco, and boil them for about
ten minutes. Every morning, one hour before lunch, drink a
cupful of this infusion. It is a simple depurative tea that
cleans out the human machine or body most excellently . . .'

This infusion is of course recommended for skin complaints
(it seems more active than the infusion made with flowers, but
it is less pleasant to the taste – the doctors of the Salernitan

school use only the flower, saying 'The leaf smells bad and the flower smells good').

The fresh leaves, crushed with olive oil, butter or lard and applied to haemorrhoids, will relieve the pain.

Flowers From the end of May to July, they are produced in crowded, flat-topped clusters, or false umbels, creamy-white in colour, with a sweetish scent. They are picked while in full flower and dried in the shade as rapidly as possible (below 30°C) in order to prevent their turning black. They are sudorific, diuretic, febrifuge and anti-rheumatic.

The infusion (10 to 20 grammes to 1 litre of boiling water; leave to infuse for five to ten minutes; 3 or 5 cupfuls per day) is recommended for bronchial catarrh, bronchitis, eruptive fevers (measles, scarlet fever, etc.), rheumatism, gout. One of the best ways of preventing influenza or a cold from developing is, at the first sign of infection, to take a very hot cupful of this infusion – or even slightly stronger if needs be (30 grammes to the litre) – whilst keeping warmly covered in bed, thus inducing a very heavy sweat.

To keep 'in good voice', many ancient herbalists suggested drinking, first thing in the morning, half a glass of white wine in which about 4 grammes of powdered elder flowers had macerated all night.

Used externally, the decoction (50 grammes of dried flower to a litre of water; boil for five minutes and leave to infuse for five or ten minutes) is used as an inhalant for head colds, hoarseness, laryngitis, as an eyewash for conjunctivitis, as a compress for chilblains and erysipelas.

Elder flowers are also used to lend fragrance to wine (mixed with must they give the taste of muscatel) and cider; they similarly transform the taste of apples stored in contact with them; lastly they give an excellent home-made vinegar, known as elder-flower vinegar, which is 'less upsetting to the stomach and healthier than ordinary vinegar', with a subtle taste that appeals particularly to the gourmet.

Here is the recipe for it: put 500 grammes of recently-dried elder flowers into a bottle with half litre of wine vinegar; seal hermetically and leave to stand in the sun for eight to ten days; strain through a fine cloth, pressing well, and then strain through a filter-paper; store in a well-stoppered bottle. (You can use the same method to make vinegar with the flowers of sage and rosemary, pinks, red roses and tarragon leaves.)

Bark   Either in spring before flowering, or in autumn when the leaves are falling, take a knife and gently scrape away the outer grey bark from the young branches in order to remove strips of green bark which lies beneath.

It is employed, preferably fresh (when it is more active), for its strong diuretic and mild laxative properties, prepared by decoction (2 handfuls to a litre of water which is boiled until reduced to half; sufficient for three doses to be drunk first thing in the morning), and used as a remedy for dropsy, urine retention, acute nephritis with oedema, renal colic, rheumatism, gout.

The same afflictions can also be treated by a wine made from the bark: pour 1 litre of boiling wine on to 150 grammes of fresh second-layer bark; cover and leave to infuse for forty-eight hours; strain and sweeten if required; one wineglassful a quarter of an hour before meals, midday and evening.

Berries   The Romans used them for dyeing the hair. Fresh, dried or in jam, they are purgative (one tablespoonful per day). In certain regions they are macerated in spirits or alcohol (45°) (60 to 100 grammes of fresh berries to 1 litre; macerate for fifteen days; press and strain through a cloth) and this tincture is taken as a purgative, 15 to 30 grammes three times a day.

Root   It is also the second layer which is used, in the same proportions and to treat the same conditions as listed above.

In homoeopathic medicine the elder, *Sambucus*, is prescribed particularly for glottal spasm.

There is another smaller variety of elder (rather more than 2 metres high, whereas the common elder grows to a height of up to 8 metres) which has more or less the same uses (the root is the part generally employed: 20 to 30 grammes to a litre of water; cold-soak for an hour; boil for one minute; leave to infuse for ten to fifteen minutes; 3 to 5 small (coffee) cupfuls per day). This is the dwarf elder (*Sambucus ebulus*), sometimes called danewort, Dane's blood, wallwort or ground elder.

ELECAMPANE
Inula helenium.   Aunée (Fr.), Hélen's elecampane, Scabwort, Wild sunflower, Horse elder

Two legends link the elecampane with the beautiful Helen of Troy. One legend has it that she was holding a bunch of elecampane when she was carried off by Paris, the other that the plant was born of the tears she shed.

Hippocrates, Dioscorides and Galen note its beneficial effects on the uterus, the urinary passages and the respiratory apparatus, and it was subsequently discovered to act on the digestive organs. An ancient herbal summarizes its uses as follows: 'It will cause asthmatics to spit and soothe persons suffering from lung disease. It is very useful in sicknesses of the stomach. It is also laxative; it breaks up thickened matter and removes obstructions. For this reason it induces menstrual discharge and suppressed voidances.' Its uses today are still much the same.

The elecampane is a handsome plant with yellow flowers, a kind of small-scale version of our garden sunflower. It grows in copses and damp, shady places, along rivers overhung by alders, in ditches, on the borders of woodland, but it is gradually disappearing and is today mostly found only in gardens – or at the herbalist's.

Its thick hairy stem often reaches a height of over a metre: its long oval leaves are green and ridged with ribs on the upper surface, whitish and covered with soft down on the underneath; its hard, horny root, brown on the outside and white on the inside, can weigh several kilos; it is the only part of the plant that is used, crushed after drying which gives it a greyish colour and an odour of violets.

The highly aromatic infusion (40 to 50 grammes to a litre of water, leave to infuse thoroughly) or the rather bitter decoction (30 grammes to a litre; soak the roots in cold water for at least one hour, bring to the boil and boil for one minute, leave to infuse for ten minutes), 3 cupfuls per day, before meals, will clear the bronchi, soothe coughs, promote expectoration (tracheitis, bronchitis resulting from influenza or not, mucoid asthma, whooping cough) and have a therapeutic effect on digestive disorders (gastritis, enteritis) – the Salernitan school used to say 'elecampane is beneficial to the entrails'.

In the treatment of anaemia in young girls of premenstrual age or suffering from leucorrhoea, the decoction (12 grammes in 125 grammes of water) taken first thing in the morning, is always, according to Doctor Cazin, highly beneficial; in the example he gives: improvement within eight days, cure in a month.

A stronger decoction – 50 grammes to half a litre of water – applied as a lotion or hot compress, will soothe itching from herpes and scabby skin disorders.

Lastly, you can prepare 'elecampane wine' which is aperient, tonic, stomachic, diuretic and a cough syrup. It is made as follows: macerate 80 grammes of root in a litre of good red or white wine for ten days, shaking the bottle frequently; strain and add sugar to taste if desired; one wine-glassful before meals, midday and evening.

ELM
Ulmus campestris.   Common elm, Field elm

In the Middle Ages the elm would stand in the village square before the feudal castle, and under its shade the local judges would mete out justice.

With its imposing height (up to 40 metres), its dark-grey bark with deep, longitudinal furrows, its leaves of a beautiful soft green, rough and harsh above, oval, assymmetrical at the base, with toothed edges, it rivals the oak and the chestnut in majesty. It is common throughout Europe and has been known since ancient times (Dioscorides, Pliny, Galen) for its astringent, depurative and anti-inflammatory virtues, which have led to its use principally in the treatment of skin conditions.

The inner bark only is used, collected in spring from two-year-old branches and dried rapidly in the sun or in shade. It is prescribed in the treatment of skin diseases (acne, furunculosis, pruritus, eczema, scabbing, psoriasis) and also for rheumatism.

Taken internally, drink one cupful, three times a day before meals, of decoction (30 to 40 grammes of chopped bark to a litre of water; cold-soak for quarter of an hour; bring to the boil and boil for eight to ten minutes; leave to infuse for ten minutes).

Used externally, bathe, or better still apply on compresses to, the affected area with a more concentrated decoction (80 to 100 grammes of bark).

EUCALYPTUS
Eucalyptus globulus. Blue gum tree

At the first sign of an influenza epidemic or any sickness in the family, my grandmother would install on the kitchen cooker and the dining-room stove little saucepans in which a decoction of eucalyptus leaves would be kept simmering day and night. We used to smile about it, but looking back I now think she saved us a lot of trouble.

Eucalyptus in fact contains a powerfully antiseptic essential oil composed principally of eucalyptol, and it is certain that this technique of permanent evaporation and fumigation is one of the best ways to ensure a healthy atmosphere in the room and protect the body against winter's contagious diseases.

The whole tree, moreover, exhales an aromatic odour that exerts a healthy influence on those regions where it is extensively grown. It is also a tree that absorbs great quantities of water, which is why, ever since it was first introduced into Europe in 1856 (its native country is Tasmania), it has been utilized to dry up and purify marshy regions that were a breeding ground for fevers. Because of this it is sometimes known as the 'fever tree', a name that is doubly apt, for its leaves, prepared by decoction (15 to 20 grammes to a litre of water; boil for one minute; leave to infuse for ten minutes; 4 or 5 cupfuls per day), are febrifuge and recommended in cases that fail to respond to quinine.

The same decoction (4 to 5 cupfuls per day as above) is also prescribed for influenza and colds, conditions of the respiratory tract, various infections (colibacillus infections, leucorrhoea), because of its antiseptic and bactericidal properties. If inhaled (two or three times a day) it will clear the bronchi and act as an expectorant (persistent cough, whooping cough); it will also relieve congestion and combat inflammation of the mucosa in throat troubles.

The dried leaves, smoked like cigarettes, give good results in cases of asthma.

Eucalyptus is also aperitif and digestive when taken as a wine: macerate 30 to 40 grammes of leaves in a litre of good wine (red or white) for ten to fifteen days, stirring from time to time; press and strain; one sherryglassful before or after meals, according to whether it is to stimulate the appetite or aid digestion.

EYEBRIGHT
Euphrasia officinalis. Euphrasy

Who is right: Doctor Cazin, who considers this plant 'almost totally without virtue' and who criticizes the famous doctors who have praised its effects, or the Abbé Kneipp who declares it to be 'a medicinal plant that strengthens the sight; when all other means have been tried and failed, it will often bring relief to the eyes; I have many times prescribed it with success'?

Not having had the opportunity to test its efficaciousness for myself, I have thought about it carefully and decided in favour of the Abbé because of the weight of the evidence that supports his view.

Eyebright is certainly not able to 'remove all obstacles to the sight', as Matthiolus claimed; it can neither cure cataract nor blindness, and it is doubtful whether 'if the herb was but as much used as it is neglected, it would half spoil the spectacle makers' trade' (Culpeper). On the other hand, long usage and recent studies by German pharmacologists both confirm its therapeutic virtues in the treatment of various eye conditions, notably conjunctivitis, watering of the eyes, mild or chronic ophthalmia, weakness of the eye and failing eyesight.

It is also prescribed for other conditions: in some regions of France it is used as a cough remedy; the Americans use it as a treatment for head colds; the Abbé Kneipp recommends it as 'a good stomachic, aiding digestion and increasing the production of gastric juices'; and *Euphrasia* is a homoeopathic remedy for head colds, eye discharge and nasal catarrh in the early stages of measles, and conjunctivitis when 'the nasal discharge is watery and the watering of the eyes is irritant'.

Eyebright (its scientific name is derived from the Greek *euphraino* – I gladden – one of the Three Graces was called Euphrosyne) is a partially parasitic plant that grows in sunny meadows, grassy clearings, marshes and thickets, preferring poor soils. Its brownish stems, often very branched and hairy, grow to a height of from 5 to 30 centimetres according to situation; its leaves are opposite, oval and pointed, toothed and downy; the flowers, which are unstalked and so form 'ears' at the tip of the stems, are small, pale blue or white, with the upper lip shaped like a helmet and the lower lip divided into three lobes characteristically marked at the base with a yellow spot, darker towards the middle, which looks rather like an eye (a resemblance that, according to the doctrine of signatures so dear to alchemists, proclaims the fact that eyebright acts upon the sight).

The flowering stems (which bloom from June to September), dried in the shade, are the part of the plant that is employed.

Taken internally, for eye conditions, coughs, head colds, digestive difficulties, a mild decoction (30 to 50 grammes to a litre of water; boil for one minute; leave to infuse for five minutes; one cupful three times a day between meals).

Used externally, for eye conditions ('this remedy cleanses the eyes and strengthens the vision,' says the Abbé Kneipp): boil 50 grammes of dried plant in half a litre of water for one minute, then leave to infuse for at least half an hour; strain through a fine cloth; soak a compress, large enough to cover the eyes and temples, in this liquid, and apply the compress for twenty to thirty minutes morning and evening (preferably while lying down), continuing treatment for ten to fifteen days; suspend treatment for ten days, then repeat.

Inevitably the eyebright – like the celandine – has its own charming but fanciful little legend: it was said that the linnet used it to improve its eyesight . . .

F

FENNEL
Foeniculum vulgare or **Anethum foeniculum.**   Hinojo

The common fennel is so well known that there is no need to
describe it. A native of southern Europe, it grows wild on
banks and embankments, on stony ground and rubble in the
Mediterranean areas of France and Italy; but it is cultivated
almost everywhere – even in England and Germany – as a
vegetable garden plant, its leaves being used as a vegetable,
grated fennel root as a salad, and a few fennel seeds or the familiar
dried stalks lending their characteristic flavour to Mediterranean specialities such as red mullet with fennel or the *loup
grillé* of the Côte d'Azur.

There are records of the use of fennel in cooking dating back
to ancient times: the Egyptians, Greeks and Romans incorporated it in their dishes; Hippocrates and Dioscorides recommended it to wet-nurses to activate the secretion of milk, as
well as to persons threatened by blindness; the Chinese and
Hindus used it to neutralize snakebite and scorpion stings;
lastly magicians and sorcerers regarded it as a beneficent herb
and believed that sprigs of fennel, hung from the rafters, would
drive the evil spirits out of a house, whilst the seeds, inserted in
the keyholes, would bar the way to ghosts.

Outside the kitchen – where you can use the leaves (either
fresh and finely chopped like chervil, or dried and powdered)
or the seeds (dried and ground like pepper) for sprinkling on
stews, fish and farinaceous vegetables which are thus rendered
more digestible – fennel has many other uses.

The dried seeds are prescribed for stomach pains, aerophagia,
digestive difficulties, sluggishness, lack of appetite, inflammation of the internal mucosa (bronchitis, gastritis, enteritis,

cystitis, etc.), as an infusion (25 to 40 grammes to a litre of water; leave to infuse for ten to fifteen minutes; one cupful to be taken after the two main meals of the day).

'Fennel seeds', writes the Abbé Kneipp, 'should be in every family medicine chest, for they are a remedy for conditions that occur very frequently; I am speaking of griping pains and flatulence ... A spoonful of fennel should be cooked in a cupful of milk for five to ten minutes and given immediately to the afflicted member of the family, to be drunk as hot as possible ... It generally brings about a rapid improvement, the warmth spreads through the body, easing griping pains and expelling flatulence.' According to Oertel-Bauer[1] this same treatment is also 'a sure and certain remedy for influenza'.

Used externally, the decoction of seeds (30 to 50 grammes to a litre of water; boil for about five minutes) is used in the steam treatment (the head held over the steaming decoction, with a towel over the head forming a kind of tent) of conditions of the eyelids and the eyes; it is also used, lukewarm or cold, for bathing the forehead and the temples, three times a day, to 'strengthen the nerves' and combat chronic headaches and migraines.

Again with the seeds you can prepare an excellent appetite stimulant and tonic recommended for anaemia and general debility: 60 to 80 grammes of seeds macerated for eight to ten days in a litre of good wine (red or white); strain; one wineglassful after meals, midday and evening.

A decoction of fennel root (20 to 30 grammes to a litre of water; boil for five minutes; leave to infuse for a further five minutes) equally stimulates the appetite (one wineglassful before each meal); it is also an excellent diuretic, prescribed by Dioscorides for 'those who can only urinate drop by drop', and recommended by numerous specialists for disorders of the gall-bladder (calculus and biliary insufficiency) and kidney and bladder conditions (one wineglassful after each meal).

1. *La Santé par les plantes*, ed. Alsatia.

FIG
Ficus carica

If there is one tree that can be said to 'belong to the history of humanity', it is certainly the fig. It shares with the vine and the olive the honour of being the most frequently mentioned in the Bible.

It is thought by some that Adam and Eve used its leaves to cover their nakedness (others maintain that this earliest garment was borrowed from the vine). The Egyptians believed that its fruit followed the acorn as the food of our most distant ancestors, and they held the fig in veneration, making use of it in several remedies.

The Hebrews, the Greeks and the Romans cultivated the fig tree – it is said that Romulus and Remus, the future founders of Rome, were left abandoned under a fig tree where they were found by the wolf that suckled them – and if historians are to be believed, many wars have been fought for no other end than the conquest of lands producing such delicious fruit.

Eaten all the year round, fresh or dried in the sun, by Mediterranean peoples, the fig was also used by them as a valuable general remedy. The Old Testament tells us it was used as poultices to cure abscesses on the gums and inflammations of the mouth; it also reports what must be considered one of the oldest cases of healing: in those times, we read in the Book of Isaiah, Hezekiah King of Judah was 'sick unto death' of a serious tumour and Isaiah the prophet had said 'Let them take a lump of figs, and lay it for a plaister upon the boil, and he shall recover', and this being done, he was cured.

Plato called figs the 'philosophers' friends' because they 'strengthen the intelligence' (in the light of recent knowledge, figs are now in fact recommended in cases of physical and nervous debility). Dioscorides recommends eating figs with hazelnuts as a protection against possible poisoning. The Salernitan school declares that the fig 'is nourishing, fattening (we know now that 100 grammes of fresh figs give 100 calories and 100 grammes of dried figs 250 calories), relaxes the bowels, relieves the chest and heals many tumors', uses which are given in the old pharmacopoeia that classes the fig among the four fruits that relieve the chest (together with the date, the jujube and raisins), and prescribes it as a remedy for coughs, persistent colds, lung diseases in general, throat conditions and constipation.

We would do well to retain many of these ancient and long-standing usages.

For constipation: wash five or six dried figs, put them in a bowl and cover with tepid water; leave to soak overnight and eat the figs first thing in the morning, drinking also the water (it is the seeds – or pips – that have a stimulant and laxative action upon the bowel).

For throat irritations (especially angina), inflammations of the mouth (dental abscesses, stomatitis, gingivitis): gargle or mouthwash, using a hot decoction obtained by boiling 5 or 6 figs in a litre of water or milk for a few minutes.

For pulmonary complaints (cough, chronic bronchitis, whooping cough, catarrh, pneumonia, tracheitis): drink the same decoction in the course of the day.

To soothe pain from burns, abscesses, boils (and bring these latter to a head more quickly): apply poultices of figs (fresh or dried) cooked in milk (for dental abscesses, half a hot cooked fig is the only practicable and effective poultice).

For chilblains and haemorrhoids: roast some figs, crush to a powder and mix with honey to make an ointment which should be applied lightly to the affected areas. (This powder, used like coffee, is also prescribed for pulmonary complaints.)

Dried figs have also long provided an excellent health beverage, which is made as follows: into a small cask put 1 kilo of figs, a few juniper berries and 10 litres of water; leave to macerate for a week; pour into bottles and secure the corks with wire; leave for a further week before using.

Lastly, if you are fortunate enough to live in a region where fig trees grow, remember that an infusion of fresh leaves (25 to 30 grammes to a litre of water) is used as a cough remedy and acts on the circulation of the blood (thus easing difficult menstruation). The milky sap that runs out when a branch is snapped will, if applied morning and evening, cause corns and warts to disappear.

FLAX, COMMON
Linum usitatissimum

The common flax ranks with hemp as the most ancient of our textiles. Both originated from Central Asia, and it is known that flax was cultivated from earliest antiquity in the East, in Egypt and throughout Europe. Even though it has since been superseded by cotton and synthetic fibres, it has forever made its mark on our vocabulary, giving us such words as linen, linoleum, linseed, etc.

The seed is the only part that is used in medicine (and in industry too, a quick-drying oil being extracted from it that is used in the manufacture of paints and varnishes, objects – such as surgical probes and instruments – made of rubber and linoleum). The seed is as brown as the flowers are blue, and highly emollient, being rich in oil and gum.

Taken internally, it is prescribed for all inflammatory conditions of the digestive and urinary tracts (gastritis, enteritis, cystitis) as well as for constipation: macerate 15 to 20 grammes of flax seed in a litre of cold water for six hours – or better still, all night; strain; one glassful to be drunk first thing in the morning on an empty stomach, and 4 or 5 cupfuls during the day, between meals. (Several authorities, including Doctor Leclerc, advise against taking the seeds themselves as is often recommended, for they might possibly cause intestinal obstruction.)

Another prescription, pleasanter to the taste, consists of pouring half a litre of boiling water on to 15 grammes of seeds and 8 grammes of pieces of liquorice, covering and leaving to macerate for two hours; strain and drink preferably not too soon before or after meals, sweetening with honey.

Used externally, a mild decoction (50 grammes of seeds to a litre of water; boil for barely two minutes) is employed as a lotion in the treatment of scurfy skin conditions, pruritus, eczema. Added to the bath water, it softens the skin and has a sedative soothing effect on persons of nervous disposition.

Poultices of linseed-meal, obtained by crushing the seeds (it is advisable to do this oneself, so as to be certain that the product is fresh and will not therefore cause cutaneous eruptions due to the prussic acid formed during fermentation), are prescribed for both internal inflammatory conditions (bronchitis, neuritis, enteritis, muscular and articular pains, contusions) and external (boils, abscesses, carbuncles, skin irritations).

The poultices are prepared by gradually adding boiling water to the meal in a bowl or basin, stirring constantly, until it acquires the consistency of a smooth paste, and then spreading this about one centimetre thick on a muslin cloth. According to Doctor Cazin, the poultices should be applied lukewarm, unless otherwise indicated, and not 'as hot as you can stand'.

FUMITORY
Fumaria officinalis.   Earth smoke

There are various theories about how the fumitory got its name, some saying that it derives from the fact that the ancients believed it was born of the 'vapours of the earth', others that it was so named because its juice, formerly employed to improve and clear the eyesight, 'would bring tears to the eyes just like smoke', others that its name simply describes the appearance of the plant when seen in the distance, when its wispy grey leaves look like smoke rising from the ground.

However, nobody disputes its properties, which have been recognized for centuries. Everyone is agreed that it is aperient, tonic, depurative, diuretic and cholagogue, and it is therefore used in the treatment of liver disorders (especially jaundice), sluggish digestion, arteriosclerosis, arthritis, urine retention, skin conditions (scabbing, eczema). It is prepared either by infusion or as a mild decoction (20 to 30 grammes to a litre of water; leave to infuse for fifteen minutes), one cupful to be taken three times a day before meals.

But the fumitory has one unusual characteristic of which you should take account, according to the effect you require: whilst it is aperient, tonic and depurative for the first eight days of treatment, it afterwards becomes sedative and hypnotic, with a tendency to induce sleep and slow down the circulation. Therefore if you are taking it to stimulate the digestion, cleanse the liver and eliminate toxins from the body, you should continue treatment for eight days, then suspend treatment for ten days before resuming it again; on the other hand, if the sedative and hypnotic action is required, treatment should be continued without a break for twenty days.

The fumitory is also employed externally. It was formerly

used to make a toilet water for purifying the skin, and young peasant girls used to boil it in milk with which they would then wash their faces 'to remove summer tan from their complexions'. Today it is used as a lotion or compress to clear up skin conditions (60 grammes to half a litre of milk; boil for five minutes and leave to infuse for ten to fifteen minutes).

The whole stems are picked in the month of June when the flowers are starting to open; they should be dried in the shade, as rapidly as possible. The plant is easy to identify: its stems are angular and branching, and grow to a height of 25 to 30 centimetres; its grey-green leaves are much divided, shaped something like a hen's footprint; its small pinkish-white flowers tipped with purple form loose terminal spikes.

G

GARLIC
Allium sativum

You should never go a day without garlic. So I am often told
by an old peasant who claims he owes his remarkable health and
vigour to eating garlic, and says: 'My father lived to the age of
eighty-nine and my mother lived to be ninety-two, and they
had always eaten plenty of garlic; from my earliest childhood
they taught me to consider it as indispensable a food as bread.
Garlic is a real shield against illness and old age.'

Modern scientific knowledge confirms that garlic is
indeed one of the most remarkable 'food-remedies' we
possess.

Originally from Asia (where it is still liberally used, particularly in China), garlic has throughout history held an
important place in most lands, both medicinally and in the
realms of religion and magic.

The Egyptians raised it to the rank of divinity; they hung
necklaces of garlic around children's necks to drive out worms
(a practice also known to our grandmothers in certain regions);
the pharaoh Cheops had a daily ration of garlic distributed to the
workmen employed in the construction of the Great Pyramid
to give them strength and protect them from epidemics; the
papyri have revealed some curious prescriptions: to prevent a
snake emerging from its hole a clove of garlic should be placed
at the opening (Ebbers papyrus), and to distinguish a woman
who will bear children from one who will be infertile a pessary
of garlic should be administered (Kahoun and Carlsberg papyrus), a method also mentioned by Hippocrates in his treatise
On Sterile Women: 'Take a clove of garlic, clean it, remove the
skin and insert as a pessary, and the following morning

discover whether the woman's breath smells of garlic; if it does, she will conceive; if not, she will not.'

The Greeks, who call it 'stinking rose', used a great deal of garlic, especially the Athenians, but those who had eaten garlic were nevertheless forbidden to enter the temples of Cybele, mother of the gods, doubtless because the odour is unfavourable to magic practices: did Hermes not advise Ulysses to resort to garlic to escape from the spells of Circe, who had turned his companions into swine? Before trying their strength in the stadium or the arena, Greek athletes and wrestlers would chew a few cloves of garlic to give themselves strength and courage.

The common people and soldiers and reapers of Rome always ate garlic, because it was held to be a powerful tonic. It was mixed with the mash of fighting cocks, and Galen called it the 'peasants' theriac', theriac being considered as a panacea in the medicine of ancient times.

Lastly, in France, Charlemagne (or his son Louis the Pious) advises growing garlic in his Capitularies; the monks of the Middle Ages grew plenty of garlic in their monastery gardens; it was also used as an antidote by heavy drinkers who, to prevent drunkenness, macerated a few cloves of garlic in their huge pitchers before swigging their wine, or else rubbed garlic vigorously on their bread; and if, as is said, the grandfather of the future Henri IV rubbed the infant's lips at birth with a clove of garlic and made him swallow a few drops of Jurançon wine, it was probably both to ensure that he would grow up to be a real drinker and also out of respect for the magical protective powers of garlic. Belief in this magical power extended as far as Sweden, where a clove of garlic was fastened round the necks of livestock to protect them against the trolls, the mischievous goblins that came by night to take milk from the cows and hurt the horses.

It goes without saying that because of its numerous properties, today confirmed by science, garlic constitutes one of the major assets of popular medicine. As well as being *de rigueur* in any kitchen (and quite essential to some dishes, such as ailloli, brandade[1] and gigot), prescriptions for the use of garlic outside the kitchen abound. To enumerate them all would be of interest only from the folklore point of view, so I shall mention only those endorsed by the centuries, first warning my readers that garlic is not to be recommended to persons suffering from skin disorders (eczema, etc.) or to nursing mothers, for it affects the milk and causes colic in new-born infants.

To lower tension: one clove of garlic crushed and left to macerate overnight in a glass of water to be drunk first thing in the morning.

To stave off a head cold: several times a day breathe in crushed or chopped garlic. In the days of the great epidemics of plague, cholera, typhus and typhoid fever, the remarkable antiseptic and bactericidal powers of garlic were used to advantage, all those who were in contact with the sick being advised either to chew garlic or rub it on their masks.

To aid digestion, inhibit fermentation and relieve flatulence: mild infusion (5 to 10 grammes to a litre of water), with the addition of a little liquorice and angelica, one cupful to be taken after meals.

For worms and dropsy: a decoction of 25 grammes of garlic to a glass of water or milk (simmer gently for twenty minutes) to be taken twice a day. For oxyuris it is recommended that treament be continued for three or four days, when the moon is on the wane, treatment to be repeated for several consecutive lunar months. One can also give lukewarm enemas, morning and evening, with a decoction of six to eight cloves to half a litre of water, or else rub the belly with a liniment prepared by crushing two cloves of garlic in 2 or 3 spoonfuls of olive oil.

For whooping cough, coughs, bronchial catarrh and chest complaints in general; pour 250 grammes of boiling water on to the appropriate quantity of crushed garlic (for adults, 50 to 60 grammes; for children up to the age of one year, 15 grammes; from one to five years, 25 grammes; from five to

1. Salt cod pounded with garlic, oil and cream. (*Translator's note.*)

twelve years, 40 grammes); leave to macerate for twelve hours; to be taken every two hours, in the following amounts; one small (coffee) spoonful up to the age of five years; one dessert-spoonful from five to twelve years; one tablespoonful for twelve years and over.

For hoarseness and loss of voice: eat a clove of garlic four or five times a day (Dioscorides prescribed a cocktail of milk (or water), garlic and honey for clearing the throat).

You can also gain the benefits of garlic by incorporating it freely (preferably raw, as cooking causes it to lose part of its volatile principles) in your daily food: chopped up finely in soup, on steak or vegetables, in salads (either in the dressing or else rubbed on to croûtons of bread), and by choosing garlic cheese; or else by taking 30 drops of tincture of garlic in a little water four or five times a day. The tincture is made as follows: chop up 50 grammes of garlic very finely and leave to macerate for ten days in a decilitre of spirits or brandy; press and strain through a fine cloth and store in a well-corked bottle.

Garlic is also employed externally.

Garlic vinegar (obtained by macerating 30 grammes of crushed garlic in half a litre of vinegar for ten days) is used for disinfecting and dressing ulcers and septic wounds. It also soothes rheumatic pains.

The unguent – variously known as 'garlic oil', 'curé's mustard' or 'devil's mustard' – is prepared by simply crushing garlic with lard and oil. It is rubbed or massaged on to the affected area to soothe sprains, muscular and rheumatic pains, neuritis; applied to the soles of the feet and on the spine, it has a decongestant action upon the lungs in cases of asthma, whooping cough and catarrh.

Garlic can also be used as a substitute for glue (simply rub the parts to be glued with a clove of garlic cut in half, and hold in place until the juice has dried), and it constitutes an excellent corn cure: each evening rub the corn with a crushed clove of garlic, avoiding the surrounding skin, or else lay a sliver of garlic on the corn, keeping it in place with a plaster or bandage;

renew the poultice daily until the corn or callous drops off (generally after eight to ten days).

Garlic has of course one disadvantage when taken internally, namely the 'anti-social odour' that Horace referred to nearly two thousand years ago when he wished his patron Maecenas, if he gave in to the gastronomic fashion of the day: 'May your mistress push away your kisses, and flee far from you!'

Here are a few practical ways of suppressing the effects of the 'stinking rose': the old fashioned suggestions are to chew for some minutes and then swallow one of the following: a piece of apple, some parsley, a raw green bean, a little aniseed or coffee; the modern methods are to rinse out the mouth with water to which has been added chloramine, peppermint essence or a chlorophyll product.

The old peasant I mentioned earlier has another answer to the problem, one long since adopted in the Midi. 'If everybody ate garlic,' he says, 'then nobody would find it objectionable.'

GENTIAN
Gentiana lutea. Yellow gentian

According to Dioscorides, the first man to employ the plant was Gentius, King of Illyria, who in the second century B.C. joined forces with Perseus, King of Macedonia, against the Romans, who conquered him and led him captive to Rome, but Doctor Leclerc declares that its discovery was due to a physician of the same name in ancient times.

In the Middle Ages the gentian was held to be a panacea, and it was incorporated into all the miracle cures of that time with their wondrous-sounding names. It was used for disorders of the stomach, the liver, the heart and the bowels; it was believed to neutralize poisons and prolong life; until cinchona (quinine) was discovered, it was the gentian that was used with success against attacks of tertian and quartan ague (in certain mountainous regions where it grows, gentian vinegar is still made and used as a febrifuge and preventive medicine against contagious diseases).

Today the gentian is considered to be 'the most perfect pure bitters', non-astringent and therefore tonic without being irritant. It is recommended for loss of appetite (it is in fact an ingredient in various alcoholic beverages – aperitifs and liqueurs – commonly consumed both in bars and at home),

stomach trouble, weakness of the digestion, sickness and fainting, general debility and also, according to some, problems of libido. It increases the secretion of saliva and gastric juices, prevents or cures spasms and acts as a nerve tonic.

The root is the only part used. It often grows to the thickness of an arm (the gentian lives for over fifty years!) and is collected in the autumn. It should be cleaned – but not washed, so that it absorbs no moisture – and cut into rings, then put to dry on a warm stove or in the sun.

It is prepared either as an infusion (3 or 4 grammes to a cupful (100 grammes) of boiling water; leave to infuse for ten to fifteen minutes; to be taken three times a day before meals) or by cold maceration (3 to 4 grammes to 100 grammes of water or wine; leave to macerate for four hours; three times a day before meals, warming slightly before taking); or as a tincture (30 to 50 grammes of root in a litre of alcohol (45°) or spirits; leave to macerate for fifteen days; strain; 20 to 30 drops in a glass of wine, before meals or, for feelings of sickness or indigestion, 10 drops on a lump of sugar); or as a wine (30 grammes of root in 40 grammes of alcohol or 45 grammes of spirits; leave to macerate for twenty-four hours; then add a litre of red or white wine; leave to macerate for ten days; strain through a fine cloth; one small glassful before each meal).

The other gentians – which generally have blue flowers – are not used.

GOLDEN ROD
Solidago virgaurea.   Aaron's rod

The basic tenets of homoeopathic medicine today are those of the great Greek physician Hippocrates, who more than 2,000 years ago advocated the treatment of disease by fasting – to eliminate accumulated waste from the body – and simple eating. Golden rod, or *Solidago* as it is called, accordingly features regularly in the homoeopathic prescriptions, since it is known to stimulate the action of the liver and the kidneys and thus assist elimination of waste matter and impurities.

Because of its diuretic and vulnerary properties, golden rod has long ranked among the best herbal remedies for urine retention and inflammation of the genito-urinary or digestive organs. Whilst there is no proof that the prescription given by Arnauld de Villeneuve, the sixteenth-century physician and alchemist (8 grammes of powdered plant infused overnight in a glass of white wine, to be drunk slightly warmed each morning on arising for ten to fifteen days), will 'unfailingly break up the stone in the bladder', there is no doubt that golden rod is extremely useful in the treatment of gravel, inflammation of the kidney due to renal calculus, kidney and bladder complaints, dropsy, albuminuria, cystitis, enteritis; its action against fluid retention also recommends it in the treatment of hepatic insufficiency, and for rheumatic and arthritic conditions (many even advocate it as a depurative in the treatment of skin diseases).

It is prepared either by decoction (50 grammes of dried plant to a litre of water; cold-soak for five minutes; boil for five

minutes; leave to infuse for fifteen minutes; 3 or 4 cupfuls per day, between meals), or as a syrup (100 grammes of plant to a litre of water; boil for ten minutes; leave to infuse for twelve hours; press and strain through a cloth; dissolve 100 to 200 grammes of sugar over a low heat or by *bain-marie*; 2 coffee-spoonfuls per day, between meals). It is preferable to take short courses of treatment, from eight to ten days, suspending treatment for the same length of time before continuing again, in order to avoid tiring the kidneys.

The flowering tips are the part of the plant that is used,

picked when coming into flower (July–August) and dried in the shade. Golden rod grows wild in woods and copses, in dry meadows and on banks and hillsides. It is distinguished by its erect stems (40 to 80 centimetres in height) reddish at the base, green and slightly downy towards the tip, which bear short flowering branches only on the upper half; its leaves are lance-shaped, slightly downy, paler on the under surface, and arranged alternately on the stem; the golden-yellow flowers form a spray or cluster at the tip of the stems.

GROUNDSEL
Senecio vulgaris.   Birdseed, Ragwort

Emerson was right when he defined a weed as 'a plant whose virtues have not yet been discovered'. I myself have noticed that ever since I told my neighbours about the therapeutic properties of groundsel, not only have they stopped cursing it for invading their flower beds, but they are little short of delighted when they find a plentiful supply of it in their gardens.

They know now that they have at hand one of the best – if not the very best – remedies for female disorders since, without the slightest harmful side-effect, it regularizes and induces menstrual discharge, soothes the accompanying menstrual pains, and is as helpful to young girls in the difficult stage of puberty as to those women who endure almost unbearably difficult and painful menstruation. Senecio is in fact the homoeo-pathic remedy prescribed for delayed or totally suppressed menstruation, as well as for painful and irregular menstruation in young girls.

The decoction is prepared in the amounts of 40 to 50 grammes of fresh or dried plant (discarding any flowers that have already turned into white down) to 1 litre of water; boil for two to three minutes; leave to infuse for ten to fifteen minutes; 4 to 5 small coffee cupfuls during the day.

Groundsel is very common in gardens and ploughed fields. Its height varies from 15 to 30 centimetres; its stems are angular and branched (a branch bearing a terminal cluster of flowers joins the stem at the axil of each leaf); the leaves are alternate, deeply cut (resembling the leaves of the dandelion); the flowers are small, yellow and form terminal cymes; the flower-heads comprise a great number of florets which are succeeded by seed covered with fluffy pappus (the Latin name of the plant, *senecio*, derives from *senex*: old man, alluding to this hoary head of seed-bearers).

Groundsel was formerly employed as a remedy for epilepsy, cholera, jaundice; cooked in milk, it was used on poultices for haemorrhoids, boils and milk retention in the breasts. It was also prescribed as a dental remedy, owing more to magic than to medicine however, given by Pliny as follows: 'If you uproot this plant with your bare hand and then three times touch the tooth which is painful, spitting on the ground each time, then replace the plant in the ground, and if the plant takes root again, that tooth will give no more pain . . .'

H

HARICOT, COMMON
Phaseolus vulgaris. Haricot bean, French bean, Kidney bean

The haricot comes to us from tropical America via Italy – Catherine de Medicis is said to have brought it to France as one of her wedding gifts on the occasion of her marriage to the future Henri II in 1533 – and the Cuban poet José-Maria de Heredia says that its names derives from the Mexican *ayocolt*.

The beans have their place in every kitchen, but it is the pods, rich in active principles, which are used medicinally. Reduced to ashes, together with the stalks, they were formerly prescribed for kidney complaints and dropsy (the distilled flower water being used as a beauty preparation 'for cleaning the face of freckles and blotches').

The pods are indeed highly diuretic and lower the blood-sugar level. They are still employed in country areas, with excellent results, in the treatment of kidney and bladder disorders, dropsy, albuminuria and diabetes: soak 3 or 4 handfuls (about 100 grammes) of finely chopped dried pods in a litre and a half of water for two hours; boil until reduced to half the volume by evaporation; drink between meals during the day.

HART'S-TONGUE
Scolopendrium vulgare, Asplenium scolopendrium, Phyllitis scolopendrium, Scolopendrium officinale. Spleenwort

Four centuries ago the root of hart's-tongue was used for the same purpose as 'the Pill' today: uprooted on a dark moonless night and hung like an amulet around the neck, either alone or together with a piece of a mule's spleen, it was believed to prevent conception.

However, it is probable that the effects expected of the leaves were more reliable: they were held to be 'good for persons able to urinate only drop by drop' and 'of great help in cases of jaundice and for removing obstructions of the spleen', properties that have been confirmed by long popular usage and that are still valid today. An infusion of hart's tongue (30 to 40

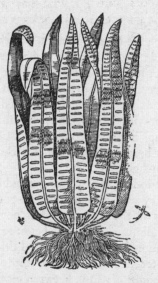

grammes of leaves, either fresh or dried in the shade in autumn, to one litre of boiling water; leave to infuse for five to ten minutes; 3 cupfuls per day, between meals) is recommended for liver and spleen disorders, pulmonary congestion, gravel, nephritis, rheumatism, diarrhoea.

Hart's tongue is a plant you will have seen many times. It grows in cracks in damp rocks, in wells, beside streams, and is recognizable by its leaves shaped like thongs or long tongues, cut away in a heart shape at the base, with parallel linear sori of spore-cases on each side of the central rib on the underside (the spores play a part in the reproductive cycle, hart's-tongue being a member of the fern family).

HAWKWEED

Hieracium pilosella.   Mouse-ear hawkweed

I am often surprised by the astonishment of learned men and I am more and more convinced that they would often have saved themselves a lot of trouble in their researches if they had paid some consideration to the age-old saying, 'God has always put the cure alongside the ill', instead of mocking its *naïveté*. The case of the hawkweed is a striking example.

Let me quote what Professor Binet has to say about it: "The time has passed when people thought that sparrowhawks ate this plant to strengthen their eyesight. On the other hand, the watery extract of this latex plant is an effective treatment for undulant fever in humans and epizootic abortion in cattle. Its antibiotic activity has been tested and confirmed on cultures of *Brucella*. What an odd discovery, to find growing along the paths frequented by grazing stock a plant so active in the treatment of infectious abortion, the disease that is so dangerous to cattle and sheep!'

Coincidence, the eternal sceptics will say. Maybe, but if so it is an oft-repeated coincidence: the eucalyptus, for example, thrives in marshy regions, and happens to cure marsh fever; the Alpine yarrow, a kind of wormwood that grows at altitudes of 3,000 metres, is a sovereign remedy for 'mountain sickness'; etc.

How much sooner we might have discovered the specific property of hawkweed, which nineteenth-century texts either omitted or declared consigned to oblivion. We would doubtless have made the discovery sooner had we taken the trouble to consult old herbals (we would have read that, infused in white wine, it was the 'proven remedy' for tertian fever, which calls to mind undulant fever), or had we inquired into the much despised 'old wives' remedies' (we would have learnt that in the country it is held to be a febrifuge).

There is no reason why tomorrow should not bring another of those sudden 'discoveries' that would in fact only confirm popular usage (hawkweed extract is indeed already accepted as exerting a favourable action on atheroma or hardening of the arteries).

It is prescribed for the following: dropsy, gravel, oedema in connection with heart complaints, fever, congestion of the liver, jaundice, gall-stones, uraemia (it lowers blood urea levels), enteritis, uterine inflammation, 'whites', excessive menstrual discharge. It is diuretic, decongestant, febrifuge, astringent and haemostatic. It is prepared by decoction (40 to 50 grammes of dried plant – leaves and flowers – to a litre of water; boil for five minutes; 3 or 4 cupfuls per day, between meals).

It should be gathered during the flowering season (May–September) and dried in the shade. You will find it on roadsides, dry slopes, in dry waste places. Its leaves are ovate and hairy, woolly on the under surface, green on the upper surface, with long white hairs on the ribs and margins; they appear in rosette formation around the base of the flowering stems; the stems rarely grow to a height of more than fifteen centimetres, and bear florets resembling those of the dandelion: they are the same shape and colour – but generally tinged with red at the edges – and are also succeeded by a fluffy ball of seeds. When picked the stem exudes a white latex that turns brown on exposure to the air.

HAWTHORN

Crataegus oxyeantha.   May bush, Whitethorn,
Sharp-spined hawthorn, Bird eagles

Each spring as I round the last bend in the lane leading to our mill, I am reminded of Proust's little path 'buzzing with the fragrance of hawthorn' and I recite to myself that telling phrase which so clearly paints the scene: 'The hedge formed as it were a succession of chapels that were bedecked with flowers, like a wayside altar.'

It is all there, even the sacred character of the hawthorn which can be traced back to the beginning of time. Through the length and breadth of Europe, it has always been considered the foremost 'protecting plant'.

Long before our own era, at wedding feasts in Athens, each guest carried a sprig of hawthorn, token of happiness and prosperity for the future of the newly married couple. In Rome it was the practice for the bridegroom to wave a twig of hawthorn as he led his bride to the nuptial chamber, and sprigs of hawthorn were attached to the cradle of a new-born child to protect him from sickness and evil spells.

The advent of Christianity only served to confirm these superstitious beliefs. The hawthorn was reputedly used for Christ's crown of thorns, and indeed the plant is supposedly referred to in Holy Scriptures long before the Passion, for the famous 'burning bush' by which Moses first spoke with God on Mount Horeb is thought to have been another variety of hawthorn, the *Crataegus pyracantha*, a native of the lands around the Mediterranean and introduced into France in 1629.

At the time of the Crusades, a knight setting out for the Holy Land would offer his lady a sprig of hawthorn, tied with a pink ribbon, as a token that he would 'live in hope'. For centuries the torches that lit the nuptial chamber were of hawthorn wood specially kept for this solemn occasion. In numerous regions it was a springtime custom to plait crowns of hawthorn and leave them for the fairies or angels who came by night to dance around the fragrant bushes, and who, it was hoped, would show their appreciation by showering their blessings on those who had taken this trouble on their behalf.

In Burgundy, mothers carry their sick child to a flowering hawthorn, for they believe that their prayers will ascend better to heaven in company with the fragrance of the flowers. In Normandy, even today, it is believed that lightning will never strike hawthorn (or a house protected by hawthorn) since lightning is the work of the devil and cannot strike the plant that touched the brow of Christ, a belief that is shared in Brittany, where the robin is also venerated because, it is said, it was when breaking off a thorn from the crown of Jesus that a little blood stained its breast.

To turn now to the therapeutic properties of hawthorn, we find that they are no less remarkable than its magic powers. The ancients utilized it as a remedy for gout, pleurisy, vertigo, insomnia, angor; and modern science confirms that its chemical components are in fact antispasmodic, sedative, diuretic and above all constitute a remarkable regulator of arterial blood pressure as well as a valuable heart stimulant with excellent sedative effects upon the cario-vascular system, and therefore on palpitations, angina pectoris, and disturbances of circulation whether resulting from the menopause or not.

Long before its name appeared in the classic pharmacopoeia

it was already a homoeopathic remedy known under the name of *Crataegus oxyacantha*), Doctor Ch. Fiessinger described hawthorn as the 'valerian of the heart', a telling phrase subsequently used by Professor Binet. As for Doctor Leclerc, in his 'précis' he writes: 'The knowledge I have acquired of hawthorn, based on more than twenty years' clinical observation, has convinced me that its lack of toxicity makes it possible for it to be administered over a long period of time, even to patients with kidney malfunction, without fear of accumulation in the body.'

So whenever it is necessary to combat any of the above listed symptoms, to re-establish the equilibrium of the sympathetic and parasympathetic nervous system on which depend the proper functioning of all our organs and our rest, you can take an infusion (one good coffeespoonful per cup, two or three times a day, one cupful to be taken last thing at night in cases of insomnia) of hawthorn flowers or petals (the simplest way of gathering the latter is to shake the branches and catch the falling petals in a box or on a cloth). This infusion also has an elective action on simple angina and is claimed to prevent it from developing if taken as soon as the first symptoms appear.

The little ovoid berries, glossy red in colour, are also valuable. Picked in September to October, dried in the sun or a low oven, they should be crushed as required to make the following decoction: 10 grammes to a litre of water, to be drunk in the course of two days as a remedy for certain forms of albuminuria; 20 to 30 grammes to a litre in the treatment of diarrhoea, dysentery and calculi; 50 grammes to a litre as a gargle (with the addition of honey) for sore throats and angina.

The decoction of flowers and berries (20 grammes to half a litre of water) is used as a lotion for facial blotches and acne rosacea.

Lastly, hawthorn is recommended – although this particular usage is less reliable than the above-mentioned, owing more to magic than to medicine! – for transforming the mood of a husband. Kabyle women invoke its powers, requesting it to 'stop my husband from beating me and change him into a donkey that I may make him carry the straw . . .'

HEATH
Erica vulgaris

Whilst one might question its actual power to break up or dissolve stones in the bladder, as indicated by the name given to it by the ancients (*erica* derives from a Greek word meaning 'to break up'), there is no doubt at all about its antiseptic and diuretic properties, and its consequently beneficial effects on the urinary tract.

It is employed with success in the treatment of nephritis, cystitis due to inflammation of the prostate or due to an infection ('Cloudy and offensive urine becomes clear, loses its bad smell, and increases in quantity' says Michel Compain), as well as gravel, albuminuria and even rheumatism (it has the further merit of stimulating the appetite).

The flowering tips – so appreciated by bees – are the part used. They are dried and prepared by decoction: 30 to 40 grammes to a litre of water, boil until reduced by a third, to be drunk a cupful at a time in the course of twenty-four hours.

Added to the bath, the flowering tips (which can be used in place of hops in the preparation of beer) are 'good for toning up the muscles'. These baths, several times a week, are recommended to anyone suffering from gout, paralysis and rheumatism.

HEDGE-MUSTARD
Erysimum or Sisymbrium officinale.   Wiry Jack

To his friend Boileau – who was suffering from loss of voice – Racine wrote:

Syrup of erysimum is certainly no quack remedy. M. Dodart, to whom I spoke of it three days ago, assures me that M. Morin, who told me about it, is without doubt the cleverest doctor in Paris, and by no means a charlatan. This doctor assures me that if the waters of Bourbonne do not cure you, this syrup certainly will. He cited the case of a cantor of Notre Dame, who had lost his voice for six months as a result of a cold, and who thought he would have to retire. This doctor started treating him with an infusion of a herb called, I believe,

erysimum, and it did him so much good that not only can he speak, but sing, and his voice is as strong as ever before. I told this story to the court physicians, and they admit that this plant erysimum is very good for the chest.

Before these praises from so illustrious a pen, various writers had already praised the virtues of this plant, recording cures obtained in cases of hoarseness – in preachers – which had been previously treated in vain by 'a multitude of remedies'.

Hedge-mustard is thus the specific for the vocal chords, and if you are in a profession that obliges you to make great demands on your voice (lawyer, singer, teacher, politician, etc.)

you will derive the greatest benefit from either the infusion (40 to 60 grammes of dried leaves to a litre of lukewarm water; leave to macerate overnight; strain and drink 4 or 5 cupfuls during the day between meals, first warming slightly and sweetening with honey) or from the juice of the fresh leaves (15 to 30 grammes) mixed with milk and sweetened with honey.

The infusion of leaves – preferably fresh – is also prescribed (6 grammes to a cupful of boiling water; leave to infuse for twenty minutes) for engorgements of the liver and more particularly for hepatic colics, for it suppresses the spasmodic reflex that arises in an effort to expel calculi, and consequently relieves the pain.

Do not imagine that a plant endowed with such virtues must be rare: on the contrary it is common everywhere, along hedges and walls, by the roadside, in waste places. Its angular stems have an untidy look about them (they spread and twist in every direction), and reach a height of 40 to 70 centimetres; its dark bluish-green leaves are deeply cut – a bit like thistle leaves – at the lower part of the stems, smaller and arrow-shaped towards the tips; its very small yellow flowers with four petals (it is one of the Cruciferous plants) are arranged in slender spikes along the stems and bloom from May to September, and are succeeded by the characteristic long thin seed pods pressed tightly to the stem.

HOLLY
Ilex aquifolium.   Holm, Hulm, Hulver bush, Needleleaved holly

Like mistletoe, holly is reputedly a plant of good omen, and for the same reasons: because it is always green, because it appears invulnerable to the march of time signalled by the changing seasons, and because it symbolizes life in the midst of the seeming death of winter. It consequently always held a place in the ceremonies that marked the winter solstice, and the protective virtues attributed to it are in fact at the root of our own traditional use of holly at the end of the year.

It also renders many other services: 'Some use to tie the branches with their leaves upon their Bacon and Martinmas Beefe', writes Matthiolus, 'to keepe Rats and Mice from them by their prickles; the branches with berries are used at Christ Tide to decke up our houses withall, but that they should defend the house from lightning, and keepe themselves from witchcraft, is a superstition of the Gentiles, learned from Pliny' (Parkinson); holly faggots are used for sweeping chimneys; the inner-bark is used to make bird-lime for poaching birds; its wood, which is very hard, polishes well and is easily stained black, is employed in cabinet-making; it is used for making goads, whip handles, riding-switches.

It also has its place as a home remedy. Its leaves – which become progressively less prickly as the tree ages – are febrifuge, diuretic and resolvent, and are therefore prescribed for catarrhal complaints and engorgements of the respiratory tract (persistent cough, bronchitis, pneumonia, influenza), facilitating elimination of the secretions that characterize these conditions, and for dropsy, rheumatism and fevers. They are employed fresh or dried, prepared by decoction (30 to 50 grammes of finely-chopped leaves to a litre of water; cold-soak for one or two hours, then boil for ten minutes; leave to infuse for a further ten mintues; sweeten – preferably with honey – for its taste is very bitter; 3 or 4 cupfuls per day).

In regions where intermittent fevers are rife, two wineglass-fuls a day of holly wine are prescribed. This is made as follows: 50 grammes of chopped fresh leaves macerated for twenty-four hours in a sufficient quantity of alcohol (45°), rum or brandy; then add a litre of white wine; leave to macerate for a further twenty-four to forty-eight hours; strain.

The berries – much prized by birds in wintertime – are sometimes prescribed as a purgative (ten to twelve berries macerated in 100 cubic centimetres of water for twelve hours), but I would not advise you to try them, for they often induce nausea and vomiting, and in any case there are other plants which are equally effective in this field but do not have the same drawbacks.

As for the small holly known as knee holly, Jew's myrtle or butcher's-broom (*Ruscus aculeatus*), it belongs to a different family, and all it has in common with the holly is the fact that it is also evergreen, with prickly leaves (small, oval, like box leaves, with a single terminal thorn) and red berries.

It grows in the undergrowth, copses and hedges (it rarely reaches a height of more than 80 centimetres whereas the holly can grow to the height of a tree). In certain regions the young shoots are eaten as salad, in omelettes or like asparagus (it belongs in fact to the same Liliaceae family as the asparagus) and, almost everywhere, its glossy green branches with their sprinkling of little scarlet balls are used for their decorative value.

Its root – which is actually a rhizome – was long ago praised by Dioscorides as a diuretic for dissolving stones in the bladder. Prepared by decoction (40 to 60 grammes of dried root to a litre of water – with the optional addition of a few pieces of liquorice; boil for five minutes; leave to infuse for ten to fifteen minutes; to be drunk as desired) it is prescribed for dropsy (Doctor Leclerc quotes cases of spectacular cures), complaints of the urinary tract, jaundice and gout.

HOLLYHOCK
Althaea rosea.   Rose-mallow

The hollyhock is a native of China and the Mediterranean region, brought into Europe in the sixteenth century.

Medicinally it serves as a substitute for the common mallow, being in fact simply a larger and more robust variety of that plant, and sharing the same properties.[1] Most gardeners, who grow it for its ornamental value, are unaware of its humbler connections...

1. See page 198.

An infusion of the flowers, picked in dry weather when they are fully in bloom and dried in the shade below 55°C (30 to 40 grammes to 1 litre of boiling water; leave to infuse for ten minutes), can be freely taken as a drink for coughs, bronchitis; as a gargle and mouthwash for aphtha and mouth ulcers; as a lotion to remove facial redness and blotches.

The dark purple flowers can be used to colour wine, but today, alas, chemical colouring matter is preferred.

HONEYSUCKLE
Lonicera periclymenum.   Woodbine

Having been prescribed for centuries as a 'vulnerary detergent' medicinal plant, the honeysuckle gradually went out of use, so much so that in 1837 Roques observes: 'Doctors have left honeysuckle in the hedgerows, and rightly so. Fortunate are those who, recovering from illness, can breathe its sweet fragrance in some pretty country spot! The pure air, the balmy scent of its flowers are also valuable remedies in themselves.'

Today we might say: 'Peasants have nevertheless continued to use honeysuckle, and rightly so,' for in the light of recent knowledge we now know that it is rich in salicylic acid (the essential element in many patent medicines, notably aspirin[1] and, as Professor Binet points out, 'also in antibiotic substances, active against colibacilli and staphylococci'.

Country folk are obviously not much concerned with these highbrow scientific notions: if they use a plant it is because of the results they get (regardless of chemical analysis), and this is why they have remained faithful to the honeysuckle.

With the leaves – gathered before the plant comes into flower, and dried – they make an infusion (10 grammes to a litre of water; leave to infuse for about ten minutes) which they know to be a good treatment for kidney stones and sluggishness of the bowels, or which they use as a gargle for angina.

1. See *Meadowsweet*, page 207.

With the flowers – picked when fully in bloom and dried in the shade – they prepare an infusion (10 to 15 grammes to a litre of water; leave to infuse for ten minutes; 2 or 3 cupfuls per day) that is an effective remedy for bronchial complaints (coughs, asthma, catarrh) and also has an anti-spasmodic action. Together with peach-blossom (3 grammes of each infused in a cup of boiling water), honeysuckle flowers are also recommended for children's coughs (notably whooping cough).

With the bark – gathered in springtime – and the root – gathered in autumn – they make a decoction (20 to 30 grammes to a litre of water; boil for three or four minutes; leave to infuse for ten minutes) that, taken in the amount of one cupful before meals, is tonic, diuretic (gout) and cholagogue (liver complaints).

HOP
Humulus lupulus

Cultivated for the manufacture of beer, to which it lends aroma, flavour and digestive and sedative qualities[1], the hop grows wild in hedgerows, copses, beside streams and on the edges of forest and woodland.

It can climb to a height of 6 metres; its leaves, three- or five-lobed, resemble vine leaves; it bears both male and female flowers, the latter during fructification, developing into an ovoid cone-like head of yellow-green scales covered with a resinous yellow dust, bitter and aromatic, known as lupulin. These cones are the part of the plant that is collected before maturity (August to September) and dried in the oven or stove, for use by brewers or for medicinal purposes.

1. Gerard writes: 'The manifold vertues of Hops do manifest argue the wholesomenesse of beere . . . for the hops rather make it a physicall drinke to keepe the body in health, than an ordinary drinke for the quenching of our thirst.' (*Translator's note*.)

The medieval pharmacopoeia pronounced them 'useful for suppurating abscesses and tumours that are in the liver and the spleen' and recommended them for melancholia and vapours due to depression. Today we acknowledge them to be aperitif, tonic, diuretic, depurative, digestive, sedative and anti-spasmodic.

The infusion (15 to 20 grammes of dried and crumbled cones to a litre of boiling water; leave to infuse for ten minutes) 'regenerates and purifies tired blood'. Taken in the amount of 3 ordinary glassfuls per day, before meals, it acts as a good general tonic for convalescents. One cupful taken after meals is a remedy for slow and difficult digestion. Doctor Leclerc observed that hops combat any tendency of the digestive tract to go into spasm or become too flaccid, thereby 'maintaining well-balanced digestive activity'.

He also confirmed its equilibrating activity on the male re-productive organs, recommending it in cases of painful priapism, onanism, persistent spermatorrhoea, and also as an anaphrodisiac. In this domain the decoction should be em-ployed (40 grammes of dried cones to a litre of water; boil for two minutes and leave to infuse for five; 3 cupfuls per day, the last to be taken before retiring).

For insomnia, nervous spasms of the stomach, the bowel and the heart, menstrual spasms and pains, an infusion of 3 table-spoons of crumbled cones in a cup of boiling water should be taken once a day.

In certain countries, notably in the north, the east and in England, a pillow filled with hops is considered good for sleeplessness and nervous irritation.

HOREHOUND
Marrubium vulgare. Hoarhound, White hoarhound

One enthusiastic doctor has nominated it as one of the best plants in Europe, adding 'there are few that are as effective against such a great number of different complaints'. This is perhaps an exaggeration, since there are indeed other plants that can claim the same merits, but the great advantage of horehound is that it is to be found almost everywhere in Europe. Although not very common growing wild in England, it is, however, cultivated.

You will find it growing along roadsides, in waste places and dry sunny pastures in lowland and mountain. It looks like the white dead-nettle and mint, which in fact belong to the same family, the Labiatae. Its angular, greyish hairy stems grow to a height of up to 80 centimetres; its opposite leaves are oval in form, rugose, woolly, ash-green in colour, with toothed edges (when crushed they exhale a slightly musky aromatic aroma); its small creamy-white flowers are grouped in clusters at the axils of the leaves, and they bloom from June through into autumn.

Its scientific name is said to derive from the Hebrew *marob* which means 'bitter juice' and this seems likely since, together with coriander, succory chicory, nettle and horse-radish, it was one of the five 'bitter herbs' ordered to be eaten by the Jews at their Passover feast, commemorating the exodus of the Israelites out of Egypt.

Since ancient times it has been a popular pectoral remedy as well as being used as a salve in the treatment of dog bites; it was one of the ingredients of theriac and other secret preparations, because of its noted 'softening' action and virtue as an appetite stimulant.

It is in fact currently prescribed for numerous conditions: chronic bronchial catarrh, wet asthma, bronchitis, persistent coughs, whooping cough, gastritis, enteritis, loss of appetite, weakness of the heart and circulation, malaria, painful menstruation, leucorrhoeia, liver complaints. This may seem a lot, but the plant is known to be expectorant, disinfectant, tonic, decongestant, diuretic, stimulant, hepatic, and to fortify the mucous membranes.

It is prepared as an infusion (30 grammes of flowering plant, picked when the flowers are beginning to open and dried in the shade, to a litre of water; cold-soak for ten minutes; warm, but withdraw from the heat before it reaches boiling point; leave to infuse for fifteen minutes; 4 or 5 glassfuls per day, which should be taken lukewarm if treatment is for a respiratory complaint). It is also made into a wine (macerate 60 grammes of dried plant in a litre of previously sweetened Spanish or Bordeaux wine for eight days; strain; one sherryglassful before the two main meals of the day).

A home-doctor of the Belle Epoque – when the canons of feminine beauty were different from ours – gives this warning about the infusion: 'It should be taken only in moderation for it can bring about a considerable loss of weight.' This additional virtue of horehound is more likely to be appreciated today and it is in fact prescribed (one litre of Infusion per day) for obesity.

HORSE CHESTNUT
Aesculus hippocastanum

Some fifty patent medicines turn to good account its incomparable action on the venous circulation, and it has long been known under its scientific name as a homoeopathic remedy, advocated in the treatment of haemorrhoids and varicose veins – for which it is also the allopathic remedy – as well as of a very painful kind of lumbago (lumbo-sacral myalgia), pains that are alleviated by cold and aggravated by heat, and of acute attacks of rhinopharyngitis.

Ever since a physician named Bachelier introduced it here at the beginning of the seventeenth century (it is actually a native of India), we have assiduously discovered other uses for it than those for which it seemed to have been created: to lend its magnificent and ornamental presence to our surroundings (gardens, avenues) and provide fruit that, reduced to flour mixed with oats and administered in the amount of 100 grammes per day, eased broken-winded horses, a purpose for which it is still used by the Turks, and to which it owes both its scientific and common name.

Chomel, in the reign of Louis XV, classified horse-chestnut powder among the errhine substances, namely those which are snuffed up the nose in order to increase the natural secretions and produce sneezing; the bark of its branches was prescribed as a febrifuge in place of quinine which was unobtainable under the Continental System;[1] the chestnuts, containing saponin, were macerated and used for laundering, and also made into soap; its flour gave an excellent wood size which, being bitter, also kept away woodworm and which, mixed with tallow, was used to make candles that were longer-lasting but unhappily gave less light than ordinary candles.

Popular medicine made use of its virtues long before it was scientifically established that a principle of horse-chestnut acts as a venous tonic and thins the blood.

Taken internally, a decoction of the outer covering of the fruit, dried and crushed (30 grammes to a litre of water; boil for five minutes; leave to infuse for the same length of time; 1 or 2 cupfuls per day, between meals) is recommended for disturbances of circulation, congested conditions of the venous system (varicose veins, haemorrhoids), enlarged prostate.

The prescription for external use is simply that you should always carry one or two horse chestnuts in your pockets, re-placing them once they have become as hard as rock. This is the classic country remedy for rheumatic pains and painful haemorrhoids. Does it work through auto-suggestion or through the evaporation and absorption by osmosis of an essential oil medicinally employed in the treatment of gout? What matters is that it does work, and you risk nothing by trying it.

1. The plan of Napoleon Bonaparte for cutting off Great Britain from all connection with the state of Europe; instituted by the Berlin Decree (1806) which declared the British islands in a state of blockade. (*Translator's note.*)

It appears that sweet chestnuts share the same virtue, if one is to judge by a letter written by Madame de Sévigné in October 1671: 'The other day I had three or four basketfuls to hand: some I boiled, some I roasted, some I put in my pocket...'

HORSETAIL, FIELD
Equisetum arvense.   Shavegrass, Bottlebrush, Pewterwort

It is a common enough plant – you will find it growing everywhere – and yet quite extraordinary.

Extraordinary because of its history, for it existed in the earliest ages of the earth. It grew in abundance and left us a

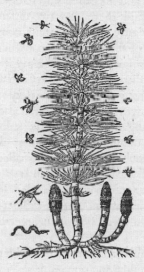

precious heritage in the form of thick layers of coal in which impressions have been found that show that it has not changed in shape: hollow stalk, slender and straight, jointed at regular intervals, with sheaths at the joints from which spring the coronas of leaves, also segmented, like long needles; but instead of measuring 30 to 120 centimetres as they do today, they grew to the height and size of a fir tree.

Extraordinary by its very nature, since it does not produce flowers but reproduces by means of spores on the fertile stem, like mushrooms, ferns and mosses. The stalks which we see throughout the summer, beside streams, in the damp places and sandy soils it prefers, are sterile. They have been preceded in the spring by other fertile stems, which rarely grow to a height of more than 20 centimetres, and are different in every way: they are reddish and bare, terminating in an egg-shaped head of spores which give them the appearance of drumsticks poking out of the ground; it is only when the spores have reached maturity that these stems, which ensure the future of the species, wither, and the others start to develop, so that in fact one might easily think there were two different plants.

Extraordinary, lastly, because of its composition. It is an absolute reservoir of silica; its ashes contain as much as 80 per cent, and if we examine the rib of the leaves through a magnifying glass we can distinguish little crystals of this mineral to which we owe, among other valuable stones, quartz, amethyst, agate and opal. However, this is not all: it also contains calcium, sodium, iron manganese, potassium, sulphur, magnesium, tannin, a complex of alkaloids and a bitter glucoside.

The Romans – including Pliny, who called it the 'hair of the earth' – considered it a general tonic and restorative and recommended eating the young shoots as a salad. It was employed by artisans for polishing wood used in cabinet-making and marquetry, and by housewives for scouring wooden, pewter and brass vessels.

But it is undeniably in the realm of health that it has rendered and continues to render incomparable service, for not only is it one of the most powerful natural remineralizing agents known to us, its silica being directly assimilable by the body – for which reason it is prescribed for tubercular patients, along with other treatments, as well as for persons suffering from debility, anaemia or recovering from illness – but it is also an excellent diuretic – depurative, and a vulnerary (internal and external) that many have termed 'irreplaceable'. (Galen said it 'doth perfectly cure wounds, yea, although the sinues be cut asunder.')

It is therefore prescribed, as diuretic and depurative, in the treatment of urine retention, dropsy, generalized oedema, kidney and bladder disorders (gravel, calculi, renal colic, cystitis, etc.), albuminuria, rheumatism, gout, skin complaints (eczema, acne, scabbing, pruritus); as internal vulnerary in the treatment of haemoptysis, metrorrhagia, inflammation of the mucosa of the stomach and the bowel (gastric ulcer, diarrhoea), inflammation of the genito-urinary organs and respiratory tract. It is prepared by decoction (40 to 50 grammes of dried plant – gathered in July to August – to a litre of water; cold-soak for a minimum of three hours; heat and simmer gently for twenty to twenty-five minutes; leave to infuse for ten minutes; 3 or 4 cupfuls per day).

This decoction, taken regularly for two or three weeks, will cause white spots on the fingernails to disappear, these being caused – according to the eminent specialist Henri Mangin[1] – by 'some degree of organic demineralization, attributable to a loss of silica and lime'. The biologist C. Louis Kervran considers horsetail of 'great importance in dietetics', stressing its 'swift action': breaking nails, a sign of decalcification, become normal again in a fortnight if horsetail extract is taken, and in a slightly longer time if the less concentrated decoction is taken.

Horsetail is also prescribed for incontinence of urine, generally in association with other plants (to a litre of water allow one tablespoonful of powdered horsetail, one tablespoonful of St John's Wort, one coffeespoonful of powdered oak bark, one coffeespoonful of powdered rhizome of tormentilla; boil for fifteen minutes; 2 cupfuls per day, preferably taken in the morning). *Equisetum* is in fact the homoeopathic remedy for this condition which Doctor Thibault describes as 'always

1. *Étude clinique et psychologique des ongles*, ed. Joseph Charles, Paris.

difficult to remedy', adding 'it seems as if *Equisetum* achieves markedly better results among girls than among boys'.

Used externally, the more concentrated decoction (double the amount of plant and decrease the volume of water by half) is employed as a lotion and on compresses to heal troublesome sores, varicose ulcers, bleeding haemorrhoids, as well as in the treatment of scabbing, eczema, pruritus, etc. Sniffed up the nose, it will at once arrest nasal haemorrhages.

For perspiring feet, make a daily application of tincture of horsetail, obtained by macerating 500 grammes of plant in half a litre of alcohol for two or three weeks, shaking the jar from time to time; press and strain through a fine cloth.

HOUSELEEK

Sempervivum tectorum.   Roof sempervivum, Jupiter's Beard, Sengreen

Before it became an almost traditional feature of our rockeries, this succulent plant which grows everywhere, on roofs, old walls, rocks, was already held in a certain esteem in country areas, as much for its medicinal qualities as for the protection it was believed to afford against evil spells – indeed it was connected with the most powerful of the ancient gods, as indicated by its name, Jupiter's beard.

It looks like an artichoke, with its fleshy leaves forming rosettes from the centre of which rises a thick stem terminating in a cluster of small pinkish-red flowers. It is the strongest leaves, taken from heads that have not yet put forth a stem, that are medicinally employed fresh.

Crushed and applied to the forehead as a cold poultice, the leaves relieve migraines and the headaches that often accompany fever. The same poultice, only hot, is prescribed for haemorrhoids, scabbing, ulcers, burns.

A fresh leaf, peeled on one side, will arrest bleeding from a cut. Applied and kept in place on a corn, renewed morning and evening for several consecutive days, it will soften the corn and make it easy to remove.

The juice extracted from the fresh leaves is used to make an unguent (equal quantities of juice and pure pork fat, combine over a low heat) which will soothe haemorrhoids, contusions and burns.

HYSSOP
Hyssopus officinalis.   Pettigrew

It owes its name to the Hebrews – they called it *Ezob* – for whom it was a sacred plant and as such repeatedly mentioned in the Bible: it enters into the water of purification as God commanded Moses it should be made (Numbers 19: 6, 18); it is one of the plants of which Solomon spoke with his customary wisdom (1 Kings 4: 33) and it is to a branch of hyssop that soldiers affixed the sponge soaked in vinegar which they held out to the dying Jesus (Gospel according to St John).

It grows wild on the stony sunny soils of the Mediterranean coast, on old walls and ruins, and the favourably exposed slopes of the Alps. It is a common garden plant, cultivated almost everywhere as an aromatic and medicinal plant, but also for its ornamental value.

Botanists classify it as a sub-shrub. Its angular hairy stalks form bushy clumps and grow to a height of 50 to 60 centimetres; its leaves are opposite, hairy on both surfaces, and lance-shaped; its flowers are generally mauvey-blue (sometimes pink or white); they are grouped at the tips of the stems, at the axils of the leaves, in tufts arranged at one side.

The whole plant exhales a pleasant aromatic odour, comparable to that of savory or rosemary, only a little more camphor-like. Much used in cooking during the Middle Ages (its leaves, chopped like parsley and chervil, lent a pungent flavour to soups, roast meats and stuffings), it is rarely used in the kitchen today, except in the Midi. On the other hand, its medicinal uses have not diminished or varied.

Hippocrates prescribed it for the treatment of pleurisy and bronchitis; the Salernitan school said that it 'doth successfully purge phlegmatics' (in other words that it evacuates mucus) and 'boiled together with honey, helpeth pulmonic persons'.[1]

Today it is prescribed for all complaints of the respiratory tract (influenza, colds, bronchitis, asthma, pleurisy), for it eases tightness of the chest and, as Doctor Leclerc stresses, 'cleanses the lungs' by facilitating expectoration.

It is taken either as an infusion (20 grammes of flowering tips, picked when coming into flower and dried in the shade, to a litre of boiling water; leave to infuse for five to ten minutes; 2 or 3 cupfuls per day), or as a syrup (pour a litre of boiling water on to 100 grammes of flowering tips and leave to infuse, covered of course, until cold; strain and gently re-heat; adding

1. Gerard states: 'A decoction of Hyssope made with figges, water, honey and rue and drunken, helpeth the old cough.' (*Translator's note.*)

1,600 grammes of sugar; 60 to 100 grammes to be taken, a spoonful at a time, per day). It is advisable not to exceed these amounts, for hyssop can act as an irritant on nervous subjects.

Externally the stronger infusion (50 grammes to a litre of boiling water) is employed on hot compresses in the treatment of wounds, sprains and bruises.

I

IVY, COMMON
Hedera Helix.   Climbing ivy

The ivy was reputed to be the 'enemy of the vine', or rather to prevent drunkenness, which is why Bacchus is always represented with a crown of ivy, why the poets of ancient times, imitating the Roman god of wine, wore ivy wreaths on their heads when they were at a banquet, and why in the taverns of the Middle Ages wine was often drunk from goblets carved out of ivy wood.

Its blackish berries, infused in white wine, were prescribed against the plague; above all, for centuries they furnished peasants with a powerful purgative, whilst the leaves were crushed and used as poultices or fomentations to facilitate suppuration and hasten the healing of sores and wounds (Leonardo da Vinci noted that wounded boar in the forests roll on ivy to heal themselves) and in many regions, particularly in Italy, mothers used to plait caps of ivy for their infants, to reduce inflammation when their heads were covered with impetigo.

Various popular remedies recommend drinking an infusion of ivy leaves for neuralgia and rheumatic pains, bronchitis, whooping cough and inflammation of the mucous membranes. This treatment is probably satisfactory, but because these conditions can all be successfully treated with other plants, I am inclined to advise against the use of ivy internally, however small the dosage prescribed, for it has been shown as Professor Binet has stressed, that 'ivy has the power to destroy the red blood corpuscles in the human body'.

On the other hand, it can be used externally with complete safety and to great advantage. The leaves in fact act as a sedative and highly effective regulator of the sensitivity of the peripheral nerves.

They are therefore prescribed for rheumatism, neuralgia, the after-effects of phlebitis, painful and swollen legs, neuritis, and especially sciatica. They are employed fresh (they are fortunately green all the year round, and ivy is to be found almost everywhere), either chopped and applied directly to the skin, kept in place with bandages, or as poultices (2 handfuls of leaves, finely chopped, mixed with 4 handfuls of bran and quarter of a litre of water to form a paste; warm on a low heat for ten minutes; then spread on a gauze pad and apply to the affected area, keeping in place for at least half an hour); or lastly on hot compresses soaked in a decoction obtained by boiling 150 to 200 grammes of chopped leaves in a litre of water for ten minutes. These same compresses are also recommended for painful areas of cellulitis, both for their soothing effects and their action on the condition of cellulitis itself.

Ivy leaves can render other services: they are a sovereign remedy for corns on the feet (after soaking in a long hot bath, apply a leaf previously soaked for two to three hours in lemon juice or macerated for one or two days in vinegar; cover with a bandage, and repeat daily until the corn is ready to come away easily in a hot bath); their juice, applied as a lotion or on compresses to the forehead and the temples, will soothe headaches and migraines; prepared by decoction (50 to 80 grammes of leaves to a litre of water; boil for ten minutes) they are used as a gargle and mouthwash to cauterize aphtha.

I will add two practical and proven remedies for use in completely different fields: (1) if you have bad toothache and no painkiller to hand, boil a glass of red wine together with 20 grammes of chopped ivy leaves, a good pinch of coarse salt and half a glass of vinegar, and rinse the mouth with this preparation; (2) if you want to remove stains from black or coloured woollen fabric, soak in water in which you have previously boiled a big handful of ivy leaves for a quarter of an hour.

IVY, GROUND-

Glechoma hederacea. Gill-go-over-the-ground, Alehoof, Haymaids, **Nepeta glechoma,** Benth

All that this plant has in common with the previous one is its name, which was given to it because it also has long pliable stems and glossy green leaves.

It grows in abundance in copses, along hedges, at the edge of meadows, in cool shady places. Its main quadrangular stem spreads over the ground, sending up stalks from 10 to 15 centimetres in height which bear slightly hairy leaves in op-

posite pairs, heart-shaped and obtusely crenate at the margins; the small violet-blue flowers, which sometimes have a pinkish tint, are grouped three or four together in the axils of the upper leaves.

The part used is the flowering herb, dried in the shade at a temperature of below 35°C. It can be gathered throughout the flowering season which starts in April and continues into summer. There is nothing against using it fresh, when this is possible; on the contrary one benefits the more by its characteristic aromatic odour – a combination of mint and citronella – which is released when one crushes the leaves.

Ground-ivy was formerly added to beer so that it would keep during long sea voyages.

It was thought to possess beneficent powers (it was made into crowns which were worn while dancing around the Midsummer bonfires, on St John's day), and it was held to be both a 'specific or preventive remedy for stones' and a sovereign treatment for the eyes: in the days when cockfighting was as popular as football is today, if a cock was wounded in the eye its owner would be advised to chew one or two leaves of ground-ivy and spit the juice into the damaged eye, to make it heal rapidly.

The properties of ground-ivy are actually much the same as those of hyssop. It is an excellent expectorant and remarkably beneficial to the mucous membranes, much to be recommended for its cleansing and purgative action on the lungs, stomach, bowel and kidneys.

It is prescribed in cases of bronchitis (5 grammes infused in a cupful (100 cubic centimetres) of boiling milk; leave to infuse for ten to fifteen minutes; to be drunk at bedtime) for it promotes expectoration; for bronchial catarrh, asthma, whooping cough (40 to 50 grammes of dried plant to a litre of water; cold-soak for a few minutes, then bring to boiling point – but do not boil – and leave to infuse for ten to fifteen minutes; 3 or 4 cupfuls per day, between meals). This infusion is also prescribed – because of its action on the mucous membranes – for gastritis, enteritis, hepatic and urinary complaints and intestinal disorders in general.

It is also made into a syrup, which has the same uses and is taken in the amount of 40 to 60 grammes per day between meals, and which is prepared as follows: pound in a mortar 10 handfuls of fresh plant, moistened with 250 grammes of the herbal infusion; cover and leave to macerate for ten to twelve hours; press and strain through a fine cloth; boil up the resultant liquid for a moment; strain; add an equal weight of sugar and simmer gently until of a syrupy consistency; store in a well-corked bottle.

Externally, the infusion is employed as an inhalant in the treatment of head colds and complaints of the respiratory tract; as a gargle and mouthwash for sore throats and inflammation of the buccal mucosa; as a lotion and on compresses to cleanse suppurating wounds and sores and ulcers (poultices of fresh crushed plant have the same effect).

The juice squeezed from the fresh plant, sniffed up through the nose, is a popular remedy for migraine and prolonged headaches.

Oil of ground-ivy (put 8 to 10 handfuls of fresh crushed plant in a litre of olive oil; leave to macerate for a month in a glass jar exposed to the sun, shaking occasionally; strain) is applied as a lotion and on compresses to sores and ulcers, as a pack in the treatment of bronchitis and attacks of gout; a few drops in the ear will soothe earache.

J

JUNIPER
Juniperus communis

This aromatic conifer, a member of the pine family, with its sharp evergreen needles and pyramid-shaped outline, is widely distributed in many parts of the world. It is common in downland, marshy ground, on hillsides and dry mountain slopes. The tree itself grows to varying heights, up to 36 feet in Norway and Sweden, but only to about 6 feet in England. It is a tree of many uses, a 'universal remedy', and a blessing to mankind.

In Mediterranean lands, where it grows to a height of from 12 to 15 metres, its wood, which 'lasts for over a century without rotting', is used in building (Hannibal, according to Pliny, commanded that the beams of the temple of the Ephesian Diana should be of juniper). The alchemists used it for heating their retorts, declaring that lighted coals covered with juniper ashes 'would keep their fire for a whole year'. Branches of juniper, hung on the door of the house, were reputed to keep snakes away by their odour, and they were burnt in public squares, streets and houses during epidemics of plague and cholera: they were used in the same way by Hippocrates to protect Athens against one of these scourges, and in the hospitals of Paris during the smallpox epidemic of 1870.

Lastly, its fruits, known as 'juniper berries', have long held a place in both home cooking and gastronomic specialities. They are put into *choucroute*, salt meat and fish, marinades, *courts-bouillons*. They are used for seasoning thrush, woodcock, grilled fish, sauces; to lend aroma to gin (Great Britain), *pégnet* (Belgium), *schiedam* (Netherlands), *aquavit* (Denmark) and in the manufacture of the spirits appreciated in northern countries which, they say, preserve the inhabitants of these damp lands from rheumatism and gout.

These two conditions are in fact included in the long list of complaints for which the juniper is prescribed, both for external and internal use.

Internally it is considered as a specific for complaints of the urinary tract and the bile ducts (gravel, calculi, renal colic, cystitis, prostatis, cirrhosis, albuminuria, diabetes) for it is antiseptic and increases the volume of urine, to which it gives an odour of violets. It is also prescribed for arthritis and chronic rheumatism (it promotes elimination of uric acid), bronchial catarrh (it controls secretions), intermittent fevers (it encourages sweating), in cases of general debility, sluggishness of the nervous system and the stomach; lack of appetite (it is tonic and aperitif), digestive troubles and intestinal fermentation (it is digestive and dispels flatulence), skin complaints (it is depurative). Under the name *Sabina juniperus* it is a homoeopathic remedy prescribed for women in cases of metrorrhagia and threatened miscarriage during pregnancy.

It is the berries – that is to say the fruits, containing 3 hard little seeds, which remain green for the first two years and only mature, acquiring a bluish-black colour, in the third year – which are employed; they are picked in October to November and should be dried in the open air, being turned over frequently. You may choose from the following methods of preparation:

INFUSION   30 to 40 grammes of crushed berries to a litre of boiling water; leave to infuse for ten minutes; 3 cupfuls per day.

WINE   50 to 60 grammes of crushed berries in a litre of good white wine; leave to macerate for fifteen days, stirring occasionally; strain; sweeten with honey if desired; one wineglassful first thing in the morning or 1 or 2 glassfuls during the day well away from mealtimes.

TINCTURE   macerate 100 grammes of crushed berries in

half a litre of alcohol (45 or 50°) for four or five days; strain; 15 to 20 drops per day, either on a lump of sugar or in half a glass of water.

The Kneipp treatment, prescribed by the famous Abbé, is currently practised in Germany and consists of eating progressive amounts of berries: four the first day, increasing by one a day up to fifteen, then reducing by one a day to four again, the course of treatment thus lasting for twenty-three days. Chewing juniper berries is also recommended to persons in contact with sickness or who wish to protect themselves against fevers in swampy countries.

Externally, the decoction of young branches or crushed berries (250 grammes of branches or 100 grammes of berries to 2 litres of water; boil for an hour and a half to two hours) on compresses will soothe sciatic pains, rheumatism and lumbago. It is also used for bathing long-standing ulcers and atonic wounds and sores, promoting healing.

Frictions with the tincture described above or with oil of juniper (100 grammes of crushed berries to half a litre of olive oil; leave to macerate for fifteen days to a month in a transparent jar or bottle, shaking occasionally and making sure that the mixture is exposed to the heat of the sun) will soothe neuralgia and rheumatic pains, lumbago, sciatica, stitches in the side, and muscular pains in general. You may of course follow this treatment by applying a pad of cotton wool soaked in either of these preparations to the affected area, covering it with a piece of woollen cloth and keeping it in place with a bandage.

Fumigation and vapour treatment with juniper (boiling the berries in a saucepan as with eucalyptus, or throwing the berries on to the fire) are excellent ways of disinfecting rooms and the people in them; Doctor Cazin recommends 'breathing in through the nose' juniper vapour or smoke as a remedy for chronic head-cold, and the Abbé Kneipp sang the praises of juniper in these words:

I cannot understand the father or mother who, whilst carefully seasoning the family's meat and *choucroute* with salt and juniper, and meticulously filling their homes with the fragrance of juniper, will let the body, which is the dwelling place of the soul, wallow in filth and dust. This dwelling place too, from time to time during the year, needs fumigating and vapourizing with juniper: this cleanses the body and soothes the respiratory apparatus.

K

KNAPWEED, BLUE See CORNFLOWER

KNOTGRASS
Polygonum aviculare. Birds' knotgrass, Knotweed, Iron grass, Ninety knot, Pink weed, Sparrow tongue, Doorweed

Knotgrass belongs to the same family as bistort;[1] it has the same properties and shares the same medicinal uses, but it has the advantage of adapting well to every type of soil and climate – so well, in fact, that it has virtually spread across the entire world (in China and Japan a blue dye comparable to indigo was extracted from its leaves), and is readily available to everyone.

You must have trodden upon it hundreds of times, on footpaths and quiet roads and in courtyards (it even grows between the paving stones), without noticing it, for there is nothing very eyecatching about its appearance. Its branching wiry stems spread along the ground, having nodular joints at the axils of the leaves which are alternate, small, narrow and pointed; its flowers, white or pinkish, are clustered in groups of two to four in the axils of the leaves and not very noticeable.

The stems – for which birds show a particular liking – are the part of the plant which is gathered during the flowering season (June to September) and utilized, fresh or dried in the shade, both in human and veterinary medicine (breeders employ it successfully in the treatment of diarrhoea in pigs and all farm animals).

The ancients praised knotgrass as a remedy for the spitting of blood and held it to be the specific for diarrhoea, an opinion confirmed by several modern authorities who all acknowledge

1. See page 52.

that cases of diarrhoea which have resisted all other treatments will respond rapidly to the astringent action of knotgrass, as country folk have always known.

The decoction (20 to 30 grammes of fresh plant or 50 grammes of dried plant to a litre of water; boil for ten to fifteen minutes; leave to infuse for the same length of time; 4 or 5 cupfuls, altogether about half a litre, per day) is prescribed as a remedy for diarrhoea, dysentery, enteritis, catarrhal conditions of the respiratory, digestive and urinary tracts, cystitis due to the presence of calculi (knotgrass is also a good diuretic), gout, skin diseases, arthritic complaints, prolonged or over-heavy menstrual discharge, spitting of blood, haemorrhages due to gastric ulcers, congestive disorders of the circulation (varicose veins, haemorrhoids, phlebitis); it is also recommended as a tonic in pulmonary tuberculosis.

Externally, poultices of crushed knotgrass (previously

washed in boiled water) arrest bleeding from wounds and promote the rapid healing of sores (the plant is rich in tannin and silicic acid).

L

LADY'S BEDSTRAW

Galium verum.   True bedstraw, Yellow bedstraw, Maid's hair, Hundredfold, Cheese-rennet, Gailion, Pettimugget, Wild rosemary

Lady's bedstraw (not to be confused with other species common in Britain, such as hedge bedstraw and goose-grass or cleavers) acts as sudorific, antispasmodic, milk diuretic and astringent.

It is a common herb growing in meadows and pastures, in hedges, on the edges of woodland and on downs. Its stems are slender and square (30 to 50 centimetres high); the leaves are slender, whitish on the upper surface, and arranged around the stem in whorls of from six to eight; its small (2 to 3 millimetres across) golden-yellow flowers are borne in terminal panicles. The whole plant exhales an aromatic odour not unlike the scent of honey or lime blossoms.

It was formerly regarded as a remedy for epilepsy, but today it is prescribed only for disturbances of nervous origin (stomach pains, insomnia, vertigo, hysteria) and as a diuretic employed in the treatment of dropsy, obesity and skin diseases.

It is taken as an infusion (20 to 30 grammes of dried leaves and flowering tips to a litre of water; 3 cupfuls per day between meals).

One of its local names, cheese-rennet, derives from a former use of the flowers in the north of England to curdle milk for making cheese, instead of using rennet.

LAUREL

Laurus nobilis. Bay, Sweet bay, Noble laurel, Roman laurel

Its traditional double role is perfectly described by Doctor Leclerc who introduces it as a plant that both 'crowns the heads of heroes and flavours the stews of the plebs'.

It is a native of the Mediterranean shores where, according to legend, it came into being when the nymph Daphne was turned by the gods into a fragrant laurel tree to save her from the amorous pursuit of Apollo, god of light (he drove the chariot of the sun) and the arts. The Greeks and Romans therefore naturally dedicated it to the sun and believed that it protected them against thunderbolts ('for which reasons', says Matthiolus, 'Tiberius Caesar wore a head-covering of laurel whenever it thundered').

Like the olive, the laurel was a symbol of peace. In Rome

the people would wave its branches as a sign of rejoicing; it decorated the palaces of emperors and great pontiffs; it adorned the statues of Jupiter at the news of a victory; it crowned conquering generals, and poets and happy lovers.

This tradition came to us along with the plant itself, which adapted well to our less clement regions. In the Middle Ages, too, artists and poets, learned men and new university graduates were given crowns of laurel leaves and berries, whence the name *bacca laurea* (modern French *baccalauréat*) given to the school-leaving certificate that has latterly been subjected to so many ups-and-downs).[1]

The laurel has also always had an important place in cooking, its aromatic and antiseptic properties making it a highly valued ingredient of sauces, *courts-bouillons*, marinades, as well as in medicine, which makes use of both leaves and berries (which look like small olives; they succeed the little greenish-white flowers in the axils of the leaves, and become blue-black when fully mature), the former for its properties as a stimulant, antispasmodic and stomachic, the latter because they are diuretic, febrifuge, expectorant and antirheumatic.

The infusion (30 to 40 grammes of fresh or dried leaves to a litre of boiling water; leave to infuse for five to ten minutes; 2 or 3 cupfuls per day, immediately after meals if required mainly to aid the digestion, or else three hours after meals) is prescribed for stomach pains, dyspepsia, flatulence, influenza, chronic bronchitis. One may also chew a bay leaf before meals: it promotes salivary secretion and therefore aids the digestion (the Pythonesses (or priestesses) of the temple of Apollo at Delphi also chewed bay leaves, but for a different purpose: to put themselves in a favourable state to deliver their oracles).

The decoction of the pitted and crushed berries (20 to 40 grammes to a litre of water; boil for five minutes; leave to infuse for ten minutes; 2 or 3 cupfuls per day, before or between meals) is recommended for dropsy, fever, rheumatism.

1. The English title 'Poet Laureate' is similarly derived from the aurel crowns of ancient Rome. (*Translator's note.*)

As a treatment for chronic rheumatism you can try a ten-day course of the following old prescription which has been praised by Doctor Cazin: 30 grammes of laurel berries, 30 grammes of box wood to 1·5 litres of water; bring to the boil and simmer gently until reduced to a litre; lastly add the peel of a lemon (chemically untreated, of course); 3 glassfuls per day.

The leaves, dried and powdered, constitute an excellent preventive medicine against intermittent fevers: 1 gramme of powder, macerated for eight to ten hours in a glass of cold water, is administered two hours before the start of the expected bout of fever. This same powder, sprinkled on atonic ulcers, swiftly cleanses them and promotes healing.

An excellent unguent used as a massage in the treatment of rheumatism is prepared by macerating for several hours in a *bain-marie* crushed fresh leaves and crushed dried berries in double their weight of pork fat.

LAVENDER

Lavandula spica or **Lavandula vera.** True lavender, Official lavender

For thousands of years lavender has been used not only for its fragrance but also as disinfectant, vulnerary, sedative, stimulant, tonic and carminative.

Long before anyone thought of making bath-salts, deodorants, or insecticides to protect clothing, the Romans used lavender in their bath water (its name in fact derives from the Latin *lavare*, to wash); sachets of lavender were placed in chests and cupboards; lavender oil was brushed over bedsteads to rid them of bed bugs and applied to the heads of children to kill lice and their eggs.

Long before the discovery of the existence of the microbes responsible for infections and the invention of antivenom serums, lavender was used, as an oil, tincture or essence, to heal sword wounds and burns, whilst huntsmen in the regions where it grew would save the life of a dog stung by a viper by immediately rubbing the bite with a handful of lavender crushed between their fingers.

Once again modern analyses have shown empiricism to have been right, for the essential oil extracted from lavender is a powerful antiseptic (in the smallest quantities it will kill the diphtheria bacillus, typhoid bacillus, Koch's bacillus as well as streptococcus and pneumococcus) as well as a remarkable neutralizing agent of venom, which accounts for the interest taken in it by Saint Hildegard, the Benedictine abbess as famed for her visions as her learning, who devoted an entire chapter to it in her famous medical treatise, and the constant use made of it in folk medicine.

It is the flowering tips and above all the little blue flowers, picked before fully in bloom and dried in the shade, that form the base of various preparations.

A mild infusion (5 grammes to a litre of boiling water; leave to infuse for five minutes; 2 or 3 cupfuls per day, between meals) is sedative and antispasmodic, and therefore prescribed for disorders of nervous origin (insomnia, poor digestion, migraines, irritability); a stronger infusion (20 to 30 grammes to a litre of boiling water; leave to infuse for five minutes; same posology) is stimulant, sudorific, tonic, disinfectant and diuretic, and therefore prescribed for complaints of the respiratory tract (coryza, acute laryngitis, bronchitis, whooping cough, asthma), chills, infectious diseases (influenza), feverishness, tiredness, chlorosis.

For eruptive fevers and infectious diseases, you can also use a classic remedy composed of five flowers, in the following amounts: 10 grammes of lavender, 5 grammes each of borage, marigold, broom, pansy; one tablespoonful to a cupful of boiling water; leave to infuse for ten minutes; 3 or 4 cupfuls per day.

Lavender oil (a handful of fresh flowers in a litre of olive oil; leave to macerate for three days in the sun, in a transparent bottle or jar; press and strain through a cloth; add another handful of fresh flowers and repeat the operation until the oil is highly perfumed, which indicates that it is saturated with the active principles of the plant) is prescribed, internally (5 or 6 drops per day on a lump of sugar) for migraines, vertigo, digestive disorders of nervous origin; externally, as a lotion or on compresses, it is employed as a remedy for burns, dry eczema bronchitis, congestion of the lungs.

The tincture – which is prepared by macerating 100 grammes of fresh flowers in half a litre alcohol (45°) for fifteen days or so – used as a lotion or friction several times a week, strengthens the hair; as a friction it is also effective against rheumatism, and on compresses is prescribed for contusions; as a gargle and mouthwash (a few drops in a glass of tepid water) it is prescribed for paralysis of the tongue.

Lastly, also externally, an infusion (15 to 30 grammes of flowers to a litre of boiling water; leave to infuse for ten minutes) is used as a douche in the treatment of leucorrhoea or 'whites', and in the treatment by inhalation of throat and bronchial complaints.

LEEK
Allium porrum

The leek can by no means be dismissed as 'the poor man's asparagus'[1]: well prepared it is a gastronomic delicacy in its own right, and in terms of nourishment is in fact far superior to asparagus, by virtue of its wealth of active principles essential to our health. It is one of the many health-giving foods (garlic, corn, carrots, cabbage, turnip, onion, etc.) which, eaten regularly, kept our grandmothers fit, unaware that they were applying dietetics principles.

It is not known where the leek originated, but we do know that it has been cultivated for thousands of years since, 2,000 years before our own era, the Egyptians used it to treat burns

1. Anatole France: *Crainquebille*.

and bites. We also know that it was valued not only as a food but for its medicinal virtues by the Greeks and Romans: Pliny recounts how Nero ate leeks 'for certaine daies in every moneth for to scoure his throat, and cleare his voice, and to take it with oile; on which days he did eat nothing else, not so much as bread'; and the Salernitan school gives us two of its common usages – to restore fertility to sterile women (leeks to be eaten in quantity) and to arrest nose-bleeds (the juice of leeks snuffed up the nostrils).

Our humble peasant classes have always eaten leeks and used them, both internally and externally, to remedy their ills. Tradition, founded on successive generations of experience, has taught them that leeks are diuretic, pectoral, antiseptic, emollient, and they continue to sue them in the treatment of many conditions.

INTERNALLY For obesity, kidney complaints (nephritis, gravel), intestinal disorders (diarrhoea, dysentery, enteritis), hoarseness, coughs: drink plenty of leek stock, obtained by simmering gently for three hours eight or ten leeks, cut into pieces, in 2 or 3 litres of water (Matthiolus says that 'the leek provoketh urine and maketh healthy bowels'). For infantile diarrhoea, give the child a coffeespoonful of this stock every five minutes and apply a hot compress soaked in the stock on his stomach every hour (naturally, apart from the stock, he should be given no other food). For enteritis in adults, drink a cupful of stock every half hour and abstain from all other food and drink.

For gravel, urine retention, diabetes: either boil a kilo of white leeks, chopped in pieces, in 2 litres of dry white wine until reduced to half the volume, and strain; one wineglassful first thing in the morning every day for a month; or macerate 4 or 5 grammes of crushed leek seeds in a litre of dry white wine for four or five days; strain; one wineglassful first thing in the morning for a month.

For colds, coughs, whooping-cough, hoarseness, bronchial

pains and engorgement: either cook a few leeks in water; extract the juice by squeezing in a cloth when they are almost soft; add honey, and take the syrup thus obtained at the onset of a bout of coughing as well as morning and evening (one table-spoonful); or cook a few leeks in very little water; reduce to a pulp when they are cooked, adding 2 spoonfuls of honey; a tablespoonful to be taken at the start of an attack (it used to be said that partridges ate leeks to render their cry more piercing).

For the accidental swallowing of a needle, pin, nail: give the person boiled leeks to eat as soon as possible; their fibres will sheathe the sharp point of the object and prevent it from damaging or perforating the stomach or the bowel; until the object has been expelled in the normal way, the person should remain on a diet of leeks and limit his liquid intake as far as possible. I speak from first-hand knowledge, for when I was about ten years old I swallowed a nail 4 to 5 centimetres long and – without pain but not without trepidation (I could see myself on the stretcher!) I evacuated it three days later thanks to this technique, which incidentally was advised by our family doctor. (Doctor Pierre Fournier also recommends this method, with leeks or asparagus or, if neither of these is to hand, with little pieces of cotton wool 'neither bigger nor thicker than a little finger nail' soaked in oil: 'Above all, do not panic!' he writes. 'If you do this, and do it promptly and properly, the child will be in no danger'.)

EXTERNALLY For bee or wasp stings, or itching caused by harvest-bugs: cut a leek in half and rub briskly on the affected area; the acid from the leek decomposes the poison, reduces the swelling, and stops the pain in a few minutes. Leek leaves, macerated in vinegar for twenty-four hours, and applied for several consecutive nights to corns on the toes and the sole of the foot, will render them easy to remove.

For abscesses, boils, carbuncles, whitlows, gatherings, to bring them to a head more quickly: either cook in hot ashes for fifteen to twenty minutes the white part of a leek, wrapped in wet paper or a cabbage leaf; mash together with unsalted lard and apply as a poultice, to be renewed several times a day; or else cook some finely-chopped leeks in lard for fifteen to twenty minutes; mash to a paste and apply hot, renewing the application several times a day.

For pleurisy, cramping pain in the side: cut up and pound in a mortar, adding a little wine vinegar from time to time, the white part of a fat bunch of leeks; transfer the mixture to a pan and cook, sprinkling with vinegar as necessary to prevent it from sticking to the pan; spread this preparation on a cloth and apply hot to the painful area, keeping in place with a bandage; retain for twenty-four hours.

Finally, here is a household recipe, invented or handed down by the chemist Raspail whose name is commemorated by the famous boulevard: soak a bunch of leeks, chopped into pieces, in half a bucket of water for a week; strain and use the infusion for washing any paintings, mirrors, lamp shades, etc. that one wishes to protect from being dirtied by flies.

LEMON
Citrus medica or Citrus limonum.

The lemon tree is probably a native of Medea, in other words that part of the present state of Iran situated between the Tigris basin and the Caspian Sea (cf. Arab. *laimùn* and Persian *limun*, meaning citrus fruits).

Mentioned by Virgil for its properties of sweetening the breath and steadying the pulse rate of trembling old men, the lemon is today medically recognized as an antiseptic and hypotensive prescribed for arteriosclerosis.

Yet for a long time it was chiefly employed only as a moth-deterrent and antidote. According to Parkinson, Matthiolus says that, 'the whole fruit or the branches of the trees laid in presses, Chests, or Wardrobes, keepeth cloath, or strike Garments from Moth and Wormes, and give them a good sent also.' Also that 'these seedes are very effectuall to preserve the heart and vitall spirits, from the poyson of the Scorpion or the venemous creatures'. This property was supposedly discovered by the Egyptians in the following manner: a governor had condemned two evil-doers to be thrown to the snakes; as they were being led away to their torture, a woman, feeling pity for them, gave them some lemons which they ate as they went on their way, and when they were 'attacked and bitten by the famished creatures', they were none the worse for it. The governor in astonishment inquired into the reason for this extraordinary resistance and, on being informed of the incident of the lemons, submitted the two men to the same torture the following day, 'having first given lemons to one of the evil-doers and to the other not': the latter was struck dead on the spot, whilst his companion escaped unharmed.

Whether the story is true or not, the lemon came to be included in most of the complicated mixtures held to be antidotes, and to be used in the kitchen to attenuate the effects of high meat or fish that was almost as high. It must certainly have prevented many cases of poisoning, as indeed it does today when we add a few drops of lemon juice to oysters and shellfish (we now know that the smallest amount of lemon juice can kill the bacillus of cholera, diphtheria and typhoid; in the space of a quarter of an hour, it rids oysters of 92 per cent of their bacteria).

The lemon is thus antiseptic and bactericide, but it is also antiscorbutic (the English navy was the first to distribute daily rations of lemon to crews remaining at sea for more than fifteen days), anti-rheumatic, diuretic, astringent, vermifuge, refrigerant, febrifuge, tonic, hepatic, antineuralgic, and more besides.

It is therefore only to be expected that it features in many home remedies that date from a time when fruits still grew as nature intended, which is not the case today. Now we have to be careful to use only lemons that have been 'biologically' cultivated, in other words that have not been treated with pesticides and have not been subjected to that fearful preservative, diphenyl, which, not content with poisoning the peel and rendering it unfit for consumption, also contaminates the outer part of the pulp. You can purchase fruit that is free from chemicals at health food stores.

To quench the thirst, especially when the patient is feverish, prepare a lemonade by mixing the juice of a lemon with half a litre of slightly sweetened water, kept at room temperature.

For liver complaints, pour a litre of boiling water sweetened with a tablespoonful of honey on to a lemon cut into rings (and unpeeled); leave to infuse and drink warm, in small cupfuls, in the course of the day.

For influenza, colds and chills, go to bed and drink the juice of a lemon in a cup of very hot coffee; this beverage induces perspiration (it is a popular febrifuge in Greece, while in Guadaloupe they take the powdered bark from the root of the lemon tree).

For worms (oxyuris), children should be given the pips of a lemon crushed in honey first thing in the morning for several days – a remedy they will take willingly.

For sore throats, angina, aphtha, stomatitis: gargle or rinse the mouth (several times a day) with the juice of a lemon in a glass of warm water into which has been stirred a coffeespoonful of honey; you can also apply compresses of slightly salted lemon juice to the throat.

To check a head cold or a runny nose, inhale through the nose some lemon juice, diluted in water to start with, then pure.

To arrest nasal haemorrhages, apply a wad of cotton wool soaked in lemon juice.

To relieve headaches and migraine: either cut a lemon in half, apply a half to each temple and keep in place with a scarf for ten to fifteen minutes; or apply compresses of slightly salted lemon juice to the forehead.

For neuralgia and rheumatism, gently rub the painful areas with half a lemon.

To aid the digestion and relieve stomachache, put a tablespoonful of lemon juice in a glass of hot water; sip it slowly over the space of twenty minutes.

I come now to the uses of the lemon in beauty treatments and about the house.

Beauty: a mixture of equal parts of lemon juice, glycerine and eau de cologne (or rose water) used as a hand lotion each evening will keep hands soft and smooth; lemon juice applied morning and evening every day for a week will prevent nails from chipping; slightly salted lemon juice used as lotion three times a day will cause freckles to disappear; lastly, lemon juice applied on a pad of cotton wool as a lotion several times a week is recommended for oily skins (leave to dry for twenty minutes before applying makeup) and for wrinkles (it will also lighten the complexion).

House: sachets of dried lemon peel hung inside cupboards will prevent moths; ink or vegetable stains on the fingers can be removed with lemon juice; to remove rust stains from white linen, place a ring of lemon sandwiched between two layers of cloth on the stain, apply a very hot iron, and repeat until the stain has disappeared; to clean blackened copper, rub with half a lemon which has been sprinkled with coarse salt; to clean silver jewellery, rub with a slice of lemon, then rinse in hot water and dry with a chamois leather.

LETTUCE
Lactuca sativa.

For me, the tranquil happiness that one feels when one gets away from the world of illusory honours and false pleasures is admirably expressed by the reply made by the emperor Diocletian, after his abdication, to a friend who was begging him to return to power: 'My friend, if you could see what fine lettuces I am growing, you would not urge me so hard to take up that burden again.'

I often think of his remark as I tend my own, and reflect that for that alone, if for no other reason, the lettuce deserves a place in the honours list of plants; but it can happily justify its place of honour with other claims, for all that some might doubt them.

Since ancient times, the lettuce has been known above all for its narcotic properties which, on the one hand, facilitate sleep (which no one is likely to complain about in this day and age) and, on the other hand, exert a sedative action on sexual drive (which, in this time of eroticism-worship, will not be to everyone's taste).

Hippocrates prescribed it as a sedative. Galen (according to Matthiolus) declared: 'Approaching the age when one no longer sleeps as well as in youth, I was greatly angered at being unable to sleep; I have found no better remedy for this trouble than eating lettuce of an evening.' Suetonius reports that a statue was raised to Musa, physician to Augustus, for having cured the emperor of melancholy by making him eat lettuce. The Pythagoreans called it the 'eunuchs' plant' and Dioscorides recommended its juice to temper lust. In the Middle Ages it was believed to increase milk in wet-nurses and nursing mothers and 'quench the fires of lechery'. In the course of centuries it thus acquired the reputation of sapping virility and diminishing fertility, and was shunned as the 'enemy of pleasure and poison of love'.

Common sense of course disposes of any such notion. As Doctor Cazin says: 'One has only to see villagers eating their big platefuls of lettuce salad every evening surrounded by their large families' to realize that it isn't a helping, or even two, of salad that is going to jeopardize your amorous reserves: if it is true, as some like to maintain, that various hermits did indeed rely on lettuce to help them through the rigours of celibacy, they must have eaten enormous quantities of it, and when it is nowadays medically prescribed for priapism, spermatorrhoeia or involuntary sexual excitation in women, it is in the concentrated form of Lactucarium (lettuce-opium), in other words the juice or milk latex that is collected from the stems, the posology in such cases being in no way comparable to the feeble amounts of active product contained in a good helping of salad.

So there is nothing to worry about: you can enjoy your lettuce – its leaves moreover contain a kind of antidote to its anaphrodisiac effects: vitamin E, called the 'fertility vitamin' – it will improve your digestion, regularize your bowel functions because of its roughage, and enable you to sleep well.

For insomnia a decoction is also recommended: one lettuce, simmered gently in half a litre of water for fifteen to twenty minutes; drink a large bowlful at bedtime for several days. This decoction – which has the advantage of not clouding the mental faculties, as opium does, nor causing constipation – is also prescribed for gastric spasms, palpitations, congestion of the liver, nervous coughs (whooping cough, bronchitis) – 3 cupfuls per day, between meals. (One may, according to season, substitute the seeds – lettuce seed was one of the four 'cold seeds' of the ancient pharmacopocia 20 to 30 grammes to a litre of water; boil for ten to fifteen minutes; 3 cupfuls per day.)

Externally, the decoction of fresh plant or seeds is employed as a lotion or on compresses as a remedy for acne, erysipelas, boils, skin inflammations in general, and ophthalmia. Lastly, it is used, in a possibly stronger amount, as a soothing toilet water that makes the skin satin smooth and soothes sunburn.

LILAC

Syringa vulgaris.   Common lilac

A native of Asia Minor, the lilac was only introduced into France in 1597 and has retained its Persian name, *Lilâk*, virtually unchanged.

In the nineteenth century some doctors noted that it was a particularly effective febrifuge in the treatment of intermittent fevers. Experiments undertaken by several of their colleagues led to contradictory results: on the one hand, spectacular successes that led to the claim that it was an 'indigenous substitute for quinine'; on the other hand, a series of failures led to the conclusion that it 'should never have been brought out of the obscurity where it belonged' . . . so that in the end it has been largely forgotten and is only rarely used medicinally.

However, I shall side with Doctor Cazin who, basing his judgement on personal observations, sometimes negative and sometimes positive, says that he believes the lilac is deserving of attention, a 'coin in our treasury of indigenous medicinal plants'. So there are two prescriptions for use of the treatment of fevers, particularly malaria: either an infusion of fresh leaves (5 grammes to a cupful of boiling water; leave to infuse for five to ten minutes; 2 or 3 cupfuls per day), or a decoction of fruit (30 grammes of still-green capsules to 700 grammes of water; boil until reduced to 500 grammes; to be drunk in small cupfuls in the course of the day).

The flowers are used in Russia to make an unguent recommended for rheumatism in the joints: macerate 100 grammes of fresh flowers in half a litre of olive oil for fifteen days, in a glass jar (covered with a paper, like a jam jar) exposed to the sun; press and strain; apply to the affected areas twice a day – rubbing well in until the unguent is completely absorbed.

LILY, MADONNA
Lilium candidum

The madonna lily is a native of the eastern Mediterranean: according to legend, two drops of milk fell from the lips of the infant Hercules while he was nursing at Juna's breast: one spread across the sky, and became the Milky Way; the other fell to earth, and from it was born the madonna lily.

The flower has been known since ancient times; it features among the allegorical signs in the Egypt of the Pharaohs; King Solomon compares a young maiden to the 'lily of the valleys'; Jesus speaks of the lilies of the field, who 'toil not, neither do they spin', In Hebrew, the same word *schscham* designated both the lily and the colour white, whence the Christian name 'Suzanne'; the Greeks called it the 'flower of flowers', and sewed its petals end to end to make ephemeral precious cloths; the Romans made lirium from it, the most popular of the many perfumes which they used in profusion; the Church associates it with the Virgin Mary, image of majesty and purity like the lily itself, whence its place in the decoration of churches and in processions.

The medicinal use of the lily also apparently dates back to ancient times. Its petals, fresh or macerated in alcohol (my grandmother used to put them in the *eau-de-vie* she brought back from her village), are an excellent antiseptic and promote speedier healing of sores and burns – which is only natural, for today we know that they contain boron, which gives the famous botacic acid.

The bulb of the lily, cooked in the oven, in hot ashes, or in milk with rye flour (one large tablespoonful of flour and one glassful of milk to two bulbs) is employed as a warm poultice (to be renewed three times a day) to subdue the stabbing pains of abscesses, boils, whitlows and carbuncles, and bring them quickly to a head, and to heal chilblains and chapped skin. Used raw, the crushed bulb applied for several consecutive days will get rid of corns on the feet.

The lily is also used as a beauty treatment: for blotchiness and redness of the face, apply lily water as a skin lotion morning and evening, letting it dry on the skin; it is obtained by boiling 120 grammes of bulbs in half a litre of water until reduced by a third. For wrinkles, massage in gentle circular movements with the juice of a white lily bulb.

LILY-OF-THE-VALLEY

Convallaria majalis. Convallaria, May lily, Conval lily, Lily confancy, Wood lily

As has often been the case, empiricism was ahead of science:

several centuries before scientists established the presence of a glucoside – given the name of convallamarin – which 'constitutes a very powerful cardiac remedy' – country folk used to make an infusion of lily-of-the-valley flowers for people suffering from a 'weak heart'.

It must be pointed out that this 'discovery' of the therapeutic virtue of lily-of-the-valley might have been made much sooner had we taken the trouble to consult our ancient and much-scorned herbals, for Matthiolus, in the sixteenth century, wrote that lily-of-the-valley will 'strengthen the heart and combat spasms and palpitation'.[1]

However, it is now recognized that its effects are those of a sedative restoring the equilibrium of the sympathetic nervous system and exercising a tonic and regulating action upon the heart. The infusion (1 or 2 grammes of dried flowers to 100 grammes of boiling water; leave to infuse for five minutes; sweeten liberally, preferably with honey, for it is very bitter; to be taken once a day, between meals) is therefore prescribed for cardiac complaints of nervous origin (palpitations) and cardiac oedema (according to Doctor Fruictier, this infusion has always been employed in the treatment of dropsy in Russia).

The flowers, dried in the shade and reduced to a powder, were also formerly considered as 'cephalic'. Ancient herbals specify that this powder 'is a very powerful sternutatory prescribed for clearing the brain in paralysis and inflammations of the head, vertigo and other conditions caused by immoderate cold and damp in the brain'.

There is no reason to suppose that this remedy, too, will not one day be rediscovered: Doctor Cazin, who has tested it, says: 'This powder, taken like snuff, has relieved long-standing headaches and cured cases of chronic inflammation of the eyes

1. Culpeper writes: '. . . the syrup helps much to procure rest and to settle the brain of frantic persons, by cooling the hot temperature of the head . . . The distilled water of the flowers is very effectual . . . and is recommended to take freckles, spots, sunburn and morphew from the face and other parts of the body.' (*Translator's note.*)

and ears, vertigo caused by suppression of nasal mucous, etc.,
by promoting the expulsion of natural secretions through the
nostrils.'

LIME, COMMON
Tilia europea.   Linden

Dedicated to Venus, the lime tree has always been used in
medicine just as it has in witchcraft: Pliny refers to the beneficial effects of lime-bark vinegar on skin blemishes; Saint
Hildegard warded off the plagues in the Middle Ages with a
ring embellished with a green stone beneath which was a
fragment of lime wrapped in a spider's web, and many herbals
praised the action of lime flowers on epilepsy (some even claim
that persons sitting under the shade of the tree were cured!),
paralysis, vertigo and oedema. Its importance was such that
by royal command lime trees were planted along roads and
avenues, and the harvest reserved for the use of the hospitals.

The flowers, gathered when fully in bloom (June to July) and
dried in the shade below 35°C, are known for their sedative,
cooling and antispasmodic properties. In infusion (one good
pinch to a cupful (100 cubic centimetres) of boiling water;
leave to infuse for five to ten minutes; three times a day, after
meals) they are prescribed for digestive complaints of nervous
origin, migraines, palpitations, vertigo and angor, nervous
predisposition, insomnia; they are given as a drink to assuage
the thirst of feverish patients.

They also have a place, according to Doctor Leclerc, in the
treatment of arteriosclerosis, thinning the blood and thereby
improving circulation: one cupful of infusion (as above) to be
taken four times a day, between meals.

Externally, the decoction (40 to 50 grammes of dried flowers
to a litre of water; simmer gently for fifteen to twenty minutes)
used daily as a skin lotion will clear impurities from the skin,
'remove wrinkles and freckles from the face', encourage hair

growth. Added to the bath (200 grammes to 2 litres of water) it
has a sedative effect on nervous and over-excited children.

The sap-wood of the lime tree – which is that part of the
trunk or branches between the hard wood and the bark – is
also used medicinally: it promotes the draining of fluids and
therefore gives excellent results in the treatment of the following: calculi (kidneys, bladder, liver), renal or hepatic colic,
rheumatism, gout, sciatica, excess of urea, albumin and cholesterol, and diabetes. Studies have established that the most active
product is that furnished by the wild lime trees of Roussillon,
for the quality of herbal infusions – like wine – is affected by the
nature of the soil.

LIQUORICE
Glycyrrhiza glabra

'The use of this root is so common that it is included in every
herbal infusion, either to cover with its sweetness the unpleasant
flavour of the other ingredients, or to lend its own particular
virtue of soothing the acrid humours that excite coughs . . . '

These lines from an old pharmacopoeia have the merit of
giving the essential concerning this shrub, namely that the part
used is the root, and that it is a pleasant demulcent as well as
an excellent cough remedy. Its efficacy in this respect was known
to the Greeks and the Romans, to Theophrastus and Saint
Hildegard, who employed liquorice to cleanse the bronchi and
clear the voice – it was often called 'Scythic' because the
ancients declared that the Scythians, those redoubtable warriors
of antiquity, could, by chewing liquorice, go for ten days
without eating or drinking, for it assuages both hunger and
thirst.

Fact or fiction? What is certain is that liquorice grows wild
in the southern parts of Europe (France, Spain, Italy, Russia) and
in the Middle East, namely in that area of the Caucasus and
Iran occupied by the Scythians, and that it is thirst-quenching:

combined with barley and couchgrass, it was the principal ingredient in the drink called 'cure-all' that not so long ago was to be found on the bedside table of every hospital patient; it was also used to make liquorice-water, the famous popular drink known under the name of coco (apparently because it was originally sold in cups made from coconut shells), which itinerant salesmen peddled in parks right up to the early years of this century. I recall, too, the sticks and ribbons of black liquorice we smuggled into school as children.

You are unlikely to come across this shrub growing wild, so I shall only give you a very brief description of its appearance – 1 metre to 1·50 metres high, leaves composed of numerous leaflets like acacia leaves, small reddish flowers arranged in spikes, succeeded by pods of seeds – and come without further ado to the ways in which its root is utilized both medicinally and in the home.

Dried liquorice root is sold both in herbalists' and grocers' shops. It is advisable to peel it immediately before use, in order to remove the bitter outer bark. It is recommended as a remedy for colds, bronchitis, bronchial catarrh, sore throats, laryngitis, gastritis, stomach ulcers, and prepared by decoction (40 to 50 grammes to a litre of water; boil for ten to fifteen minutes; drink as required). As a mouthwash, a concentrated decoction (200 grammes to 1 litre) is prescribed in cases of glossitis, when the mucous membrane of the tongue is scarlet, covered with clotches and very painful cracks.

Apart from liquorice water ('coco') – which is made either with the powder sold in the shops, or by macerating 50 grammes of root to a litre of water for twenty-four hours with a pinch of aniseed or fennel and a few slices of lemon – you can make an excellent refreshing beverage, equally suitable for sick or healthy persons (as a cool summer drink it is more thirst-quenching than any of the bottled drinks on the market) in the following way: macerate 30 to 40 grammes of liquorice root (peeled) for twenty-four hours in 1 litre of cold water; boil 20 grammes of dried couchgrass roots in 1 litre of water for fifteen to twenty minutes, and when cold mix together the two infusions and sweeten to taste, preferably with honey. When serving, a slice of lemon or a sliver of lemon peel may be added to each glass – not that this is necessary, but it makes it look prettier.

LOOSESTRIFE, PURPLE   See PURPLE LOOSESTRIFE

LUNGWORT, COMMON
Pulmonaria officinalis.   Beggar's basket, Jerusalem cowslip

In pursuance of the doctrine of signatures, because its leaves are spotted with blotches of a paler colour that call to mind the appearance of a diseased lung, it seemed obvious that the lung-wort must be the specific for lung complaints; the plant was accordingly so named, and formerly widely employed in the medicines and syrups prescribed for all chest complaints, from simple bronchial inflammation to serious conditions that would today be labelled 'tuberculosis'.

It is unlikely that lungwort ever cured consumption, as was often claimed long ago. On the other hand it most certainly has

a beneficial action on complaints of the respiratory tract for, through its active principles (tannin, silica, potassium nitrate, iron, lime, mucillage), it fortifies the bronchi, relieves inflammation, promotes perspiration (it is closely related to borage), soothes coughs and acts as an expectorant.

The whole plant – leaves and flowers gathered in May to June and dried in the shade – is therefore recommended for coughs, bronchitis, bronchial catarrh, influenza, hoarseness, pharyngitis, prepared as a mild decoction (30 to 40 grammes to a litre of water; bring slowly to the boil, boil for two to three minutes; leave to infuse for ten minutes, 3 or 4 cupfuls per day, at regular intervals; sweeten, preferably with honey which strengthens its soothing action). In several regions chest sufferers are given regular doses of an infusion made with a mixture of equal parts of lungwort, plantain and coltsfoot (*tussilago*), using the same proportion of plant, the same method of preparation and the same posology as for the above-mentioned decoction.

Lungwort is easy to find (it grows among sunny undergrowth, in clearings, thickets, beside streams, in damp places with a chalky soil) and equally easy to identify: its oval, hairy leaves, spotted with paler blotches, are grouped at the base of the stem in a close tuft and alternate on the flowering stems, which are also hairy and grow to a height of 20 to 30 centimetres; its bell-shaped flowers with five petals are borne in clusters of five or six at the summit of the stems, like the flowers of the cowslip; they are among the earliest spring flowers, and have the characteristic of being of different colours: pink, mauve and blue, according to their stage of development; in fact the new bright-pink flowers become blue after pollination, and flowers of both colours, as well as of intermediate shades, are generally to be found on the same stem.

M

MAIZE

Zea mays.   Indian corn (in USA corn)

Despite its synonym, maize is in fact a native of South America. Its grains serve as food for both man and livestock; the Indians eat them green (as we eat peas), the Americans eat them boiled and buttered (corn-on-the-cob being especially popular), and in Europe maize is often made into a flour (such as polenta).

But it also provides us with one of the best natural diuretics with the following particular advantages: it triples or quadruples urinary secretion in the space of twenty-four hours; it exercises a sedative effect on the urinary and biliary tracts, it thins the bile and promotes the elimination of phosphates (the most frequent of all forms of lithiasis, together with calcium and magnesium), it exerts a favourable influence on arterial pressure (it is hypotensive), it is not irritant and there is no danger of its causing the slightest mishap.

It is therefore recommended for gravel, renal colic, chronic or acute cystitis, albuminuria, chronic cholecystitis, cardiorenal oedema, dropsy, prostate complaints, gout, rheumatism and, in general, all catarrhal conditions of the bladder or diseases that require the volume of urine to be increased.

The part of the plant that is used is the 'tassel' that is borne at the summit. These stigmas, commonly referred to as the beard of maize, are gathered when the grains are ripe. Once dried, they are prepared by decoction in the amounts of 20 to 50 grammes to a litre of water; boil for five minutes; leave to infuse for ten to fifteen minutes; to be drunk as wished – usually not more than a litre per day, taken in small coffeecupfuls, between meals.

MALE FERN

Dryopteris filix-mas, Aspidium filix-mas, Polypodium filix-mas. Male shield fern

It is hard to imagine a present-day president of the republic or minister of health paying a fortune to a healer for one of his secrets in order to publish it so that everyone could benefit – and it would certainly raise a general outcry among those who have the monopoly of healing.

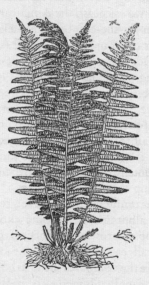

Yet on occasion that is exactly what kings once did: Louis XVI paid 1,800 francs for 'a famous remedy for tapeworm, which the dame Nouffer, after the death of her husband, has practised for twenty years, in Morat, in Switzerland, on a great number of patients, and always with very happy and very swift success.' After several physicians had been commissioned to verify the efficacity of this remedy, the King entrusted Turgot with the task of making it known to the people; but, as Doctor Cazin wryly observes, its 'importance diminished as soon as it became familiar' . . .

This remedy was actually only a 'secret' insofar as – each age proudly and stupidly scorning, in the name of progress, the practices of previous epochs – people had forgotten that the male fern was a vermifuge commonly employed since ancient times and known, among others, to Dioscorides, Galen and Avicenna, who used it as a remedy for 'broad or thin worms', in other words tapeworm and ascaris. Dame Nouffer's remedy in fact consisted of administering to the patient – who had eaten only bread sops the day before – 12 grammes of powdered male fern root (or rather rhizome) in 190 grammes of lime-blossom water, and then two hours later giving him a purgative drink made from plants.

This treatment being strictly unsuitable for children under the age of three, persons suffering from heart or liver complaints, pregnant women or persons in frail health, various other formulae have been put forward which are less risky but still effective. I shall mention two: that of Michel Compain: decoction of 15 to 50 grammes of rhizome to a litre of water, boil until reduced to half a litre; to be taken first thing in the morning; one hour afterwards take a decoction of alder buck-thorn, 10 to 15 grammes in 500 cubic centimetres of water, boiled until reduced to 250 cubic centimetres; and that of Hector Durville:[1] decoction of 15 grammes of rhizome in a litre of water, to be drunk during the day for two or three days (this part of the treatment, alone, is effective against ascaris and small worms); then on the third and fourth day, first thing in the morning, take a decoction of 15 to 20 grammes of rhizome in half a litre of water and, two hours later, 40 to 50 grammes of castor-oil.

Nevertheless, I should add that these treatments should only be employed as a last resort, when other vermifuges, easy to administer and with no unpleasant side-effects, have failed;

1. *Bréviaire de la santé et de la médicine par les simples.* H. Durville, ed., Paris.

I am thinking particularly of pumpkin seeds, which I mention further on, and which generally give excellent results.

But the male fern rhizome has other uses: its decoction (150 to 200 grammes to a litre of water; boil for ten minutes and leave to infuse for a further ten minutes), applied on hot compresses, will relieve pain from rheumatism or neuritis; as a foot-bath, it is prescribed for cramp and attacks of gout; added to the bath water, it is active against arthritis and rheumatism.

The leaves, dried, are used in country areas to fill mattresses and pillows which are considered to have the same anti-rheumatic virtues and to cure children with rickets or subject to bed-wetting. It is the leaves which distinguish the male fern from other types of fern that are apparently identical but in-active: their leaflets, arranged alternately along the central rib, are themselves divided, and the smallest divisions are *rounded* and not *pointed*.

Superstitious beliefs – which still persist in regions where magic has not yet been ousted – decree that the leaves of male fern should be cut only on Midsummer night, whilst reciting special formulae designed to drive off the spirits that guard them. It was also once believed that if a pregnant woman trod upon a male fern, she would miscarry.

MALLOW, COMMON
Malva sylvestris. Wild mallow
Malva rotondifolia. Dwarf or round-leafed mallow

The virtues of the common mallow have been praised from ancient times – when it was grown as a domestic plant – to the present day. Pythagorus and his disciples regarded it as good for moderating the passions and clearing the stomach and the mind. Cicero, in one of his letters, relates that he was copiously purged by eating a stew of common mallow mixed with beet. Horace and Martial say that it develops the intellectual faculties and encourages the practice of virtue. Pliny declares that 'any person taking a spoonful of common mallow will that day be spared from all maladies that might come his way'.

The common mallow and dwarf mallow – which grow in the same situations (waste places, waysides) – differ only in their height (the former growing to a height of 1·50 metres, the latter to barely 15 centimetres) and in the shape of their leaves (common mallow leaves being kidney shaped, the margins broken up into five lobes; dwarf mallow leaves being almost

round and scarcely lobed at all). Both have hairy stems and leaves, and lilac-pink flowers with five petals, their respective diameters measuring 4 centimetres and 1·5 centimetres; lastly, both have disk-shaped fruits, sometimes called 'cheeses' because of their shape, consisting of numerous one-seeded portions which separate at maturity.

The flowers and the leaves, dried in the shade, are used for their high mucilage content which, next to marsh mallow root and linseed, is used to make the emollient most frequently employed in the treatment of acute inflammation of the respiratory, gastric and urinary tracts, the skin and the eyes. Indeed the medicinal properties of the common mallow are much the same as those of the marsh mallow (see below) – they belong in fact to the same family of Malvaceae – so I shall give only a brief summary of its uses and posology.

Internally, in the treatment of coughs, bronchitis, asthma, stomach complaints, constipation, inflammation of the urinary tract: infusion of flowers and leaves (15 to 20 grammes to a litre of water; cold-soak for ten minutes; heat to boiling, but do not boil; leave to infuse for ten to fifteen minutes; to be drunk as required). The stronger infusion (10 grammes to a cupful of water) is laxative.

Externally, in the treatment of skin or eye irritations: apply the infusion as a lotion or on compresses, or poultices of leaves and flowers previously softened in very little boiling water; for inflammation of the mouth and throat: the infusion used as a mouthwash or gargle; for toothache and painful gums chew a few flowers previously softened in hot water; for bee or wasp stings: apply fresh leaves crushed in olive oil.

MALLOW, MARSH
Althaea officinalis.   Official mallow, Mallards, Guimauve, Schloss tea

The marsh mallow is unusual inasmuch as it gives its name to a substance which has absolutely nothing to do with it, as any real plant expert or herbalist knows. In fact, marshmallows – which for children of my generation was both a sweet and a cough-cure – are made with gum arabic and sugar, to which are added stiffly beaten egg whites with orange flower water, but do not contain even the tiniest fragment of the plant. The latter, however, is a well-known pectoral remedy, which might explain why its name came to be given to marshmallows.

The marsh mallow is a decorative and deservedly popular garden plant. Its tall downy stems reach a height of 1·50 metres to 2 metres; its handsome leaves are opposite, soft and hairy, with three or five lobes; its large pale pink flowers with violet-purple centres have five petals, and are produced in small clusters from the axils of the stem leaves, at the summit of the stems. It also grows wild, in damp uncultivated places and salt-marshes near the sea.

Its scientific name, which derives from a Greek root meaning 'to heal' or 'to cure', indicates that the ancients considered it a panacea. All parts of the plant contain a significant amount of mucilage, and all parts are used: the root (long, with tap-roots, white both outside and inside) which is gathered in autumn and strung up to dry in an airy dry place; the leaf, which is collected in June, before the plant comes into flower; and the flower, which is picked in July and, like the leaf, dried in the shade.

The principal virtue of the marsh mallow is that of being 'the most emollient of all the mucilagenous plants', and it is for this softening action that it has constantly been employed through the ages. (It has also, it is true, been used to cheat justice in an age when it was common practice to subject people to trial by red-hot iron; its sap, mixed with plantain seeds and white of egg, was used to make a protective unguent with which the accused coated their hands, the better to withstand the ordeal ... and demonstrate their innocence, for their burns would only be slight; in the Middle Ages, marsh mallow seeds crushed in oil were also believed to keep away snakes if rubbed on the body).

Internally it is used to soothe irritation and inflammation of the mucosae (bronchitis, colds, irritant cough, laryngitis, tracheitis, gastritis, enteritis, constipation, cystitis, catarrhal conditions of the bladder and urethra), either in infusion (30 grammes of leaves and flowers to a litre of boiling water; leave to infuse for ten minutes; 4 or 5 cupfuls in the course of the day), or decoction (macerate 30 grammes of root, chopped into small pieces, in a litre of cold or tepid water for one to two hours before heating gently to a temperature of about 50°C, 3 cupfuls per day). It is recommended to sweeten with honey which increases its soothing action.

Externally, the decoction of root (slightly stronger: 50 grammes to a litre) is used as a gargle in the treatment of sore throats, angina, tonsillitis; as a mouthwash in the treatment of dental abscesses, stomatitis, gingivitis, aphtha; as a tepid enema for intestinal inflammation or constipation; as a hot compress for boils, abscesses, erysipelas, inflamed sores. It is prescribed for sinusitis: as a very hot inhalation, the head covered by a towel, then on compresses to soothe and relieve congestion, applied to the painful areas.

Although it will doubtless appear archaic and too simple for this progressive day and age, I will mention to mothers that the best way of soothing sore gums and helping infants to cut their teeth is to give them a stick of marsh mallow to suck. It is not only cheap but endorsed by centuries of usage.

MARIGOLD

Calendula officinalis or **Calendula arvensis.** Marygold,
Garden marigold, Calendula, Pot marigold

Olivier de Serres recommended the subjects of good King
Henri IV to deck their gardens with marigolds because 'they
are plants that keep their flowers well into winter' and he de-
plored the fact that these flowers were 'little used in medicine
despite all the properties that have been attributed to them'.

He might well express the same regret today for, apart from
its continued importance as a homoeopathic remedy, prescribed
for both internal and external use (*Calendula* is known as 'the
homoeopathic antiseptic'), the marigold is hardly used outside
the folk medicine. Doctor Cazin, after repeated evidence of its
efficacity, sadly observed: 'The ancients might have exaggerated the virtues of the marigold, but today we underestimate
them.'

These virtues – which have been described as just as brilliant
as the colour of its flowerheads – render it valuable in the treatment of many complaints: it is used as a sudorific and diuretic
for influenza, fevers, rheumatic pains, gout; for preventing
inflammation and promoting healing in gastritis, enteritis,
ulcerations of the mucosa of the stomach and the bowel; as a
stimulant and to relieve congestion in liver complaints, biliary
insufficiency, calculi, jaundice (it promotes the flow of bile);
as an emmenagogue and antispasmodic in the treatment of
irregular and painful menstruation, hysteria, menopausal
disorders and obesity (to help menstruation, treatment should
commence one week before the period is due).

In all these cases, the flowers are used preferably fresh, or
dried in the shade (either detaching the flower from the green
calyx or else using the whole flowerhead), and prepared by
infusion (30 to 40 grammes to 1 litre of boiling water; leave to
infuse for ten to fifteen minutes; 3 or 4 cupfuls per day).

Externally, the flowers are prescribed, as a lotion or on compresses, in the treatment of burns (they soothe the pain),

wounds (American surgeons used them during the War of Secession), milkcrust and impetigo of the scalp (this usage was mentioned as early as the twelfth century by Saint Hildegard in her treatise on medicine).

They are employed either fresh, chopped up (sometimes with the stems and the leaves), as a poultice; or as a decoction (50 to 100 grammes of plant to 1 litre of water; boil for five minutes; leave to infuse for ten minutes); or as a spirit (macerate 200 grammes of fresh flowers in a litre of alcohol (70° or 90°) for fifteen days; press and strain through a cloth; to be used neat or in boiled water on sores and wounds); or as an unguent (simmer gently, for at least two hours, 200 grammes of fresh flowers in 600 grammes of water; add 400 grammes of lard and boil again until the water has completely evaporated; press and strain through a cloth; store, corked, in a glass or earthenware pot).

They are also an excellent treatment for chilblains: as a curative: soak the affected parts in prolonged hand- or foot-baths of a decoction at 37°C (100 grammes to 1 litre of water), then cover the ulcerated chilblains with a poultice of boiled flowers or a layer of unguent; as a preventive treatment: as soon as the cold weather starts, bathe the hands or feet subject to chilblains each day (prolonged baths, always at 37°C) in 2 litres of decoction to which have been added two or three generous handfuls of sea-salt (this preparation can be used twice).

The fresh crushed leaves (or their sap) are as effective against warts as the sap of the greater celandine[1] and have the advantage of not being toxic. They will also remove corns and callouses (applications morning and evening).

The marigold owes its generic name, *calendula*, to the fact that it flowers each month at the Calends (Latin *calendulae*), meaning the first day of the month in the Roman calendar. It has to some extent been considered also a magic plant: the king Jean d'Aragon, in accordance with the recommendations

1. See page 75.

of Spanish sorcerers, advised his subjects to wear as a talisman a marigold, picked when the sun is entering the sign of the Virgin, wrapped together with a wolf's tooth in a bay leaf.

Dried marigold flowers have their culinary uses in certain regions of England and Germany, especially in soups, hence the old English name pot marigold. They have also been used to colour butter and lighten the hair.

MARJORAM, SWEET

Origanum majorana. Pot marjoram, common marjoram
Origanum vulgare. Wild marjoram

Sweet marjoram is cultivated, but common or wild marjoram grows wild more or less everywhere (dry pastures and slopes,

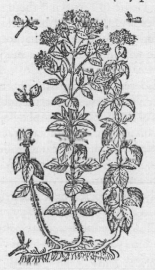

the edges of woodland and hedges). Medicinally their properties are the same, and they are administered in the same amounts.

The two varieties obviously share a certain family resemblance. The wild marjoram is to be recognized by its angular stems, which grow to a height of 30 to 60 centimetres, often reddish in colour and covered with hairs; by its ovate opposite leaves, the underside rather downy, which grow smaller and smaller towards the summit; by its slightly faded rose-coloured flowers, borne in dense opposite panicles which adorn the upper part of the stems; by its aromatic odour which resembles the scent of thyme (it contains thymol, which is lacking in the cultivated variety).

The flowering tips, fresh or dried, are used as aromatic herbs in the flavouring of many foods (salads, stuffing, *pot-au-feu*, sauces, pizza, goulash, etc.), as well as in home remedies.

Ancient texts tell us that the Greeks used to plant marjoram over tombs to give peace to the spirits of the departed, and declare that 'applied on the outside, or taken inside, it soothes the stomach and is good for pains of the liver and the spleen, because it has the virtue of fortifying them as well as clearing them'. Dioscorides says that it combats acidity and flatulence of the stomach, and Aristotle reports that tortoises which have swallowed a snake will immediately eat marjoram so as not to die.

It is now considered an antispasmodic, expectorant, antiseptic, stomachic, vulnerary, and is therefore prescribed for nervous disorders of the stomach, aerophagia, intestinal spasms, liver complaints of nervous origin, migraine, facial tics, insomnia, asthma, acute or chronic catarrh, in the treatment of bronchitis, fitful coughs (whooping cough), head colds, menstrual pains and rheumatism.

Taken internally it is prepared by infusion (40 to 50 grammes of flowering tips to a litre of boiling water; leave to infuse for five to ten minutes; 2 or 3 cupfuls per day before or after meals), or else by maceration (50 grammes of plant – preferably fresh – to a litre of good wine; leave to macerate, stirring occasionally, for eight to ten days; press and strain through a fine cloth; one sherryglassful after meals).

Externally, an unguent made with marjoram (simmer 100 grammes of plant – preferably fresh – in half a litre of olive oil, or in 500 grammes of butter or lard, in a *bain-marie*, for an hour; strain through a fine cloth) is massaged into the affected area in the treatment of rheumatic, muscular and nervous pains; bathed on the forehead and temples, it will relieve headaches; on the nose, it will cure head colds (dried leaves, powdered and taken like snuff, will also cause sneezing and clear a stopped-up nose).

In the treatment of rheumatic pains and stiff neck, in addition to the infusion, hot poultices to be applied to the painful area are also prescribed: chop up coarsely a sufficient quantity of fresh plant; wrap in a cloth which should then be placed on a hot-water bottle or a radiator until hot enough to be applied to the patient (in country areas, the plant itself is generally warmed by stirring it round in a saucepan before wrapping it in the cloth).

According to an historical chronicle, the famous German physician, surgeon Fabricius von Hilden, used marjoram to cure a head cold that was affecting the equally famous soldier and statesman Wallenstein,[1] who was so pleased that he gave him 200 gold crowns and had him escorted back to Rostock in his own carriage drawn by four white horses. Unfortunately the chronicle does not give us the prescription for the remedy he employed.

MEADOWSWEET

Spiraea ulmaria. Queen of the meadows, Bridewort, Lady-of-the-meadow, Maid-of-the-meadow, Dolloff, Elm-leaved spiraea

The meadowsweet is a queen on three counts.

Firstly because of its regal appearance: its height – it is so tall (1 metre to 1·50 metres) that it dominates all the other plants that surround it in the moist rich meadows, by the sides of streams and rivers and in the ditches where it grows; its slender stems, angular, often tinged with red; its pinnate leaves, small

1. During the Thirty Years' War. (*Translator's note.*)

leaflets alternating with large ones, their borders finely serrated, also lightly tinged with red on their dark-green upper surfaces, whilst the under surfaces are silvery and downy; its masses of minute flowers which form light delicate clusters that tremble in the slightest breeze like fragile creamy lace.

Secondly because of its perfume. Sweet and heady, it eclipses all others. From June to August, when the sun has warmed these flowering tufts all day long, this fragrance reigns over the countryside, lending the air that indefinable sweet scent that is remembered by many town-dwellers as the scent of sweet holiday evenings.

Lastly because of its many therapeutic properties which make it an unrivalled medicinal plant, its leaves, flowers and root all being used, according to the complaint for which it is prescribed.

You will find the key to this exceptional efficacity if you crush a few flowers or a leaf in your hand. You will discern a distinct odour of methyl salicylate. The essential oil elaborated by the plant in fact contains both this and salicylic aldehyde, and it is these products and their derivatives, so generously put at our disposal by nature, that have a salutary action.

A brief reminder of certain chemical and pharmaceutical developments will help you to understand the mechanism of this action: (1) it was by the oxidation of salicylic aldehyde (present in the meadowsweet) that in 1838 the Italian physician and pharmacologist Raffaele Piria discovered salicylic acid; (2) it was from this salicylic acid that in 1853 the Strasbourg chemist Charles-Frédéric Gerhardt discovered acetyl salicylic, a derivative of the former, which is the most widely-used of all medicaments, namely aspirin; the very name of this medicament evokes its close ties with the meadowsweet, for it has borrowed its scientific name, changing it from 'spiraea' to 'aspirin'.

It is therefore hardly surprising that this plant exerts the same effects and is prescribed for the same complaints – plus a few others that are not unimportant – as aspirin, but with the advantage of being a natural remedy. When it is dried, the methyl salicylate changes into salicylic acid and salicylates of sodium, potassium, magnesium, etc. These salts are the principal antidotes for, firstly, uric acid which, by depositing its crystals in the joints, is responsible for gout, and, secondly, oxalic acid which, together with uric acid, is one of the causes of renal and urinary calculi.

Consequently, meadowsweet is, like aspirin – only without fear of the side-effects often caused by aspirin on the gastric mucosa – prescribed for feverish conditions such as influenza and chills, for articular rheumatism and gout, but also, because of its diuretic virtues, for kidney and bladder complaints (gravel, cystitis, in particular), dropsy, oedema, and cellulitis which is in fact defined by one specialist as 'a condition characterized by an oedema which inundates the cellular tissue and hardens the connective fibres', hence the opinion of one of his colleagues who considers meadowsweet to be 'the best treatment for cellulitis, and the best therapeutic agent for connective and adipose tissue'.

In all these cases – as well as for cardiac complaints, arteriosclerosis, nervous diathesis, insomnia – the flowers are the part used, picked when they are fully open and dried in the shade (below 40°C) after being separated from the stems, either by hand or with a comb; they are taken in infusion (40 to 50 grammes to one litre of almost boiling water – at 90°C for the steam from the water would carry away the salicylic acid; cover and leave to infuse for ten minutes; 3 or 4 cupfuls per day, between meals). In the treatment of articular pains in particular, a three-week course of this treatment is recommended, the first cupful of the day to be taken first thing in the _____ before breakfast. I might add that compresses soaked _____ poultices made with the flowers that have _____ infusion, will relieve pain when applied _____ by rheumatism.

_____ is a popular homoeopathic remedy: _____ thritis sufferers with a marked predisposition to excess of uric acid, to sufferers from chronic rheumatism and subjects prone to gout symptoms.

An infusion of leaves, dried in the shade (same preparation, same amounts), is a sovereign remedy for diarrhoea. Lastly, a strong decoction of root (30 to 40 grammes to half a litre of water; heat gently and boil for five to ten minutes; leave to infuse for the same length of time) is an excellent detergent used for bathing sores and ulcers, the tannin it contains encouraging them to dry up more quickly.

MELILOT

Melilotus officinalis.   King's clover, King's chafer, Yellow sweet clover

The Egyptians included it in many preparations (for ear-ache, worms, blows, etc.) and named it in their magic incantations intended to ward off death. The ancients credited it with the power of allaying the furies of drunkenness. The sorcerers of the Middle Ages incorporated it in their philtres and the doctors of Molière's day used it in the treatment of a great variety of complaints, from colic to ophthalmia, from various tumours to pains in the lower abdomen, retention of urine, gout, etc. Indeed, so much was expected of it that people were inevitably disappointed and finally began to doubt the very qualities it does in fact possess.

Its virtues are such that it should be reinstated: it is anti-spasmodic, antiseptic, diuretic and sedative. It is therefore prescribed for neuralgia, nervous excitation, insomnia, gastric and intestinal spasms, pains connected with menstruation, infections of the urinary tract.

It is taken in infusion – pleasantly fragrant thanks to the coumarin[1] it contains – in the amounts of 3 or 4 cupfuls per d one of which should be taken last thing at night before (40 to 50 grammes of dried flowering tips to a litre of

   1. See *Woodruff*, page 315.

water; leave to infuse for ten to fifteen minutes). This infusion, as a lotion or on compresses, is also used for inflammation of the eyelids and rheumatic pains. (*Melilotus officinalis* is the homoeopathic remedy prescribed for the headaches that accompany hypertension and menopause.)

You will not find it difficult to find and identify the melilot, whose name evokes the attraction it holds for bees (from the Greek *méli*, honey). Formerly cultivated as a fodder plant, it grows in meadows, along roadsides, in hedgerows and in waste places. Its hollow stems grow to a height of 1·50 metres; its dark green leaves have three leaflets with toothed edges; its yellow flowers, which resemble the flowers of the bird's foot trefoil and the lucerne, are grouped at the top of the stalks.

Some *cordon-bleu* chefs place a bunch of the flowering tips of melilot inside a newly killed and cleaned domestic rabbit to lend the flesh the flavour of wild rabbit.

MINT
Mentha.   Wild mint, Round-leaved mint, Apple-scented mint, Peppermint, Curled mint, Balm mint, Brandy mint, Horse mint, Water mint, Corn mint, Marsh mint, Hairy mint, Whorled mint, Spearmint, Garden mint, Mackerel mint, Penny royal

I should have added 'etc.' to this list of the principal names and varieties of mint for, as a ninth-century monk humorously observes in his treatise on plants: 'if one were to enumerate completely all the virtues, varieties and names of mint, one would be able to say how many fish are swimming in the Red Sea . . .'

It is the peppermint (*Mentha piperata*), valued for its lingering fragrance and its wealth of aromatic essence, that takes pride of place as much in pharmaceutics and cosmetic practice as in confectionery and the manufacture of liqueurs and drinks, but all species of mint possess exactly the same properties, and because of these they have been widely used since ancient times.

The Greeks in the time of Pericles made a perfume from it; so did the Hebrews, hence the reproofs addressed by Jesus to the Scribes and Pharisees, who were paying large sums to procure it, whilst neglecting justice and mercy. The Romans used to put it in their wine to give it aroma and incorporated it in most of their sauces; Roman women would chew a paste made of mint and honey to sweeten their breath, and also to mask the odour of the wine they drank in secret at a time when the law imposed the death penalty on any woman caught taking the drink reserved for men and gods.

Pliny recommends those who study to bind their head in a crown of plaited mint, for it delights the soul and is therefore good for the mind, but he cautions lovers against using it because, like Hippocrates and Aristotle, he judges it 'contrary to procreation' (the Greeks were of the opposite opinion: they forbade their soldiers to eat mint because, they said, it so incites a man to love that it diminishes his courage;[1] I might add that in the light of modern knowledge the Greeks, not Pliny, have been shown to be right.

Mint also constitutes one of the principal weapons against vermin, especially penny royal (*Mentha pulegium*); it is strewn on the floor, placed in beds and even in sacks of grain or near cheeses, because its odour also keeps mice away. Mothers throughout the ages have found its therapeutic virtues providential: it is refreshing, antiseptic, digestive, expectorant, anti-spasmodic, tonic, cordial.

It has often been said that mint is incompatible with homoeopathy. I have been told by a doctor that in fact mint can be allowed providing it is not taken too close to other medication.

Prepared by infusion (four or five fresh or dried leaves to a

1. 'Aristotle and others in the ancient times forbade Mints to be used of souldiers in the time of warre, because they thought it did so much to incite to Venery, that it tooke away, or at least abated their animosity or courage to fight.' – Parkinson. (*Translator's note.*)

cupful of boiling water; leave to infuse for five minutes; twice a day after meals) it combats sluggishness of the stomach and bowels, prevents flatulence, stimulates the gall bladder. It is the great remedy for digestive disorders (vomiting, colic, distension, flatulence, liver pains, etc.). It also tones up the nervous system and is therefore prescribed in cases of general debility, palpitations, vertigo, hiccoughs. Its only drawback is that in some persons it can cause insomnia; in this case, prepare a weaker infusion (two leaves per cup) and take only one cupful at midday.

Externally, inhalations (40 to 50 grammes of leaves to a litre of boiling water) are recommended for asthma, persistent coughs, chronic bronchitis, together with the infusion. The fresh or dried leaves, previously softened in a little lukewarm water, are applied as compresses for migraine, facial neuralgia, rheumatic, joint and muscular pains, and gout. You may also use the following balm as a lotion or friction to rub into the affected area: macerate a generous handful of leaves in a litre of olive oil for six to eight weeks, in the sun or in a warm place; cover the jar with a paper pierced with holes and shake occasionally; press and strain through a fine cloth, and store in a well stoppered jar or bottle.

MISTLETOE
Viscum album.   European mistletoe, Birdlime mistletoe

A sacred plant for most of the ancient peoples of Europe, symbol of immortality because it remains green and living when the trees that support it seem to be dead – the mistletoe has always been closely associated with magic and medicine.

The Druids called it the 'plant that heals all ills' and, at the conclusion of the famous annual ceremony when the priests gathered mistletoe with a golden sickle, they would distribute sprigs to our ancestors who wore them around their necks as a talisman, or hung them at the entrance to their huts as protection against evil. The Teutons believed it rendered their warriors invincible, and restored fertility to sterile animals. Elsewhere magical powers were traditionally attributed to it that have survived in the form of our present-day customs and superstitions: our New Year kiss exchanged beneath the lucky mistletoe; in Austria the branch of mistletoe fastened over the bedroom threshold, to deliver the sleeper from nightmares; the sprig of mistletoe slipped under the pillow on Midsummer Night by Welsh girls who want to see their future husband in their dreams.

In the olden days mistletoe was used medicinally as the standard antispasmodic, the specific for epilepsy, convulsions, apoplexy; it was particularly recommended to persons who were victims of attacks or 'blood blows', in other words persons suffering from high blood pressure. Modern research has shown that it is in fact an excellent natural remedy for high blood pressure and arteriosclerosis because of its action upon the vaso-motor nervous system, and for this reason it is included in various patent medicines. Lastly I might mention that it features in a method of cancer treatment known as 'viscum therapy', which originated in Switzerland, based upon the findings of Rudolf Steiner, the founder of anthroposophy, and is recognized in many countries but not yet in our own.

But people had been making medicinal use of mistletoe long before modern research confirmed its efficacy. Generally the mistletoe growing on apple or pear trees was preferred, for it was believed to possess greater virtues. It is gathered when the berries are reaching maturity (October to November); the leaves and young stems, without the berries, are the part that is used, generally fresh (when they are most active) but also dried in the shade, either as they are or else powdered.

For use in the treatment of high blood pressure (and its accompanying side-effects – migraine, vertigo, arteriosclerosis, heart complaints of nervous origin, haemorrhages, troubles connected with the critical age, haemoptysis) there are three methods of preparation for preserving the active principles of mistletoe which are partially destroyed by heat: the infusion (20 grammes of chopped leaves to half a litre of water; cold-soak over night and drink during the day, before and between meals, a small cupful at a time); the wine (macerate 40 grammes of chopped fresh leaves in a litre of white wine for twenty-four hours; 2 or 3 wineglassfuls a day before meals); the powder (one coffeespoonful in a little tepid water, two or three times a day) – this powder (1 or 2 grammes a day taken in honey) is also prescribed for whooping cough and for soothing spasmodic intermittent coughs.

Externally, hot poultices of leaves and berries, boiled for a few minutes in water or milk, soothe the pain of rheumatism and gout.

MUGWORT
Artemisia vulgaris.   Common artemisia, Felon herb

The mugwort or common artemisia is named after Artemis, the Greek moon goddess identified with the Roman Diana. The plant was baptized with her name not so much because legend has it that it was created by this divinity, as because its power is identical to that of Artemis, whose chief mission, apart from the hunt, was to bring help to women in their particular maladies, as much by regularizing their menstrual cycle as by aiding them in their confinements. In short, its name – which evokes the moon and the patron goddess of the so-called weaker sex – clearly indicates its chief uses and explains why, ever since Hippocrates, Pliny and Dioscorides, it has been considered the 'female plant' *par excellence*.

For a long time it was even credited with magical virtues in addition to its indisputable therapeutic properties. For example it was held to be a talisman against tiredness: the first recorded reference is in Pliny's *Naturalis Historia*, where he advises the traveller always to carry a sprig on him, and several centuries later we find the same notion echoed in the French saying, 'He who carries artemisia on his travels will never feel weary.'

It was also believed to have the power of warding off most of the dangers that beset poor mortals. 'He who is careful to carry this herb on him always', we read in that celebrated wizard's book of spells *Les Secrets du Grand Albert*, 'needs have no fear of evil spirits or poison or water or fire, and nothing can harm him. Furthermore, if it is always kept in the house, then lightning will never strike that place nor, if it is placed at the entrance, will any venomous air infect it.' In the Middle Ages it formed one of the ingredients of the philtres that would 'untie knots'[1] and it was traditionally worn as a garland either on the head or around the waist when dancing around the Midsummer fire, being afterwards thrown into the flames to immunize the wearer against sickness in the year to come. There are still many country-dwellers who believe that a sprig of the herb carried on the person affords protection against ills.

These customs were doubtless largely kept up because the common artemisia or mugwort is easy to find. It grows wild throughout Europe – and also in the northern parts of Asia, America and Africa – particularly on waste land, embankments, among rubble, in stony places and on the banks of streams. It is easily distinguished by its height, often greater than that of a man. Its stem is stiff and angular and generally reddish in colour; its leaves are deeply incised, smooth and dark green above, but silvery-white and covered with silky down beneath; when crushed between the fingers they exhale an aromatic odour not unlike that of wormwood or bitter artemisia, to which in fact it is closely related. Its flowers are small and greenish-yellow or reddish-yellow, arranged in long spikes at the top of the stem.

We employ the flower-heads and the dried leaves, but rarely the roots which tend to go mouldy.

1. Culpeper states: 'Being made up with hog's grease into an ointment, it takes away wens and hard Knots and Kernels that grow about the neck and throat . . .' (*Translator's note.*)

Its main medicinal use is obviously concerned with difficult, irregular or painful menstruation, and the troubles associated with the menopause. The Greeks and the Romans already employed it in this way, and many countrywomen have it to thank for having passed through the difficult period of what is called the critical time of life with a minimum of trouble. The infusion of 20 grammes of dried plant to a litre of boiling water is taken daily. Treatment should be started ten to twelve days before the usual start of menstruation, after which treatment should be suspended, for if taken over too long a period it can become damaging to the nervous system.

The same infusion (a cupful to be taken midday and evening before meals) is an excellent general stimulant recommended in cases of loss of appetite, difficulties of digestion, disturbances of circulation. It is equally considered one of the best vermifuges for ascarides and oxyures, and is even sometimes employed to reduce fever.

Taken in a weaker dosage (10 grammes of plant to a litre of water, two cupfuls per day) it is both antispasmodic and sedative, and therefore recommended in cases of chronic diarrhoea, nervous vomiting, hysteria and epilepsy.

A final prescription, 'a remedy many times tested by a surgeon to the king', indicates its beneficial effect in attacks of gout: boil a handful of mugwort in half a litre of olive oil until reduced by a third, and apply this liniment to the affected area.

Lastly, mugwort has its place in culinary art by reason of its aromatic qualities and its stimulating action on the digestive functions. Whilst it is no longer employed to lend its scent to beer, having been supplanted by hops, it is still employed in certain countries, notably England and Germany, as a seasoning for meats, both tenderizing the flesh and enhancing its flavour.

There is, of course, another artemisia which is gastronomically very famous indeed: namely *Artemisia dranunculus*, or tarragon.

MULLEIN

Verbascum thapsus.   Great mullein, Common mullein, High taper, Hag-taper, Torch, Beggar's blanket, Blanket herb, Adam's flannel, Candle wick, Velvet or flannel herb, Agleaf, Hare's beard, Shepherd's club, Lady's foxglove, Cow's lungwort, Aaron's rod

Its first virtue – it has many others – is that you don't actually have to look for it: it will bring itself to your notice by its exceptional height.

In fact you would have to be particularly short-sighted or absentminded not to notice its tall flower stalks, which often reach a height of 2·50 metres, and can be seen from June to October, reaching up to the sky on sunny slopes or stony ground. The flowers themselves are packed closely together, covering about a metre of the upper part of the stalk, and bloom in turn throughout the whole summer. They are a pretty clear yellow colour, with a corolla 3 to 5 centimetres in diameter that botanists term infundibuliform, which means quite simply shaped like a funnel: *infurdibulum* in Latin.

The decorative leaves also attract attention. Mullein being a biennial plant, a basal rosette of leaves is formed during the first year from which the flower stalk grows in the second year, further leaves appearing, arranged alternately on the stalk (by which time it is not uncommon for the basal leaves to cover more than half a square yard of ground); they are ovate, broad and soft, and covered with whitish-grey woolly hairs.

Its virtues have long been known to mankind. Dioscorides prescribed its roots for pulmonary complaints; Pliny its leaves to cure bronchial complaints in humans and broken-winded horses; Saint Hildegard considered the decoction of flowers and leaves to be a specific for hoarseness.

In the Middle Ages, apart from the condition for which it is still prescribed today, mullein juice was recommended by physicians for gout and haemorrhoids. The method of preparation was curious, consisting of pounding together the leaves and flowers, then letting them rot in a wooden tub hermetically sealed with plaster and either left in the sun or buried in dung; after three months of what they termed 'digestion', the juice would be pressed out and stored in tightly corked jars, to be applied on the painful areas.

Do not worry; the prescriptions I shall give you are far less complicated but just as efficacious. They are based on the flowers (picked in dry weather the moment they come into bloom for they soon fall, dried in the shade as swiftly as possible to prevent them from turning brown) and the leaves, fresh or dried.

The infusion (3 grammes of dried flowers to 100 grammes of water, three or four times a day) has a pleasant sweet taste, for the petals contain as much as 10 per cent of glucose; it is prescribed for bronchitis, obstinate colds, asthma, chills, dry coughs; it is demulcent, sedative (being slightly narcotic); it promotes expectoration and is also sudorific. Several authorities even recommend it in cases of gastro-enteritis and kidney and bladder complaints because of its diuretic action (which others question), but above all for its beneficial action on 'all inflammatory conditions of our viscera'.

The decoction of flowers and leaves (30 grammes to a litre of water; boil for three to four minutes) employed as a gargle (every half hour) is good for throat complaints and especially hoarseness (this is Saint Hildegard's receipt).

The decoction of fresh leaves (100 grammes boiled in a litre of milk, then left to infuse for ten minutes) is in Ireland and certain regions of England believed to be an infallible remedy for tuberculosis if 2 to 3 litres are drunk daily (if using dried leaves, reduce the amount to 30 grammes to a litre).

The fresh leaves, boiled in milk for five minutes, are employed as poultices on whitlows, boils, carbuncles, ulcers, haemorrhoids, chilblains: they bring immediate relief and promote the evacuation of pus (the patient is also recommended to drink the milk for it constitutes an excellent depurative). Prepared by decoction in water (60 grammes to a litre, boil for five minutes), used as a lotion or on compresses, they are prescribed for scabbing, burns and painful ulcers. Dried, they can be used as a substitute for tobacco and are often smoked by asthma sufferers, who find they bring relief.

For haemorrhoids and chilblains you can also employ mullein oil: one part of fresh flowers to two parts of olive oil; macerate over a low heat, then cook until no moisture remains; press and strain; store in a tightly corked jar; to be used as a lotion or rubbed in lightly.

Finally, let me give you a piece of advice of capital importance, which is why I have saved it to the last: it is essential always to strain both infusion and decoction through a very fine cloth or, better still, absorbent cotton wool, to eliminate the minute hairs which cover the whole plant (flowers and leaves) and which, without this precaution, would irritate the throat.

N

NASTURTIUM
Tropaeolum majus

A hardy perennial in the Andean belt, whence Pizarro's 'conquistadores' brought it to Europe along with the gold of the Incas, over here the nasturtium is an annual. Its scientific name derives from the Greek *tropaion*: trophy, so-called because the flower and the leaf evoke the helmet and shield that compose the trophies with which monuments are decorated.

'It is more commonly used as a food than as a remedy,' notes the author of an eighteenth-century treatise. Indeed, whilst sometimes used in place of watercress as an antiscorbutic, the young leaves and flowers were in those days used mostly in salads, to lend piquancy to lettuce, and its buds and green seeds were pickled and eaten like capers, recipes which are still used today in certain regions.

But ever since Elizabeth-Christine, daughter of the famous Swedish botanist Linné, was the first to observe that at dusk on hot summer days sparks were emitted from the heart of the flower, from the stamens and the styles, scientists have turned their attention to the chemical composition of the plant (according to them, this strange phenomenon is connected with its high phosphoric acid content), so furthering our knowledge of its therapeutic virtues (we now know, for example, that it is a powerful natural antibiotic which has the merit of not destroying the intestinal flora, hence its commercialization as such by a German laboratory, and that it also possesses rejuvenating and aphrodisiac virtues, referred to by Professor Binet who calls it 'the flower of love').

It is recommended to those who suffer from chronic bronchitis, bronchial catarrh, emphysema: infusion of fresh leaves,

2 to 3 grammes to 100 grammes of boiling water, leave to infuse for five minutes; two or three times a day.

Its fruits, ripe and dried (0·60 grammes, crushed and taken in a spoonful of honey or half a glassful of sweetened water), are purgative, and have the advantage of not causing any colic.

It is above all 'the plant for the hair' – doubtless because of its high sulphur content: 100 grammes of leaves contain as much as 0·17 grammes of sulphur – for it arrests hair loss and promotes growth, toning up the scalp. Here is the prescription for a hair lotion that you can make yourself: 100 grammes of fresh nasturtium leaves, flowers and seeds; 100 grammes of fresh nettle leaves; 100 grammes of fresh box leaves; 500 grammes of alcohol (90°); chop the plants, leave to macerate for fifteen days in the alcohol; press and strain; perfume with a few drops of lavender or rosemary essence; massage frequently and briskly into the scalp or brush on vigorously with a fairly stiff hairbrush.

NETTLE
Urtica dioica.   Stinging nettle

The nettle does not deserve its bad reputation, for to spurn it and deprive oneself of its virtues on the grounds that its hairs secrete a liquid containing formic acid that irritates the skin when one brushes against them is as illogical as it would be to give up eating sea-urchins because they are covered with spikes!

Before the advent of so-called 'special feed', chopped nettle leaves used to be included in the food given to poultry and pigs (and not so long ago horse dealers used to mix them with oats to make horses more frisky and lend a gloss to their coats); they were also used in the cleaning of dairy utensils before the arrival of wonder detergents. Its seeds, mixed with mash, induce hens to lay more. Its stems, steeped like flax, provide a good yarn used by fishermen in various countries (Holland, Siberia, Kamchatka in particular) to make ropes and nets.

In certain regions of Germany, Italy and France, when it is fresh, young and tender, it has always been eaten either raw, in salad, or cooked and served like spinach, or else first boiled, then chopped and added to soup, to which it lends a pleasant taste. It has also been a fashionable beverage in its time, as mentioned in a mid-eighteenth-century text: 'It has been the fashion in Paris for some time to take a herbal tea of nettle leaves infused in boiling water like ordinary tea . . .' Lastly, it has even played a role in magic practices: in France, where it was believed to quell fear if held in the hand together with sprigs of yarrow and to enable a person to catch fish in the rivers with his bare hands if he first smeared his skin with nettle juice mixed with tarragon juice; in darkest Africa, where it is still used in the initiation test of a secret society: it is rubbed over the postulant's body and he is then sent to take a bath, which is almost unbearable torture.

The nettle has long been respected for its medicinal properties. Today it is the homeopathic remedy, *Urtica urens*, for urticaria accompanied by burning pain and severe pruritis: our great-great-grandfathers also used it in prescriptions that correspond to those maintained by popular tradition. It is considered a general tonic (anaemia, chlorosis), a depurative and regenerator of the blood (scabbing eczema), a stimulant of the digestive functions (heaviness or stomach cramps), a valuable aid in the treatment of diabetes and, because it promotes urinary secretion, in the treatment of dropsy and rheumatism. It is also used with success as a remedy for diarrhoea, enteritis and haemorrhages.

The leaves and the roots, fresh or dried, and preferably gathered in the spring, are prepared in a mild decoction, one cupful to be taken three times a day, before meals (40 to 50 grammes of leaves to a litre of water; boil for two to three minutes; leave to infuse for ten minutes; or 30 to 40 grammes of roots to a litre of water; bring slowly to the boil; boil for at least five minutes and leave to infuse for ten minutes).

For internal and uterine haemorrhages, frequent nose-bleeds, haemorrhoids, enteritis, Doctor Leclerc recommends either the juice of fresh nettles (100 to 125 grammes per day, to be taken in several doses between meals), or nettle syrup (pour a litre and a half of boiling water on to 250 grammes of fresh leaves; leave to infuse for twelve hours; strain and add 500 grammes of sugar; 200 to 300 grammes per day, to be taken in several doses between meals).

The seeds are also used. Many concur with Galen that 'taken in a draught of mulled wine, they arouse desire' and recommend them for impotency (one coffeespoonful of powdered seeds taken in jam or honey). But they are above all a common country remedy for incontinence of urine ('bed-wetting') prepared in either of two ways: (1) take 16 grammes of nettle seeds and 60 grammes of rye flour and mix to a paste with a little hot water and some honey; mould into six small cakes and bake in the oven; give the child one of these cakes to eat every evening for eight to twenty days; (2) mix 16 grammes of powdered nettle seeds, 20 grammes of powdered oak bark, 20 grammes of powdered tormentil (shepherd's knot) with 50 grammes of butter; spread this mixture on to a slice of bread, adding some sugar or jam if wished, and give it to the child to eat in the evening, in the same way as the little cakes mentioned above.

Externally, the juice of the fresh plant (leaves, young stalks or root) introduced into the nostrils on a piece of cotton wool, will arrest nasal haemorrhage almost at once.

As a scalp tonic, to combat baldness and eliminate dandruff, the following lotions may be applied daily: either a decoction in water (boil 100 grammes of roots in a litre of water for a quarter of an hour; strain), or a maceration in alcohol (macerate 60 grammes of nettle root and 60 grammes of flowering tips of marjoram for fifteen days in a litre of alcohol (45°), brandy or rum). An alternative treatment is to comb the hair each morning the wrong way, from back to front, with a comb dipped in nettle juice.

To keep your hands white, wash them each evening with a

decoction of 50 to 80 grammes of roots boiled for ten minutes in a litre of white wine to which has been added a glassful of wine vinegar.

There is lastly a treatment that may well be called heroic. It was practised in the time of Petronius by exhausted libertines in order to revive their flagging sexual appetites; it has been recommended by the Abbé Kneipp, although naturally for a very different purpose: 'If you suffer from rheumatism that fails to respond to all other remedies,' he says, 'beat or rub the affected areas for a few minutes each day with fresh nettles. Your fear of this unusual rod will soon give way to joy as you feel your condition improving.' This is no exaggeration, and it has been repeatedly verified by Doctor Cazin.

O

OAK, COMMON
Quercus robur.   Strong oak, Tanner's bark

Because of its imposing stature (it can grow to 40 metres in height and 7 metres in girth) and exceptional longevity (more than two thousand years), the oak was considered a sacred tree from ancient times to the Middle Ages: the Greeks and Romans dedicated it to Zeus and Jupiter, pronounced oracles by interpreting the sound of the wind in its leaves, and plaited crowns of oak leaves to honour victors, athletes or soldiers; the Gauls venerated it and the Druids owed it their name derived from the Celtic word *deru*: oak. Lastly it was not by chance that Saint Louis meted out justice beneath an oak tree or that it was under an oak tree that Joan of Arc first heard her voices.

Bark, leaves and acorns are used in country regions for their astringent and tonic virtues due to their high tannin content. (Oak sawdust is also used, with water and vinegar, to clean bottles.)

The bark is collected in spring from branches that are four or five years old, and dried in the sun or the shade in a draught. Chopped into pieces and prepared by decoction (80 to 100 grammes to a litre of water; boil for ten minutes) it is used as a gargle and mouthwash for inflammation of the throat (pharyngitis, tonsillitis) and the mucous membranes of the mouth; as a douche in the treatment of metritis, uterine fibroma and leucorrhoea; as prolonged hot baths for chilblains, excessive perspiration and frost-bite; on compresses applied on to hernias, inflamed glands, haemorrhoids. Milled and ground to a fine powder, called 'tan' or 'tanner's bark', and taken like snuff, it will arrest nose-bleeds; sprinkled on the sheet it will heal the bed-sores of 'patients whose skin is injured by too long a stay in bed'; lastly, it is prescribed (2 or 3 grammes of powder in a tablespoonful of honey first thing in the morning) for over-heavy or prolonged menstruation; Doctor Cazin announces that in this way he has cured uterine haemorrhages that 'had failed to respond to all other treatments'.

The young leaves, picked in the spring and dried, prepared by decoction (30 grammes to a litre of water – or 20 grammes plus 10 grammes of a mixture of equal parts of centaury and artimisia (wormwood) – boil for a few minutes; leave to infuse for ten minutes; one cupful per day, sweetened with honey) are recommended for weak or tubercular patients, and in cases of dysentery. Combined with the leaves of dead-nettle and eucalyptus (10 grammes of each to a litre of water or wine, prepared by decoction), they are employed as a remedy for leucorrhoea, one wineglassful to be taken before meals.

The acorns – which present the unusual characteristic of breathing throughout winter storage and which, according to Pliny, were used by man as food before he discovered wheat – when roasted yield the 'acorn coffee' which was the national beverage in Germany during rationing in the First World War. This coffee is stomachic; it possesses 'antiseptic and nutritive properties' that makes it suitable for persons with poor diges-tion or in cases of colic, diarrhoea and dysentery. It has, more-over, the merit of not being a stimulant.

OATS, CULTIVATED
Avena sativa.   Groats

Who, in this horse-powered technological age, ever thinks of using oats as a remedy? Dieticians, of course, value porridge oats or oatmeal as a tonic and remineralizing food, but it has practically lost its place in medicine, apart from a few rare instances and the homoeopathic use of the mother tincture, *Avena sativa*, of the fresh plant, gathered at flowering time, in the treatment of nervous prostration and insomnia, loss of appetite, exhaustion and convalescence following illness.

Oats in fact went out of favour as a medicinal plant even before the disappearance of the hackney carriage. As long ago as 1890 the good Abbé Kneipp wrote: 'I often regret that the sick, whose blood needs purifying and fortifying, are given all kinds of beverage to drink, but never a decoction of oats', and he goes on to enumerate its virtues: 'easily digested', 'a cooling drink for overheated blood conditions', 'an excellent restorative for convalescents exhausted by serious illness'.

'The preparation is simple', he added. 'Wash a litre of oats six or eight times in cool water, then cook in 3 litres of water, boiling until reduced by a half. Decant the water, mix in 2 spoonfuls of honey and cook for a further few minutes.'

You can, of course, prepare this drink – which is not only cooling and fortifying but also diuretic and slightly laxative – with porridge oats.

An infusion of oats (2 generous handfuls in a litre and a half of water, reduced to a litre, to be drunk in the course of a day) is also prescribed in the treatment of dropsy.

Roasted powdered oats are used to make a laxative coffee that relieves persons suffering from haemorrhoids or subject to constipation. 'Two or three cupfuls taken first thing in the morning, for two or three days', says Doctor Cazin, 'generally have a beneficial effect.' A little milk and sugar may be added.

For sharp stabbing pains (stitches) and lumbago, poultices of whole oats cooked with a little vinegar bring swift and marked relief.

OLIVE
Olea europaea

When the dove returned to the Ark for the second time, it carried a fresh branch of olive in its beak. In this way Noah knew that the waters of the Flood had abated on the land, and the olive tree – of which Georges Duhamel said 'where olives are not found, nor is the Mediterranean' – had the honour of becoming the first named plant in our history of the world.

The Greeks – to whom their patron goddess Pallas Athene had brought the olive at the same time as the fig – made it their symbol of wisdom and so honoured it that only chaste men and virgins were allowed to grow it. The Romans called it the 'tree of Minerva' – the Latin name for Athene – and also venerated it. Peace being a form of wisdom, those asking a cessation of hostilities would carry an olive branch, an allegorical significance that has remained as unchanged through the centuries (it features today on the United Nations flag) as has the bellicose nature of man himself . . .

But the olive tree has above all been a blessing to the people of Mediterranean countries: without much effort on their part – Virgil comments that *it asks neither bill-hook nor hoe once it has taken root* – it gives them its wood, its leaves and its fruits, in other words provides them with shelter, warmth, food and remedies. The ancients not only made great use of olive oil in their food and in the care of their bodies (they would rub it all over themselves from head to feet after bathing, to keep their muscles and joints supple, a technique also used by athletes before a race or a contest) but they also employed it internally as a remedy for liver complaints and more particularly for gall-stones.

Popular tradition, which happily ensures the survival of any simple and effective remedy, has brought down to us these doubtless somewhat improved versions of the following treatments:

For hepatic insufficiency, cholelithiasis (gall-stones), biliary or renal colic, colitis: one teaspoonful of olive oil (pure and cold-pressed, unadulterated by chemical substances designed to increase the yield or act as preservatives) to be taken first thing in the morning or else in the evening, as long as possible before or after eating (it is advisable to start by taking only half a coffeespoonful, gradually increasing to the full dosage; after taking, rinse out the mouth with mint tea or suck a slice of lemon).

For constipation: a tablespoonful of olive oil first thing in the morning or added to your soup in the evening (taken in this way it is easily tolerated): the oil stimulates a flow of bile into the intestine thereby dispersing accretions of bile sediment.

As a sedative for painful attacks of biliary or renal colic: one wineglassful of olive oil, taken a little at a time, will swiftly subdue and finally dispel the pains altogether (this dosage is the minimum; you may take up to 400 grammes of oil, at the rate of one tablespoonful every half hour); remain lying down on your right side.

For colic brought on by difficult confinement: one spoonful of olive oil in a cupful of hot milk.

To prevent intoxication if you cannot easily tolerate alcoholic drinks (prior to parties, etc.): before dining, swallow a tablespoonful of olive oil. Those who are already familiar with this 'trick' will tell you that the oil floats on the surface and prevents the fumes of alcohol from rising to the head. 'This ingenuous explanation is amusing enough', writes Doctor Fournier, 'but obviously untrue. However, the spoonful of oil is valuable, although for another reason, the real reason this time: it lines the walls of the stomach in such a way that the alcohol, taking much longer to pass into the bloodstream, has time to be broken down by the liver.'

Externally, olive oil (2 tablespoonfuls) mixed with the white of an egg is an excellent soothing ointment for burns or insect stings. Applied hot as a friction over the kidney region, it is recommended for children who wet the bed.

It has been discovered that the olive leaf, which is employed in some countries for tanning leather, acts as a hypotensive and vasodilator, and lowers the blood-sugar level. It is therefore recommended for hypertension, angina pectoris and diabetes, especially as it has the great advantage of provoking no side-effects even when taken over a long period: soak 20 to 30 grammes of chopped dried leaves in half a litre of cold water for six to eight hours; bring to the boil, then leave to infuse for twenty minutes; to be taken in the course of a day, in small cupfuls, between meals.

The leaves also possess febrifuge and astringent properties (as does the bark) and have been employed in the treatment of fevers, when quinine was not available, by the French health officials during the Spanish wars: 60 grammes of fresh leaves infused in a litre of boiling water for twenty-four hours; to be drunk in the course of the day. This infusion is also used for cleansing wounds and sores and promoting healing.

ONION
Allium cepa

The onion is commonly grown throughout Europe and eastern lands (it is thought to have come originally from Egypt); it is tonic, diuretic, vermifuge, emollient and antiseptic, and has been held in high repute throughout the ages.

Its uses are many. Like garlic, it has been put to all kinds of work. In Egypt, where it was deified, it featured in many medicinal preparations; it has been used as a prophylactic during epidemics of plague and cholera; it has been praised as an aphrodisiac (hence the traditional onion soup after a night's revels, and the custom, in some regions, of taking onion soup to a young couple after their wedding night!); it has been put forward as a contributing factor of longevity – the Bulgarians, it is pointed out, are great eaters of onions and count many centenarians among their number; it has been said that it lends colour to the hair and fosters hair-growth; it has been recommended for obesity ('You who are fat and lymphatic', we read in one treatise, 'eat raw onion, it was for you that God made it.').

I shall not pursue this list, which is of interest only from the point of view of folklore. On the practical level, the main things to know are: (1) that the onion indeed possesses the properties mentioned above; (2) that it only fully retains these properties when raw (cooking partially destroys its active principles contained in a highly volatile oil); (3) that its fresh juice is irritant and suits only a strong stomach. Hence the simple rules governing its use internally.

If you tolerate it well, eat raw onion as often as possible (in salads, hors-d'oeuvre, added (finely chopped) to soups and vegetables). It is an incomparable aid to health (Dioscorides *dixit*) and, should you suffer from any of the complaints listed below, do not hesitate to take, two or three times a day, a glassful of the following maceration: four medium onions, sliced, to a litre of hot water; leave to macerate for two to three hours.

If you find it difficult to digest, take onion wine instead (place 300 grammes of finely chopped onion, 100 grammes of honey and 600 grammes of white wine in a bottle; leave to macerate for at least forty-eight hours, shaking fairly frequently; strain; 2 to 4 tablespoonfuls per day) or else another very similar preparation (grate an onion as finely as possible; mix together with a spoonful of honey in a glass of wine; to be taken in three doses in the course of a day).

These preparations are prescribed for anaemia, exhaustion, bronchial complaints, flatulence, dropsy, oedema, genito-urinary infections (prostatitis, cystitis), arthritis, rheumatism, gout, diabetes (it lowers the blood-sugar level), gravel, retention of urine, worms (for which – especially oxyuris – a more active formula is advisable: macerate 100 grammes of finely-chopped onions in a litre of white wine for forty-eight hours; press and strain through a fine cloth; one wineglassful first thing in the morning for eight to ten consecutive days, preferably when the moon is on the wane or at the time of the new moon).

Still internally – but cooked this time – its emollient and pectoral action makes it a useful remedy for coughs and bronchitis. It can be taken either as a decoction (boil three onions cut in quarters in half a litre of water for five to ten minutes; strain; sweeten with honey; to be drunk in the course of a day, in coffeecupfuls), or as a syrup (boil 100 grammes of chopped onions in 200 cubic centimetres of water for five to ten minutes; strain; add a heaped tablespoonful of honey and boil gently until of a thick syrupy consistency; 2 to 6 coffeespoonfuls per day). In country areas, an onion baked in hot ashes or in the oven and eaten with oil or butter is a popular remedy for hoarseness.

Lastly, the onion – *Allium cepa* – is the classic homoeopathic remedy for coryza when watering of the eyes is only slight and the nasal discharge causes irritation of the nostrils and the upper lip.

Obviously, the absorption of raw onion leaves an odour in the mouth and on the breath. You can remedy this disadvantage by the same means recommended for garlic.[1]

Externally, grated raw onion applied as a poultice is prescribed in the treatment of chilblains, arthritic and rheumatic pains, burns, migraine (placed on the forehead), retention of urine (placed on the lower abdomen). Crushed in vinegar and applied daily as a lotion, it will cause freckles to disappear. Cotton wool soaked in onion juice will cure buzzing in the ears and soothe acute toothache. Cooked in hot ashes or an oven, reduced to an ointment and applied very hot, renewing the application every hour, it will bring abscesses, boils and whitlows to a head more quickly, and reduce the pain.

Raw onion also has various household uses: cut in half, it is used for cleaning windows and knife blades; it restores brilliance to patent leather belts and handbags; crushed with a little damp earth, it makes an excellent product for cleaning brasses; its juice, brushed over the brasses, will protect them from fly stains.

ORANGE
Citrus aurantium.   Bitter or Seville orange, var. amara; Sweet or Portugal orange, var. sinensis

Sometimes carried by conquerors, sometimes by pioneer

1. See page 125.

traders, the orange travelled a long way from its native land, central Asia, before reaching Europe and taking root on the shores of the Mediterranean, subsequently being used to embellish both palaces and public parks.

The virtues of the fruit itself are widely advertised, but we tend to forget that the leaves and flowers are also very useful aids to health. Yet there was a time – not so very long ago – when orange blossom could be found in two places in the middle-class home: under a glass dome in the bedroom – the garland Madame had worn on her wedding day as a symbol of her virginity; and on a shelf in the bathroom or on the marble top of the washstand – the bottle of orange flower water that was always kept at hand for those perpetual feminine malaises ranging from indigestion to the vapours. I am reminded of the following eminently quotable passage, written by Doctor Cazin, which I hope you will enjoy as much as I do: 'It [orange flower water] is in frequent use for spasms, convulsions, palpitations, precordial "anxiety", nervous colic, hysteria and that long series of nervous complaints which, in our great cities, overwhelm women who feel that they are not understood, women weighed down by happiness and boredom, their lives spent either reading the latest novels or doing embroidery that taxes only their fingers, or else lying feebly on a divan receiving idle calls that are but the palest reflection of the delights of society . . .'

Things have changed since those days – happiness now is called 'self-realization', boredom 'depression' and society 'the consumer society' – but orange-flower water (still to be bought, although not much in demand) taken as formerly in sugared water or on a lump of sugar can certainly soothe conditions of acute distress that baffle psychoanalysis, aid digestion when trouble is not organic (aerophagia, gastric and intestinal spasms) and restore sleep without resorting to sleeping pills and tranquillizers that are all to a greater or lesser degree toxic.

The leaves – picked fresh from the tree, not gathered from the ground beneath it – have the same sedative and antispasmodic properties through their action upon the sympathetic nervous system. They have been prescribed with some success in the treatment of epilepsy – milder and infrequent attacks – (a handful of leaves to half a litre of water; boil until reduced to half the quantity; to be drunk first thing in the morning). They are also sudorific – Matthiolus says that an infusion of orange leaves 'will cause the patient to sweat so greatly that it will bring out all the bad humours on his skin'. To soothe the nerves, calm palpitations and as a remedy for insomnia, take 2 or 3 cupfuls each day – one to be taken on retiring – of the infusion: three or four leaves to a cupful (100 cubic centimetres) of boiling water; leave to infuse for ten minutes; add a coffee-spoonful of orange flower water (optional).

With the peel of your oranges – providing you are certain they have not been treated with diphenyl[1] – you can make an excellent apéritif wine: macerate the peel of six oranges in half a litre of brandy or alcohol (45°) for fifteen days; add 2 litres of white wine in which you have previously dissolved 500 grammes of sugar; strain; store in tightly corked bottles and leave for at least a week before using; this wine improves with age.

1. See under *Lemon*, page 182.

P

PANSY, WILD
Viola tricolor.   Heartsease, Herb trinity, Garden-gate,
Love-in-idleness

'The over-stimulated imagination easily endows plants with feelings, easily confuses them with living creatures. Because the violet and the pansy lend themselves so wonderfully to our illusions, we have ascribed to them the modest virtues that honour the heart of womankind.' Thus a late-nineteenth-century chronicler opened his eulogy of the two best-known members of the huge family – more than 200 species – of the *Violaceae*.

Both possess medicinal properties that have earned them a place of honour in the traditional family pharmacopoeia, but it is doubtless the pansy that is used the most, for it is the plant that is automatically employed for cleansing the blood at the changing seasons and for treating all kinds of skin complaints.

It prefers sandy soils, and will be found in cultivated fields and waste places, and on hilly pastures where in June and July it covers the ground with a carpet of brilliant hues. It rarely grows to a height of more than 15 to 30 centimetres; its flowers are like a smaller version of the flowers of our garden pansy, and vary in colour to include all the shades and combinations of the three basic colours – white, yellow, purple – such as a painter might dream of.

It is picked when it comes into flower (even the roots can be kept) and dried in the shade as quickly as possible for, although taken from the ground, growth continues and diminishes its effectiveness.

It is above all else depurative and diuretic, but it also contains methyl salicylate (easily recognized by the odour it exhales and the pronounced taste it releases when chewed), and is therefore prescribed, on the one hand for skin diseases (eczema, scabbing, psoriasis, impetigo, acne in adolescents, pruritis in old persons, spots, milk-crust), generalized oedema, dropsy; and on the other hand for rheumatic complaints and especially rheumatism in the joints accompanied by fever.

It is taken in a mild decoction (40 to 60 grammes of dried plant to a litre of cold water; leave to soak for at least an hour; bring gently to the boil; boil for no longer than ten to twenty seconds; leave to infuse for ten minutes). For cutaneous eruptions and dropsy, drink 3 or 4 cupfuls per day, between meals or at least a good half hour before eating. For rheumatoid arthritis, drink – again, as long as possible before or after eating – a litre of decoction in the course of a day.

To reinforce the internal action of the decoction in the treatment of skin diseases, it is recommended to apply compresses soaked in the same decoction to the affected areas.

PARSLEY

Apium petroselinum or **Petroselinum sativum.**
Common parsley, Cultivated parsley

There is a charming legend, based on ancient superstitions, that will please those of you who, like myself, grow parsley in the garden, for it gives both an explanation as to why it is slow to sprout and a certificate of good conduct to the gardener. according to this legend, the parsley must go seven times to find the devil and return to its place before starting to grow, and it will then only do so providing it has been sown by an upright and honest man . . .

Like most of the aromatic herbs, it has been endowed with magical powers, beneficent or maleficent according to the differing epochs and countries. The Greeks featured it at funeral banquets and made it into crowns for the winners of the Isthmian games. The Romans believed it caused sterility and would bring on epilepsy in infants if eaten by nursing mothers. In the Middle Ages it was believed that your enemy was condemned to sudden death if you pronounced his name while tearing out a root of parsley, and it is probably a legacy of this ancient practice of witchcraft that even today many people refuse to transplant parsley because it 'brings bad luck'.

Fortunately for both gastronomy and health, these beliefs did not prevent parsley from rapidly winning a privileged place in the culinary art – 'parsley is in great request' notes Pliny, 'and no man lightly there is but loveth it: for nothing is there more ordinary, than to see large branches of Parsley good store, swimming in their potage'; and Galen says 'there is no herb so commonly used at table' – and retaining this place throughout the centuries, to the great benefit of our health. Such eminent specialists in nutrition as Lucie Randouin and Paul Fournier have said of it: 'One may, without exaggeration, consider it as one of the most valuable health-giving foodstuffs that Nature has generously put at the disposal of mankind.'

It is rich in iron, calcium, vitamins and various trace-elements indispensable to the body. So do not hesitate to use it freely, cooked (it is included in the traditional bouquet garni) and especially raw, added, finely chopped, to salads, soups, vegetables. Bear in mind, too, its numerous medicinal uses, so well known to our grandmothers.

All parts of the plant are used, root, leaves and seeds, fresh or dried in the shade (parsley being a biennial, the roots are collected at the beginning of autumn in the second year, at the same time as the seeds); all parts contain, in greater or lesser proportions, the same active principles – including apiol – that qualify it as aperient, stimulant, diuretic, antiseptic, pectoral and emmenagogue, in other words having the power to regulate the menstrual discharge.

The fresh leaves in infusion (15 to 20 grammes to half a litre of boiling water; leave to infuse for five to ten minutes; to be drunk in the course of a day, a small cupful at a time at regular intervals) relieve the painful cramps that often accompany menstruation; they also aid the digestion and stimulate the circulation of the blood.

The dried root, in decoction (40 to 50 grammes to one litre of water; boil for two or three minutes; leave to infuse for ten minutes, 2 or 3 cupfuls per day before meals) stimulates kidney function and is therefore prescribed for dropsy, oedema, rheumatism, retention of urine, arthritis, gravel (it is interesting to note that the Egyptians already used parsley – wild parsley, for the plant has only been cultivated since the Graeco-Roman epoch – in the treatment of complaints of the urinary tract).

A stronger dosage of fresh root (100 grammes to a litre of water; boil for five minutes and leave to infuse for ten minutes; to be drunk in one day) restores and regulates the menstrual discharge – although Doctor Leclerc preferred to employ the juice of the fresh plant (100 to 150 grammes per day), considering the decoction too mild to bring about spectacular results. An alternative method is to use a decoction of seeds (80 to 100 grammes to a litre of water; boil for five minutes and leave to infuse for ten minutes; to be drunk in one day).

Externally, the crushed fresh leaves will relieve irritation from insect stings and can be used as an emergency dressing on wounds. Cooked in wine, they are applied as a poultice on contusions and sprains (renew the poultice three or four times a day).

A wad of cotton wool soaked in parsley juice and placed in the ear will relieve toothache or earache.

Daily applications of the water in which a handful of parsley has been steeped overnight will cause freckles to disappear and clear the complexion (alternatively a lukewarm decoction may be employed in the same way, obtained by boiling a large bunch of parsley in half a litre of water for fifteen minutes).

Lastly, here are two prescriptions which I cannot guarantee will be successful, but which are worth trying since they are perfectly harmless. I came across the first in an old book of necromancy, the second in a magazine: (1) For loss of hair: pound some parsley seeds to a powder and sprinkle liberally on the head for three consecutive evenings, rubbing well into the scalp; (2) For car-sickness: the singer Mick Micheyl recommends, having tried it herself, wearing a sprig of parsley on the stomach, attaching it directly to the skin with sticky tape or a plaster.

PASSION FLOWER
Passiflora incarnata.   Maypops

Although a native of the tropical countries of America, this climbing plant has become acclimatized and will grow outdoors in well-protected positions, lending to our gardens the strange beauty of its flowers. These – with a little imagination! – evoke the instruments of Christ's Passion: the corolla is the crown of thorns, the three styles of the pistil are the nails, the stamens the hammer, while the pointed leaves represent the spear and the tendrils the whip.

It was only in the second half of the nineteenth century that its remarkable sedative action was discovered, for it has the property of calming the nerves without causing depression, and of inducing sleep yet allowing the subject to wake feeling as fit and alert as after a normal night's sleep.

It is prescribed for the following: insomnia in nervous or anxious persons and subjects with imbalance of the sympathetic nervous system; state of nerves; nervous complaints of the heart and stomach (palpitations and gastric spasms); nervous disorders connected with menstruation and menopause: in one day drink 3 cupfuls (one of which should be taken in mid-afternoon and another on retiring) or more if required, of mild decoction made with chopped plant (leaves and flowers) picked when coming into bloom and dried in the shade (30 to 50 grammes to a litre of water; heat gently; boil for one minute and leave to infuse for ten minutes).

Passiflora is the homoeopathic remedy for nervous insomnia.

PEACH
Amygdalus persica

Of its fruit I shall say only that it was not particularly valued by the doctors in ancient times or, leaving it to dieticians to debate its virtues, mention merely its tonic effects in facial beauty care (applications of crushed pulp).

Its flowers and its leaves, on the contrary, have always been held medicinally in high repute, on condition that the prescribed dosage is not exceeded for they contain – as does the kernel of the stone – hydrocyanic acid which is toxic and has caused a number of accidents, especially among children who, playing at dolls' dinner parties, break open the stones and eat the kernels.

Its uses have not changed ever since the peach tree, a native of Ethiopia and very common in Persia, was introduced into Italy during the reign of Claudius, the father of Britannicus. They are laxative, vermifuge, antispasmodic and sedative. They can be used fresh or dried; the flowers are collected in spring (you can collect those which fall when the tree is gently shaken without impairing the fruit crop since it is the sterile blossoms that drop off the branches); the leaves, which appear after the blossom, are picked in summer because in spring their active principles are not yet at their maximum and in the autumn they have almost disappeared.

The infusion of dried flowers will calm children who suffer from tantrums (a pinch of flowers to a cupful of boiling milk or water; leave to infuse for five minutes); it has a laxative and sedative action, prescribed for constipated and nervous children (15 to 30 grammes according to age, to half a litre of boiling milk or water; leave to infuse for five minutes; 1 or 2 cupfuls per day).

But it is the syrup – which was used regularly by Louis XIV and Voltaire – that is most often employed to combat constipation (its action is not harsh and is therefore suitable for sensitive bowels) in children (one coffeespoonful at bedtime, either neat or in a herbal tea), who will take it more readily than chicory syrup, and in adults (2 or 3 coffeespoonfuls last thing at night).

The syrup is made as follows: pour a litre and a half of boiling water on to 500 grammes of fresh flowers; cover and leave to macerate for at least twelve hours; boil for five to ten minutes; press and strain through a fine cloth and add 500 grammes of sugar; cook over a gentle heat until it acquires the consistency of syrup: store in a tightly-stoppered jar.

The dried leaves (30 grammes to half a litre of boiling water; leave to infuse for five minutes; to be drunk in one day) are especially recommended for conditions of the urinary tract (haematuria, nephritis). Either fresh and crushed, or dry and boiled for a few minutes together with an equal quantity of dried flowers, they are applied as poultices on the abdomen as a remedy for worms (oxyuris) in children.

PELLITORY-OF-THE-WALL
Parietaria officinalis.   Official pellitory

Like the daisy, it was once much employed in medicine, but is nowadays almost entirely neglected; it is still used only by those who know it to be an invaluable aid in the treatment of conditions of the urinary tract, namely phytotherapists, herbalists and peasants.

Dioscorides prescribed it for 'suppression of wine'; most authorities, from the Middle Ages to the eighteenth century, accorded it a place of honour 'for dispersing obstructions and aiding the flow of liquors'; then it went out of fashion, only country people remaining faithful to it because they knew it to be effective.

It has the additional advantage of being as common as its near relative the nettle, although it does not share the stinging nature of the latter. It is found throughout Europe, on old walls and in stony places. Its cylindrical stems, sometimes reddish in colour, generally grow to a length of 40 to 60 centimetres; its alternate leaves have a downy under-surface and look like a narrower version of the bay leaf; its tiny flowers are greenish-white and grouped in the axils of the leaves.

When possible, it is preferable to utilize the fresh plant for drying causes it to lose some of its efficacy, but if dried rapidly (if possible in a drying cabinet) it keeps a sufficient measure of its active principles for it to be recommended in the treatment of dropsy, cystitis, inflammation of the prostate, stones in the kidneys and bladder, gravel, nephritis, oedema, retention of urine, on which it acts as diuretic, sedative and emollient.

It is taken in a mild decoction: 30 to 40 grammes of dry plant to a litre of water; bring gently to the boil; leave to infuse for ten minutes; to be drunk, between meals, in the course of two days; add a slice of lemon, for it is particularly tasteless.

Externally, poultices of fresh plant, roughly crushed, are used to reinforce its internal action in cases of retention of urine (apply on the pubis and lower abdomen) and kidney stones (apply on the back in the region of the kidneys).

PERIWINKLE, LESSER
Vinca minor

It was granted its letters of nobility by those of Madame de Sévigné who, in 1684, wrote to her daughter, Madame de Grignan: 'Lastly, my dear, at all events comfort and cure yourself with your good periwinkle, very green and very bitter, but very good for your complaints as you already know: it will cool your inflamed chest.'

Because its creeping supple stems retain their little ovate dark

green leaves all the year round, it has naturally been associated with the idea of eternity; hence the Italian custom of plaiting it into wreaths to be laid on the tombs of children and adolescents, and in Flanders the custom of strewing it on the path of the bride and groom on their way to church, its pure blue flowers symbolizing the virginity of the bride and its leaves the ever-lasting love of the young couple.

Inevitably it has played its part in magic practices: thrown with other plants on to a burning fire, it helped to cause apparitions of absent loved ones to form in the smoke; it was incorporated in love philtres; it was rubbed on snake bites while secret formulas were recited, and it was believed to 'arrest the menstrual flow and protect pregnant women from miscarriage' if worn fastened around the thigh.

The latter belief links up with one of its major medical uses: arresting haemorrhages – 'it staunches the flow of blood from any part of the body' the ancient herbalists said – for it is astringent. It is also vulnerary, febrifuge and sudorific.

Internally, it is prescribed in a mild decoction (50 to 60 grammes of dried flowers, leaves and stems, chopped, to a litre of cold water; steep for at least an hour; bring to the boil; boil for about twenty seconds; leave to infuse for ten to fifteen minutes; 3 or 4 cupfuls per day) for haemoptysis (spitting of blood), chest complaints, malaria, leucorrhoea, dysentery, excessive menstrual discharge, anaemia (it is of interest to note that two alkaloids extracted from the lesser periwinkle are used in medicine in the treatment of leucaemia and Hodgkin's disease).

In country regions, one of the classic remedies for pleurisy is to give the patient a kind of cocktail (half a glass of white wine mixed with half a glass of periwinkle juice) and keep him well covered so that he perspires freely.

It is also used to make an excellent tonic wine (highly spoken of by Doctor Leclerc) which is given in the amount of 2 to 4 tablespoonfuls per day, before meals, for tiredness and to persons who suffer from a weak chest. There are two methods of preparation: either macerate 100 grammes of chopped leaves, preferably fresh, in a litre of Banyuls for ten days; press and strain through a fine cloth; or else infuse 100 grammes of chopped leaves in a litre of boiling red wine with 100 grammes of sugar; leave to cool, press and strain.

Externally the decoction (50 to 60 grammes of leaves to a litre of water or wine) is used as a gargle and mouthwash in the treatment of tonsillitis, inflammation of the uvula, mouth ulcers; as a lotion and on compresses for badly-healing sores. A fresh leaf, crushed between the fingers and inserted into the nostril, will arrest nose-bleed.

PINE

Pinus sylvestris.   Scots or Scotch pine, Scotch fir, Forest pine, Pinaster, Sea-pine, Norway pine, etc.

Associated, wherever any of its eighty-odd species grow, with the cults that marked the awakening of religious feeling in mankind, it was also soon employed for medicinal purposes. Formulae discovered on papyri show that the doctors of Egypt in the time of the Pharaohs prescribed it in the form of pitch and turpentine resin; Hippocrates prescribed it as a remedy for pneumonia, and Arab doctors used it as the specific for 'ulcers of the lungs', which were probably tubercular cavities.

For thousands of years it has been known for its properties as a bronchial disinfectant. These properties continue to earn it a place today in the composition of numerous medicines and home remedies.

The parts used are the buds, dried in the shade, picked in the spring just before they open; the cones, picked while still green; and the fresh needles, collected at any time of the year.

The buds, prepared by decoction (40 to 50 grammes to a litre of water; cold-soak for one to two hours; heat gently and boil for one or two minutes; leave to infuse for ten minutes; 3 or 4 cupfuls per day), are employed in the treatment of bronchial complaints, cystitis, rheumatism, gout, skin diseases (in fact, they are not only expectorant and antiseptic, but also stimulant, tonic and sudorific).

The same decoction is prescribed: as inhalations for head colds and sinusitis; as a gargle for laryngitis; on hot compresses for rheumatic or gout pains; as warm douches, morning and evening, for leucorrhoea and metritis.

The green cones and the needles are principally used to make a decoction which is added to the bath water to relieve attacks of breathlessness, soothe rheumatic pains and combat skin diseases: boil 1,000 to 1,500 grammes of needles, twigs and chopped cones in 15 litres of water for an hour and a half; add the decoction to bath water at 35°C; duration of bath: fifteen minutes.

In certain countries, notably eastern France, Switzerland, Germany and Austria, people make a syrup which is an excellent bronchial tonic. It is prepared by pouring half a litre of boiling water, either on to freshly picked buds (50 to 60 grammes), or on to four or five green cones; leave to macerate for twenty-four hours; boil for thirty to forty-five minutes; strain; add 4 or 5 tablespoonfuls of honey; heat gently until it acquires the consistency of syrup, and let it cool before bottling. The usual dosage is 2 to 3 coffeespoonfuls per day.

PINK
Dianthus caryophyllus.   Clove-Pink, Carnation, Picotee

Here is another plant that has been forsaken by modern medicine on the grounds that it is ineffectual. Yet doctors formerly included it among the cordial plants and employed it with success in the treatment of malignant fevers to promote perspiration and passing of urine, whilst also quenching the patient's thirst.

This usage certainly seems to support the story that supposedly led to the introduction of the pink into France: the Saint Louis crusaders, struck down by plague outside Tunis, are said to have drunk a certain aromatic liqueur made with pinks which reputedly alleviated their fever, whereupon they determined to bring back with them some specimens of the plant which had thus relieved their ills – which would explain

why the pink was originally called *tunica*, the name also given
to the syrup prescribed for persons 'afflicted with very malignant fevers'.

Whatever the advocates of chemically manufactured drugs
may say, the pink can still render service for feverish conditions,
when it promotes perspiration and quenches the thirst.

The rules laid down by Doctor Chomel still serve as a guide
for us to follow: 'Among the great number of species of pink
that are grown in gardens, choose those which are simplest in

form, and of these the reddest and most fragrant.' The petals
are picked and used either fresh to make a syrup or *ratafia*, or
dried in the shade to make infusions (3 to 5 grammes of petals
to 100 cubic centimetres of boiling water; leave to infuse for
five to ten minutes; to be taken twice a day).

To make the syrup: place 500 grammes of fresh petals in a
glass or china receptacle and pour on to them a litre and a half
of boiling water; leave to infuse for six hours; strain and heat in
a *bain-marie*, adding sugar until it acquires the consistency of

syrup; store in tightly corked jars. This syrup is generally taken in warm water or a herbal tea, one tablespoonful per cup.

To make the *ratafia*: macerate 250 to 300 grammes of fresh petals in a litre of spirits or alcohol (45°) for eight to ten days; press and strain through a fine cloth; sweeten to taste. It is prescribed in the amount of one liqueur-glassful as a 'very excellent remedy' for indigestion, distension and flatulence.

PLANTAIN
Plantago major, Plantago media, Plantago lanceolata, Plantago alpina, Plantago psyllium. Greater plantain, Ripple grass, Waybread, Hoary plantain, Fire-weed, Henplant, Lamb's-tongue plantain, Black plantain, Long, narrow leaved or ribwort plantain, Rib grass

Throughout the ages, the plantain has always been highly valued. Dioscorides, Pliny and Galen praised it as an astringent and vulnerary, and as a remedy for eye disorders. There are repeated references to its healing action in the plays of Shakespeare. Medical treatises, from the Middle Ages to the eighteenth century, extolled it as 'a plant that nobody should despise' and recommended it above all others in the treatment of more than twenty different diseases.

There are numerous varieties of plantain, all having more or less the same properties and similar characteristics, and therefore easily recognizable: the leaves and the flowering stems (which vary in height from 20 to 40 centimetres) all spring from a basal rosette directly attached to the stout rootstock; the leaves are ovate (fairly pointed) with strongly-developed parallel longitudinal ribs on their under-surfaces; the flowers, which appear from May to September, are borne in tall dense cylindrical spikes at the extremity of the stems, which rise from the axils of the leaves; they are yellowish-white, pink or brown in colour, according to which of the most common species they belong: the greater plantain (*Plantago major*), the hoary or lamb's-tongue plantain (*Plantago media*), and the long-narrow-leaved or ribwort plantain (*Plantago lanceolata*), which grow abundantly along waysides, in meadows and pastures and dry places, and the *psyllium* plantain which is found in the Midi.

The parts used are: (1) the leaves, fresh or dried (quickly, in the sun or drying cabinet at 40–50°C, to keep them from turning brown, which results in an unpleasant tasting infusion), picked from spring to flowering time; (2) the ripe seeds, i.e. picked when they are easily detached from the terminal spikes.

The fresh leaves – which are eaten, mixed with dandelion leaves, as a depurative salad in the spring – are known to peasants as an emergency dressing: when they injure themselves, they crush the leaves between their fingers and apply them to the wound. 'A dressing of this kind', says the Abbé Kneipp, 'is the first and often the best for it promotes rapid healing. One might say that the plantain closes the gaping wound with a seam of gold thread; for, just as gold will not admit of rust, so the plantain will not admit of rotting and gangrenous flesh.' The fresh leaves, washed in boiled water and crushed, are also used as poultices on badly healing wounds and sores, varicose ulcers, scabbing; crushed and rubbed on the skin, they soothe irritation from insect stings and bites (wasps, bees, mosquitoes) doubtless by neutralizing the poison – it used to be said that weasels, before attacking vipers, would roll in tufts of plantain to ensure themselves of total immunity.

Depurative, expectorant, astringent and restorative, the decoction (80 to 100 grammes of chopped dried leaves to a litre of water; cold-soak for ten minutes; bring to the boil; boil for two or three minutes and infuse for ten minutes; 3 to 5 cupfuls per day) is recommended for persons suffering from bronchitis, whooping cough, tuberculosis and weakness of the respiratory tract; for anaemia and in convalescence; for enteritis with diarrhoea, dysentery, chronic nephritis. A weaker decoction (50 to 60 grammes to a litre) is used as a lotion, eye-wash and on compresses in the treatment of inflammation of the eyelids (conjunctivitis, blepharitis); however, when possible the following formula is even better: 10 grammes of plantain leaves, 5 grammes of a mixture of equal parts of cornflowers and melilot flowers to 150 grammes of boiling water; leave to infuse for fifteen minutes and strain through a fine cloth.

As for the seeds – which enter into the composition of poultry feed – they are prescribed both as a gentle purgative for constipation and in the treatment of enteritis and mild diarrhoea by virtue of the mucilage they contain: 1 to 3 coffeespoonfuls in half a glass of water; leave to swell for two hours and drink immediately before the evening meal or last thing at night. The most active seeds are those of the plantain of the Midi, sold in chemists shops under the name of *psyllium*.

PLUM
Prunus domestica

We seldom make use of the laxative, febrifuge and diuretic virtues of its dried leaves taken in decoction (25 to 30 grammes to a litre of water, boiled for five minutes and infused for ten) for there are other herbal medicines that are both more active and more pleasant to the taste; but its fruits, desiccated in the sun or low oven to make prunes, are a first class energy food for athletes – who, like mountain climbers and racing cyclists, want foods that yield the highest energy content for the least weight – and are above all the ideal treatment for constipation.

'Nature', noted a Renaissance doctor, 'has allowed figs and prunes to retain their virtues when dried: both will comfortably loosen the bowels.' The decoction of prunes has thus long served apothecaries as the basis of purgative infusions, particularly for children, and prunes, cooked in a mixture of water and wine with cinnamon, lemon peel and sugar, were still in my own childhood days the traditional family dessert-remedy for sluggishness of the bowels.

People nowadays disregard this old-fashioned treatment, which is a great mistake, for prunes – untreated of course – are undeniably the most natural and delicious means of regulating bowel movements.

In cases of chronic and stubborn constipation, prunes should be taken first thing in the morning before breakfast, for it is known that this is when their action is at its best.

The best methods of preparation are: (1) Doctor Carton's, who specified that they should be freed of sugar and acids so that they become a kind of 'bolus of cellulose' that in its passage through the intestine exerts both a mechanical action and a cholagogue action: split the prunes lengthwise with a knife as far as the stone; soak in water, which softens them and restores their original water content; cook for two to three hours, changing the water three times during cooking (pour off the water and replace with hot water); eight to twenty prunes to be eaten first thing in the morning; (2) Doctor Oudinot's: split the raw prunes with a knife and soak in plenty of cold water for twenty-four hours; four to ten prunes to be eaten at breakfast. 'Some of our patients,' the Doctor adds, 'have been following this diet successfully for years.'

POPLAR, BLACK
Populus nigra

For reasons that philologists – and perhaps sociologists – are probably able to explain but which I confess are unknown to me, its name derives from the Latin word *populus* that meant both the people and the tree – perhaps because it multiplies rapidly and is to be found everywhere, because it is tall but light in weight (packing cases are made from its wood), because it is often the victim of a parasite (mistletoe) or because it murmurs and whispers a lot of the time.

There are some twenty varieties of poplar, all possessing more or less identical commercial or therapeutic properties; but it is the black poplar, with its triangular slightly serrated leaves, which is traditionally – doubtless because the most widespread – the source of raw material in popular medicine.

Its bark calcined in a sealed vessel yields the famous plant charcoal sold by chemists for the last hundred years in the form of powder or pills as a remedy for acidity, constipation and flatulence. Its buds (picked, obviously, in the spring) have been used much longer (for at least four hundred years) as a tonic, expectorant, diuretic, analgesic and as a remedy for haemorrhoids.

The oldest preparation is the ointment known as 'populeum unguen'. Apothecaries elaborated it with their own choice of numerous plants (especially bryony root and bramble leaves), but the poplar buds constituted the principal element and you can easily make it yourself by following this simple method: boil for at least two hours one part of freshly picked buds in three parts of water (for example, 200 grammes of buds to 600 grammes of water); add to the decoction thus obtained two parts of unsalted lard (which would be 400 grammes in our example) and leave this mixture over a low heat until all the water has evaporated; press and strain through a coarse cloth and store in a china or glass pot with a close-fitting lid.

This unguent is recommended, in light applications, for

burns, inflammation, chapped or cracked skin, rheumatic or gout pains, haemorrhoids.

The tincture made from the buds is also a valuable medicinal aid. It is prepared as follows: macerate 200 grammes of freshly picked and crushed buds in a litre of alcohol (90°); leave the jar in a warm place – in the sun or close to a stove or radiator – for about ten days, shaking occasionally; press and strain through a fine cloth and store in tightly corked bottles. This tincture is employed externally (compresses and frictions) for contusions and sprains, but also internally (three times a day, 10 to 15 drops in a little water or on a lump of sugar) for chest complaints (coughs, bronchitis, tracheitis), muscular and articular pains, inflammation of the urinary tract (cystitis, nephritis).

The dried buds (15 to 20 grammes to half a litre of boiling water; leave to infuse for half an hour) are prescribed, in the amount of 2 or 3 small cupfuls per day (preferably taken after meals), for rheumatism, gout, dropsy, chest complaints.

Lastly, poplar wine is an excellent tonic, antiseptic, and sedative in cases of persistent cough, tracheitis, bronchitis, bronchial catarrh; macerate 100 grammes of fresh crushed buds and 40 grammes of bitter orange peel in a litre of good red wine for eight days; press and strain through a fine cloth; one sherry-glassful before meals midday and evening.

POPPY, RED

Papaver rheas.   Corn poppy, Corn rose, Red-weed, Canker, Headache

The Egyptians made garlands of poppies (some have been found in tombs dating from the time of the Pharaohs) and used the seeds as a condiment, as did the Greeks and Romans, who added them to their cakes both for their flavour and for reasons of health: according to Dioscorides, it 'doth soften ye belly gently'. The flowers were used to make a medicinal syrup which, says Parkinson, 'is with good effect, given to those that have a Plurisie, and the dryed flowers also, either boyled in water or made into powder and drunke, either in the distilled water of them, or in some other drinke, worketh the like effect . . .'

The flowers are the part of the plant that is still used today. The petals are gathered throughout the flowering season; they should be dried immediately by laying them out, taking care not to crush them on paper (the faster they dry, the less they will tend to turn black, and for this reason they are often put in a drying cabinet), and then stored in tightly closed jars, kept in a dry place.

They are taken in infusion (5 to 10 grammes to a litre of water, 4 or 5 cupfuls per day) for heavy colds, catarrh, bronchitis, angina, asthma, colic, eruptive fevers, insomnia, whooping-cough.

The poppy promotes perspiration, soothes coughs and calms restlessness, because of its emollient properties and its mildly narcotic action (it belongs to the same family as the opium poppy, *Papaver somniferum*), which explains why its juice formerly used to be added to infants' feeds to make them sleep (which was at least better than adding brandy to the feeding bottle as they did in Normandy!).

Externally, a stronger infusion (10 to 20 grammes to a litre) is employed on compresses in the treatment of dental abscesses, eye disorders and also as a beauty lotion to combat wrinkles.

POTATO
Solanum tuberosum. Tuberous nightshade

It was a long while before the potato triumphed over prejudice and suspicion (because it is a solanaceous plant like belladonna and henbane from which the Borgias made their poison, it was suspected of being poisonous and causing leprosy!), but it has since made up for lost time: there are now some 1,600 known varieties, and it is hard to imagine a normal diet in which the potato is absent. Eaten raw, it has been the remedy for scurvy on long voyages, and popular medicine adopted it even before scientists confirmed its therapeutic usefulness.

Internally, raw potato juice is employed as a remedy for stomach ulcers, chronic diarrhoea, diabetes: three or four times a day for a month, half a glassful flavoured with carrot juice or honey for its taste is rather unpleasant.

Externally, grated raw potato is prescribed as a poultice to relieve the pain from burns and sunburn, for chilblains and cracked skin, to reduce swelling in puffy eyelids and 'untire' the eyes.

Slices of raw potato, freshly cut and applied to the temples, soothe headaches and migraines. The same application, renewed morning and evening, on atonic wounds, 'nasty' sores, 'swellings' of dubious origin, promote healing or bring about their disappearance within a few weeks.

To make the hands soft and white, rub them for several consecutive evenings with a paste obtained by boiling and mashing very white floury potatoes, adding a little milk and (optionally) a few drops of glycerine and rose water.

A country remedy for pains, sciatica, lumbago, etc., is to keep a small potato in the pocket, replacing it when it has completely dried out.

A last point, little known but important to your health: boiled potatoes should not be eaten more than twenty-four hours after cooking, for they then generally harbour a bacillus (protens) which is found in putrefied animal matter.

POTENTIL
Potentilla

SILVERWEED
Potentilla anserina.   Wild tansy, Goosegrass, Gooseweed, Goosefoot, Goosegray

CINQUEFOIL
Potentilla reptans. Creeping potentilla

TORMENTIL
Potentilla erecta. Bloodroot

The above-named are all sisters, all have the same properties (to varying degrees, admittedly), frequent the same places practically, but are distinguished by certain individual features.

ROOT   All have a gnarled woody rootstock, blackish outside for the silverweed and the cinquefoil, reddish-brown for the tormentil. The latter also has the thickest root, up to 3 centimetres in diameter and 20 centimetres in length (it is also red inside).

STEMS   Creeping stems for the silverweed and the cinquefoil, slightly downy and often tinged with red, extending for as much as a metre like the runners of the wild strawberry, and like them also rooting at intervals from the leaf knots; the stem of the tormentil is straight, slender and branched (between 10 and 40 centimetres in height).

LEAVES   The leaf of the silverweed looks like a large bird's feather; it comprises numerous deeply-toothed leaflets, their upper surface a handsome green and slightly downy, their under surface velvety and whitish in colour; the leaf of the cinquefoil has a long stalk, five divisions (sometimes seven), and is less deeply-toothed but otherwise sharing the same features as the leaf of the silverweed; the leaf of the tormentil has three divisions (sometimes five) and is narrower, with toothed borders like the others, and of a lighter green on the under surface.

FLOWERS   Bright golden yellow (sometimes with touches of greenish-white on those of the silverweed and the cinquefoil); they have numerous stamens and five petals, except for the tormentil which only has four – this being the best way of identifying it.

The 'potentil sisters' share the same preference for waste places, roadsides, hedges, ditches, moist pastures (geese are particularly fond of silverweed, and pigs will root about in the ground in search of its roots). They flower from spring to autumn, during which period are collected the flowering plant of the silverweed and the cinquefoil, the rhizome of the tormentil, raw materials which should be dried in the sun as rapidly as possible.

They are characterized by their astringent, anti-inflammatory and sedative properties, because of which they have always been employed in the treatment of intestinal disorders (tormentil derives from the Latin *tormina*: colic) and fever (a sixteenth-century treatise even declares of the cinquefoil that 'it is a marvellous fact that this plant placed beneath the sole of the foot and in the palm of the hand will reduce fevers of any kind').

So you can employ any one of the three, according to which is to hand; however, the tormentil is undeniably the most active because of its high tannin content (17 per cent in the rhizome) which makes it one of the most astringent of our plants. It is therefore to be preferred, although the silverweed and the cinquefoil obviously have the same medicinal uses (they are prepared as a decoction of dried flowers and leaves, 20 to 30 grammes to a litre of water; cold-soak for ten minutes; bring gently to the boil; boil for three to four minutes; leave to infuse for ten minutes; 3 or 4 small cupfuls per day).

Tormentil is prescribed for colic, enteritis, diarrhoea in the aged and in persons suffering from tuberculosis, catarrhal complaints (asthma, chronic bronchitis, hay fever), gynaecological disorders (cystitis, metritis, leucorrhoea), painful menstruation, passive haemorrhages, skin conditions (scabbing, pruritus, herpes, wet eczema) in decoction: 40 to 50 grammes of crushed rhizome to a litre of water; cold-soak for ten to fifteen minutes; leave to infuse for the same length of time; 4 to 6 small coffee-cupfuls per day (never use iron utensils when preparing this or the other potentils).

An alternative excellent – and less complicated – remedy for the complaints listed above, as well as a tonic prescribed in cases of fatigue and tuberculosis, is tormentil wine: macerate 60 to 70 grammes of crushed rhizome for eight to ten days in a litre of wine (sweet or dry, according to taste); 3 wineglassfuls a day, to be taken after meals.

The tincture has the same uses, and is prepared by macerating a handful – about 150 grammes – of dried rhizome in a litre of alcohol (45°) for ten to fifteen days; press and strain through a fine cloth; twenty to thirty drops on a lump of sugar.

Externally, a stronger decoction (60 to 100 grammes to a litre of water) is prescribed as a lotion or on compresses or as a gargle, for bruises, ecchymosis, purulent sores, varicose ulcers, burns, skin complaints, aphtha, pyorrhoea, gingivitis, tonsillitis, pharyngitis, softening of the gums, mouth ulcers, and to remove freckles.

Chewing a piece of rhizome of silverweed or tormentil from time to time is an effective remedy for mouth complaints and hardens the gums.

PRIMULA, OFFICINAL
Primula officinalis.   Cowslip, Paigle, Pagle

You are probably unaware, as I was myself until about ten years ago, that the cowslip has other uses besides bringing a breath of spring into dreary town houses in the form of nosegays picked on a Sunday outing in the country. Yet its leaves can be eaten as salad, in some countries its root is used to lend aroma to beer, its flowers yield a fragrant herbal tea of a lovely golden yellow colour which can advantageously substitute for the classic lime-blossom tea, and lastly its therapeutic properties are confirmed.

These properties were formerly somewhat exaggerated, and people regarded the cowslip as a kind of panacea. However, its uses are none the less valuable for being more limited than was once believed.

The root (which is actually a short rhizome, slightly reddish in colour, with long rootlets, possessing an odour of aniseed which it loses when dried), gathered either in spring before the plant comes into flower, or in the autumn, must be carefully washed before drying. Its action is anti-inflammatory, expectorant, emollient, diuretic and mildly laxative, and it is therefore recommended for clearing the bronchi, eliminating toxins, cleansing the bowels. It is prescribed for complaints of the respiratory tract (bronchitis, influenza, pneumonia, tracheitis, whooping cough), rheumatism, gout, gravel: in decoction, 20 to 30 grammes of chopped root to a litre of water; cold-soak for half an hour; heat gently and boil for two or three minutes; leave to infuse for fifteen minutes; 3 cupfuls per day between meals.

Externally, the highly concentrated decoction (100 grammes of root to a litre of water; cold-soak, then boil until reduced by a third) is employed on compresses for ecchymoses and contusions.

The flowers (golden yellow, with a yellow corolla with five spreading lobes, grouped at the summit of the stems in umbels all on the same side and exhaling a honey-like fragrance), fresh or dried, make a delicious infusion (20 to 30 grammes to a litre of boiling water; leave to infuse for ten to fifteen minutes; 3 cupfuls per day, after meals) which has a sedative action on the sympathetic nervous system and is recommended for headaches, migraines, vertigo, nervous spasms of the stomach and the intestines, flatulence, constipation, insomnia, angor. It is also used on compresses applied to the forehead for headaches and migraines, and also as a lotion to be applied daily 'to remove all blotches from the face'.

Cowslip oil (macerate a handful of fresh flowers and a handful of fresh chopped root in a litre of olive oil for six weeks, in a tightly-stoppered glass jar exposed to the sun or kept in a warm place, press and strain through a cloth and store in corked jars), used either as a friction to be rubbed gently into the skin, or on compresses, constitutes an excellent treatment for contusions, pains, swellings, symptoms of paralysis.

Lastly, I think I should warn you of a possible hazard

connected with the cowslip, which has been brought to light by modern research into allergies: placed next to the skin, as when tucked into the neckline of a dress for example, it can engender in certain subjects a dark red cutaneous eruption that gives a feeling of burning and intolerable itching: this is 'primula dermatitis'.

PUMPKIN, AMERICAN
Cucurbita pepo

A native of India, it has long been cultivated in most of the hot or temperate regions of the globe, but it was only at the beginning of the nineteenth century that the most valuable of its therapeutic virtues was discovered.

It was in 1820 that Doctor Mongenay, a doctor in Cuba, announced the efficacity of its seed in the treatment of tapeworm. Several of his colleagues tested his prescription and were so enthusiastic at their results that they communicated their observations to the societies of medicine, commenting that 'our indiginous medicinal material is not as poor as it is made out to be'.

But the saying 'no man is a prophet in his own country' is probably more true in the medical field than any other, and a few decades later Doctor Cazin – who used it with success in several cases that had resisted all other known remedies – announced in his turn: 'The humble pumpkin has the misfortune of being familiar . . . If it were to be transformed into expensive bottles with smart labels, those of our town dwellers who suffer from tapeworm would hasten to purchase it and praise its happy effects. Country doctors will simply prescribe pumpkin seed, and their patients – whose common sense has not been warped by imagination – will accept it gratefully as they do everything that is simple and close to nature.'

So here is the receipt for this vermifuge (ascaris) and taenifuge (tapeworm) which has the double merit of being neither irritant nor toxic, so that it can be administered for several consecutive days without undesirable side-effects: on the day preceding the course of treatment and throughout the three-day course itself, keep to a milk diet; pound 30 to 40 grammes of pumpkin seeds, stripped of their outer covering, to make a paste, and mix this with an equal quantity of honey; take this mixture first thing in the morning before breakfast, in three doses at twenty or thirty minute intervals: on the last day, three or four hours after the last dose, take either 40 grammes of castor oil, or a decoction of buckthorn alder (10 grammes of bark to 250 grammes of water, boil for five minutes and leave to infuse for a further five minutes). It is naturally advisable that the stools be passed into a chamber pot or similar receptacle half filled with water in order to check that the tapeworm has been completely expelled, including the head.

The seeds – which the ancients classed among the 'four major cold seeds' and advocated for quelling the ardours of the flesh – are also (pounded with sweet almond oil or olive oil) used to make a paste that keeps the skin soft and removes freckles.

The pulp of raw pumpkin, applied as a cold poultice, will immediately soothe first-degree burns, ophthalmia and headaches.

PURPLE LOOSESTRIFE

Lythrum salicaria.   Spiked purple loosestrife,
Willow-leaved lythrum

If you go fishing, you will have seen it often, for like you it frequents the banks of ponds and rivers (and similar marshy moist places). It is a sturdy plant, growing from 60 centimetres to 1 metre in height, with quadrangular stems and long, opposite lanceolate leaves. From June to the end of August it bears long spikes of reddish-purple flowers with 6 petals, in which your line may sometimes catch as you glide beneath the willows (its botanical name in fact derives from *salix*: willow, because it is generally found growing beneath them).

Collect the flowering tips and dry them in the sun or in a drying cabinet. Their astringent properties and powerful and swift haemostatic action have for thousands of years made them the remedy for acute or chronic inflammation of the gastro-intestinal mucosa.

Internally, the decoction (40 to 50 grammes of dried plant or 150 grammes of fresh plant to 1 litre of water; boil for five minutes and leave to infuse for ten minutes; 3 to 5 cupfuls per day, between meals or a quarter of an hour before) is prescribed in cases of diarrhoea (with or without haemorrhage), bacillary dysentery, spitting of blood, internal haemorrhage, excessive menstrual loss, frequent nosebleeds (epistaxis), stomach pains.

Externally, a more concentrated decoction (100 grammes to 1 litre of water) is employed on compresses in the treatment of skin complaints (eczema, impetigo, itching); as a lukewarm douche for vaginitis, vulvo-pruritus, leucorrhoea. It also acts on varicose ulcers, but for this condition it is preferable to prepare the decoction with red wine.

R

RADISH
Raphanus sativus.   Garden radish, Cultivated radish
Raphanus niger.   Black radish
Raphanus rusticanus or Cochlearia armorica.
(Horseradish) Spoonwort[1]

Whether cultivated or wild, pink or black, the radish has the same properties but in varying degrees, which is why each species has been allocated its own particular role, both gastronomic and medicinal.

The pink radish – which we munch at the start of a meal to whet the appetite, although not all of us find it easily digestible! – is advocated first thing in the morning as a treatment for jaundice and urticaria, and during the day for whooping cough.

The black radish – which is also included among the *hors d'oeuvre*, either cut in rings or grated – has a stronger taste and a more pronounced action on the bronchi, the liver and the blood. It is therefore utilized other than at table, in the treatment of various complaints.

As an expectorant and respiratory stimulant, for coughs, whooping cough, bronchial catarrh, engorgement of the respiratory tract: cut the radish thinly into rings, sprinkle with sugar and leave to macerate for twenty-four hours; press and strain through a cloth; one tablespoonful every hour or at the onset of a fit of coughing (the radish can also be crushed with an equal quantity of sugar and, when the sugar has been completely dissolved by the juice, pressed and strained).

As a hepatic stimulant and true specific for complaints of the

   1. The name is derived from the Latin *cochlear*: a spoon, from the leaf-shape. (*Translator's note.*)

gall-bladder, liver disorders, hepatic insufficiency, cholecystitis, hepatic colic: 20 to 40 grammes of freshly extracted juice first thing in the morning. (black radish extract is sold by chemists under the name of *raphanus*; it has the advantage of being stabilized and better tolerated than the fresh juice; I myself am indebted to it for the fact that I have had no further trouble with my liver ever since my one and only attack of hepatic colic a dozen years ago, and many correspondents have thanked me for introducing them to it).

As a diuretic and nerve sedative, for rheumatism, gout, gravel, sciatic pains, skin diseases: macerate 30 to 40 grammes of black radish, cut into small cubes, in a litre of white wine or beer for ten to fifteen days; press and strain: 2 wineglassfuls a day before meals.

Horseradish, cultivated or wild, has such a pungent taste that it is classed as a condiment (much appreciated in Alsace, Germany and Switzerland where it is used instead of mustard). It is the most powerful of the antiscorbutics and is utilized, like the radish, in the treatment of engorgement of the respiratory tract, wet asthma, rheumatism, gout: either in a mild infusion (20 to 30 grammes of fresh root to a litre of water; bring gently to the boil; do not let it boil; leave to infuse for twenty minutes; 2 or 3 cupfuls per day), or a maceration (20 to 30 grammes of fresh root to a litre of wine or beer; macerate for ten to fifteen days; 2 or 3 wineglassfuls per day).

RAPE

Brassica napus. Rape cabbage, French turnip

Our grandmothers, who had doubtless never even heard of the famous doctor of the Salernitan school, nevertheless shared their opinion of the rape, which they used to say has a good taste, is diuretic, a friend of both stomach and chest. They never failed to include it in their home-made soups, and thanks to the following simple, tried and tested prescriptions, they turned to good advantage its emollient, pectoral and demulcent qualities.

To soothe chest irritations (colds, persistent coughs, asthma, bronchitis, whooping cough): either drink as much as you wish of a decoction made by boiling 100 grammes of rape cut into rings in a litre of water or milk for ten to fifteen minutes, sweetening it with honey; or take 4 or 5 coffeespoonfuls daily of the syrup obtained either by making a hollow in the raw rape and filling it with castor sugar, or by crushing raw rape with sugar and squeezing out the juice through a fine cloth after a few hours. This syrup may be taken mixed with an infusion of pectoral flowers if wished.

To soothe itching and inflamed chilblains; to calm the pain in attacks of gout; to bring abscesses, boils and whitlows to a head and relieve inflammation: apply a poultice of cooked and pulped rape (preferably baked in the oven or in hot ashes, for in this way the juice remains concentrated). Applied behind the ear over the carotid artery, this poultice will relieve acute toothache.

It goes without saying that, to achieve the expected results, the rape should be – as it was in our grandmother's day – cultivated without use of chemical fertilizers and without the benefit of insecticides.

RASPBERRY
Rubus idoeus.   Wild raspberry, Mount Ida bramble

In the days when our ancestors hunted bears and drove out the plague, the raspberry was valuable to them for both purposes: as bait for the former ('bears are particularly fond of them' declares one learned treatise, 'and so they are easy to find when this fruit is ripe'); and as a protection against the latter, in the form of raspberry vinegar.

Its present uses are less spectacular: fresh or preserved, it makes a delicious dessert and also one of the best drinks, cooling and tonic, for feverish patients – raspberry syrup (one table-spoonful in a glass of water).

Here are two recipes for making this syrup: the first is an old officinal recipe, formerly used by apothecaries (put together 500 grammes of very ripe raspberries, 500 grammes of wine vinegar and 500 grammes of sugar; bring gently to the boil, stirring continuously; press and strain through a fine cloth and store in a tightly corked bottle); the second is a classic family recipe (crush the fruit and leave to ferment for five days; press and strain through a fine cloth; weigh the juice thus obtained and add sugar in the following proportion: 700 grammes to 500 grammes of juice; heat gently until the sugar has melted; do not cook; store in a tightly-closed jar).

The leaves of the raspberry have more or less the same properties as strawberry leaves, and are therefore prescribed in the same way; but they are also sudorific, and therefore recommended especially for chills and influenza (40 to 50 grammes in infusion to a litre of water; drink as desired, sweetened with honey).

The decoction of leaves (50 grammes to a litre of water; boil for two or three minutes, then infuse for five minutes) is employed as a gargle for throat complaints and on compresses for scabbing, cutaneous eruptions and inflammation of the eyes.

Lastly, Jos. Triponez recommends persons of nervous disposition or suffering from insomnia to drink, instead of tea, a home-made herbal tea 'which has a delicious aroma and is at once sedative, soporific and digestive, and suitable for all ages', made as follows: mix together equal parts of raspberry, strawberry, bramble, balm and sweet woodruff leaves, and lime blossoms; prepared by infusion, one pinch per cup.

REST-HARROW

Ononis spinosa. Spiny rest-harrow, Cammock, Wrest-harrow

This quotation from Matthiolus explains the origin of its names. 'It is called Aresta bovis and Remorum aratri because the roots are both so tough that the Plough Share cannot easily cut them, and so deeply and strongly fastened in the ground, that the Coulter happening under it causeth the Oxen to bee at a stand for the first twitch, not being able without more than ordinary strength to pull them forth . . . also called Acutella, because the thorns doe pricke those that unwarily goe by it' (Parkinson).

The rest-harrow is indeed not a very friendly plant. A dwarf shrub (20 to 60 centimetres) growing by roadsides and in barren pastures and ill-cultivated fields and waste places, it is pretty to look at, with its pink flowers (very occasionally white) streaked with red veins, like the flowers of the pea; but its branches possess sharp spines, and anyone who tries to pick it or pull up its tap-root, which may be up to 50 centimetres long, soon finds that this is no easy task.

Yet its root – which can be collected at any time of the year and dried in the sun or shade – is one of the best-known diuretics. Galen set it above all others, and today it is one of the principal weapons (secret weapons, of course) of healers, who often combine it with silver birch, horsetail and meadowsweet.

Old treatises advocate it as being 'good for breaking the stone and causing it to come away', and it is known for certain that it increases the volume of urine, lessens inflammatory conditions, hence its use in the treatment of cystitis, nephritis with renal calculus, engorgement of the prostate, dropsy, chronic albuminuria, gravel, arthritic and rheumatic conditions, oedema, skin disorders resulting from poor elimination of organic waste matter.

It is taken in decoction: 20 to 30 grammes of dried root to a litre of water; simmer gently until reduced by a quarter; add 5 grammes of fennel seeds or mint to give it fragrance (optional); to be drunk, a small cupful at a time, previously heated and sweetened with sugar, at regular intervals during the day.

The dried flowers and leaves in decoction (30 grammes to a litre; boil for ten minutes; add a tablespoonful of honey) make an excellent gargle for angina and sore throats.

RHUBARB
Rheum officinalis, Rheum palmatum

It was introduced into medicine for its root, imported from China where rhubarb grows wild (hence its name *rhababarum*: barbarous root) and where it was held in such high repute that one author actually devoted an entire treatise to it.

It adapted successfully to the European climate and, since it is easily multiplied by splitting the root, any garden worthy of the name has long contained a few heads of rhubarb that furnish the raw material (the reddish-green petioles – or sticks – of the huge leaves – which themselves are toxic) for stewed *compote*, jams and tarts – delicious! – particularly recommended for persons suffering from lack of appetite, liver problems or sluggishness of the bowels. However, rhubarb should not be eaten in too great a quantity, for it exerts, through its acids, a decalcifying action on the body (you need only consider that a well-known household 'hint' for removing lime scale from saucepans consists of boiling a few pieces of rhubarb in water!).

The root does not share this disadvantage, but it does have the same properties however – it is tonic, it promotes evacuation of bile, and it is a mild purgative that does not cause colic. You can gather it in autumn, from heads that are four or five years old (by when it can have reached a length of 60 centimetres and be thicker than a man's arm), and dry it, after first cutting it into pieces the size of your fist (it is a fine yellow in colour, not unlike the colour of bile), first on a screen or riddle, turning it over several times a day, then threaded on to a string and hung in a well-ventilated place in the shade (drying takes from six weeks to two months and causes it to lose easily two thirds of its weight).

It is employed either crushed in infusion (5 to 10 grammes to a litre of boiling water; leave to infuse for fifteen to twenty minutes; one glassful before meals); or powdered (1 to 3 grammes in a glass of tepid water or 1 to 3 grammes mixed with honey or jam; to be taken at one or two mealtimes, according to the effect desired and to individual reaction).

It is also made into a wine (macerate 60 to 80 grammes of crushed rhubarb root, 10 to 15 grammes of gentian root, 8 to 10 grammes of angelica root in a litre of good red or white wine for forty-eight hours; press and strain through a cloth) which is taken daily in the amount of 15 to 30 grammes as a tonic and 60 to 120 grammes as a purgative.

In tincture, together with gentian (macerate 50 grammes of rhubarb root and 150 grammes of gentian root in a quarter of a litre of alcohol (45°) for eight days; strain), it cures stomach cramps: 15 to 30 drops in a little water, three times a day.

Rhubarb is a homoeopathic remedy. *Rheum palmatum*, for infantile diarrhoea.

RICE
Oryza sativa

'With regard to its usages in Medicine', we read in a work, which appeared in the time of Louis XI, on indigenous and foreign medicines (rice was then included among the latter), 'it is a highly useful nourishment for persons exhausted by haemorrhages, for women who have suffered excessive menstrual loss, for persons suffering from lung disease and consumptives. We have few foods better able to sweeten and temper acridness of the blood . . .'

Today it forms the basis for most dietetically recommended diets and it is interesting to note that it holds the attention of modern medicine precisely because of its action on the blood, since it is prescribed for hypertension and azotemia or retention in the blood of nitrogenous substances which include urea.

However, we tend to overlook the usefulness of rice-water which has long been and still is the classic country remedy for diarrhoea (effective not because it 'binds' as is often thought, but because it soothes intestinal irritation).

Rice-water is made by boiling 20 to 30 grammes of rice in a litre of water for at least half an hour; it is then strained through a cloth, and can be sweetened with honey if wished. Can be drunk freely, a small cupful at a time.

There is an alternative and subtler method – but which does not give better results for all that – which consists of roasting the rice like coffee, grinding and preparing it like coffee.

Rice, ground to a powder, or ground rice added to water or milk, makes emollient poultices that are recommended for skin diseases and cutaneous inflammation.

ROSE, RED
Rosa gallica.   Rose flowers, Provence rose

Out of more than 10,000 varieties in existence at the present time, the one which is medicinally valued is the red damask rose, known as the French rose or Provence rose since it was brought back from the crusades by Thibaut de Champagne.

The long history of the 'queen of flowers' is closely tied in with the history of humanity itself, and it would take a whole book to relate it. It is believed to be the first flower ever cultivated by man; it is associated with most religions, from ancient Indian sacred rites to Christianity, including the Greeks, the Romans and the Gauls who, to demonstrate their scorn of death, would often go into battle with only a crown of roses for a helmet.

It has similarly been associated with politics – witness the Wars of the Roses which tore England apart in the fifteenth century – and with gastronomy (at the time of the decline of Rome, the people ate rose cakes, rose jam, dishes seasoned with extract of roses pounded with a pestle, and drank wine in which sachets of roses had been steeped) and the art of cosmetics (the 'beauties' of antiquity would dust themselves with rose powder after their bath, applied rose oil to lend a sheen to their eyelids, and – even in those days – chewed pastilles made from myrrh and rose petals crushed in honey to sweeten their breath).

The first to make medicinal use of the rose were the Arab doctors, who employed it as the specific for tuberculosis and pulmonary complaints. Avicenna reports the case of a consumptive, for whom funeral arrangements had already been made, who recovered his health by taking conserve of roses. Matthiolus says that rose-buds 'aid those who spit blood' and several treatises record the case of the spectacular cure of the wife of a viceroy of Portugal, who was not only saved in seven months by taking massive amounts of conserve of roses, but also acquired a new beauty from the fact that 'one saw reflected in her face the brilliant glow of roses'.

This medicament thus featured in the Codex (it was made with red rose petals, dried and reduced to a powder), but Doctor Leclerc was of the opinion that 'that preparation was a dirty brownish oil, both nauseous and bitter to the taste' and proposed in its place this ancient receipt using fresh roses: pound in a mortar the petals of roses (red roses, of course) still in bud, having first removed their unguis (the claw or narrow lower part of the petal by which it is attached to the receptacle), with three times their weight in sugar and a sufficient quantity of infusion of roses to make a paste of the consistency of honey; to be taken in the amount of 50 to 100 grammes per day. (The efficacy of this remedy is less surprising now that modern research has shown it to contain antibiotic principles.)

The decoction of leaves (30 to 40 grammes to a litre of water; boil for two or three minutes; leave to infuse for ten minutes; 2 or 3 cupfuls per day) is advocated for diarrhoea and dysentery.

Rose honey (boil 20 grammes of rose petals – taken from buds and with the unguis removed as above – in 100 grammes of honey for ten minutes; press and strain through a fine cloth) is a sovereign remedy – taken a coffeespoonful at a time – for sore throats and inflammation of the buccal mucous membranes.

The infusion of dried petals (40 to 50 grammes to a litre of boiling water; leave to infuse for ten to fifteen minutes) is employed as a lotion and on compresses for ophthalmia and conjunctivitis.

Lastly, a very good toilet-vinegar can be made in the following way: fill a jar with petals, picked in the morning before the sun has dissipated the essential substances that have become concentrated during the night, and from which the unguis has been removed; cover with a good white vinegar; leave to macerate in the sun for twenty days; strain.

ROSE, DOG-   See DOG-ROSE

ROSEMARY
Rosmarinus officinalis.   Romero

We shall never know whether it is to a botany-loving hermit

or an angel sent from heaven that we owe the recipe for the famous 'water of the Queen of Hungary' that so many women have longed to possess in their secret beauty arsenal; but what we do know for a certainty is that its principal ingredient is rosemary.

Since the end of the fourteenth century, when this recipe was communicated – somewhat mysteriously as you will be able to judge for yourself – to the queen, the mention of rosemary in every treatise is invariably accompanied by so many variations of the recipe that one is confounded. The oldest version is doubtless the nearest to the truth: I have copied it from a venerable text, modifying the spelling to make it easier to read:

In the city of Buda, in the Kingdom of Hungary, was found the present recipe in the Hours of Her most Serene Highness Princess Donna Izabella, Queen of Hungary.

I, Donna Izabella, Queen of Hungary, aged seventy-two, infirm of limb and afflicted with gout, have for one whole year used the present Receipt, which was given to me by a Hermit I had never seen before, and have not seen since, which had so great an effect upon me that I recovered my health and regained my strength, and on beholding my beauty, the King of Poland desired to marry me; which I refused for the love of our Lord Jesus Christ, believing that the Receipt had been given to me by an Angel: 'Take 30 ounces [about 950 grammes] of spirit of wine distilled four times [rectified alcohol], 20 ounces [about 600 grammes] of rosemary flowers; put all together in a tight-corked vessel for the space of fifty hours, then distil in a bain-marie. Take one dram [about 4 grammes] in the morning once a week with some other liquer or drink, or else with meat [food], and wash the face with it every morning, and rub the infirm limbs with it.'

Should you be tempted to try this astonishing elixir but lack the possibility of carrying out the final distillation, I should mention that most of the variations advanced over the centuries avoid this operation, recommending instead that the flowers or flowering tips of rosemary be macerated (still in alcohol) in a glass jar, well-stoppered, exposed to the sun for at least a month and shaken frequently, and then pressed and strained through a fine cloth. Another formula – claiming, of course, to be the authentic 'water of the Queen of Hungary' – might appeal to you equally: it consists of following the above procedure, but of using, to 2 litres of alcohol, 2 good handfuls of flowering tips of rosemary, a handful of flowering thyme, half a handful of marjoram leaves and half a handful of sage leaves.

However, rosemary was known long before Donna Izabella 'put it on the map'. The Romans considered it a sacred herb which brought happiness to the living and ensured peace to the dead in the great beyond. Hence they plaited it into crowns which they wore on certain festive occasions (weddings, in particular) and lay on tombs; they also burned it as incense during religious ceremonies. Later the Christians associated it with the Virgin Mary who was said to have rested beneath a rosemary bush during the flight into Egypt or else to have hung the swaddling clothes of the Infant Jesus on its branches, 'and it is from that time', the legend declares, 'that its flowers are the colour of the sky and appear on the day of the Passion'; this also explains the belief that families who scent their homes with its fragrance receive special protection.

All this did not prevent rosemary from being widely used in cooking and in medicine. People knew – better than they do today – that it is 'good for seasoning meats and making sauces'; it was incorporated into numerous balms used for curing wounds and pains; it was the remedy for jaundice, debility, vertigo, loss of memory; its flowers 'preserved in sugar' were believed to be 'excellent against the plague' and to sharpen the eyesight if eaten with salt only first thing in the morning before breakfast with 'their nearest leaves'.

It is now known that rosemary promotes the healing of wounds, is antirheumatic and antineuralgic, antiseptic, a general stimulant and cardiotonic, that it acts upon the bile clarifying it and increasing its flow (confirmed by intubation).

Internally, it is therefore recommended for influenzal and pulmonary complaints, physical or mental overstrain, anaemia, prostration following severe illness, dyspepsia, fermentation of the intestinal content (distention, flatulence), hepatic insufficiency, jaundice, cholecystitis, cirrhosis, gall-stones, rheumatism, gout, renal insufficiency, retention of urine, dropsy, oedema, obesity, painful menstruation, cardiac complaints of nervous origin (palpitations), vertigo, fainting, migraines; in infusion of flowering tips, fresh or dried: 30 to 50 grammes to 1 litre of boiling water; leave to infuse, covered, for ten minutes: one cupful after meals, except the condition affects the liver: in this case, one cupful in the morning before breakfast and before meals.

It is also used to make an excellent wine which is fortifying, digestive, antispasmodic and highly diuretic (especially when prepared with white wine): 200 grammes of fresh leaves or 60 grammes of dried leaves to a litre of wine; leave to macerate for fifteen days, shaking occasionally; strain; sweeten if desired, according to taste; one sherryglassful after or between meals.

The water of the Queen of Hungary – in other words spirit of rosemary – is most particularly advocated for indispositions of digestive or nervous origin: 10 to 20 drops on a lump of sugar.

Externally, it is used on compresses or massaged into the affected area in the treatment of rheumatic pains and contusions, used as a lotion once a day it acts as a skin tonic, gets rid of puffiness beneath the eyes, and has a fortifying action when rubbed into the scalp, so preventing falling hair.

Lastly, the decoction of flowers or flowering tips (50 grammes to half a litre of water or white wine; boil for two minutes and leave to infuse for fifteen minutes), applied as a lotion twice daily to the face, is reputed to combat wrinkles and remove freckles. (Annie Cordy confided to a magazine that she takes care of her complexion by spraying her face with rosemary water.)

S

SAGE
Salvia officinalis.   Red sage, Garden sage

Sage is unrivalled as the queen of medicinal plants, as the rose is the unrivalled queen of ornamental flowers. Its very name is a kind of diploma of efficacity, since *salvia* derives from the Latin *salvare*, meaning 'to save', 'to cure'.

For the Romans it was the 'sacred herb', to be gathered with a special ceremonial, without using iron tools (we now know that iron salts are a substance incompatible with sage!), 'wearing a white tunic, the feet bare and well washed', having previously offered sacrifices of bread and wine. They believed that it not only protected life but helped to give life, and therefore advocated it for pregnant women or those who wished to conceive: the latter were to refrain from sharing the conjugal bed for four days, drink a goodly quantity of sage juice, and then 'live carnally with their man', whereupon they would unfailingly conceive (a belief that is supported by the case of a town in Egypt where the women were obliged 'by those who had survived a great outbreak of plague' to swallow the same potion, and 'in this way the town was forthwith repopulated with children').

Throughout the Middle Ages it was an obligatory ingredient in medicinal preparations, and later treatises continued to give it pride of place. We read such praises as: 'The desire of sage is to render man immortal', 'it has so many virtues that it is considered by many as a universal healer of all ills'; some writers give this last-ditch remedy: 'When a baby is given up for lost by the doctor, and nobody understands the illness which is going to take its life, prepare a decoction of sage and administer a small spoonful every five minutes; you will witness the resurrection of the infant.' Lastly, closer to our own time, the Abbé Kneipp makes this recommendation: 'No man who owns a garden should forget to plant in it a head of sage . . .'

Sage, in fact, does not grow wild in our regions as it does in the southern areas of Europe where it originated, but it acclimatizes very well (I have a dozen heads in my rock garden

and bordering my garden paths, which readily withstand the rigours of the climate in Auvergne) and their ornamental value is the more appreciated as they retain their foliage throughout the winter.

The height of this hardy perennial sub-shrub – which must not of course be compared with the salvia with red flowers that is sown annually and ornaments so many flower borders in summer – varies from 30 to 60 centimetres; the lower part is woody whereas the upper part is formed of quadrangular hairy woolly stems; the leaves are opposite, ovate, long, greenish-grey and velvety; the flowers – much visited by bees – are mauvey-blue, small, grouped in clusters at the extremity of the stems; they appear in June to July, the period when the leaves are gathered and dried in the shade at a temperature not exceeding 35°C if you do not want them to lose their aromatic scent – which would be a pity, for it is particularly pleasant – and above all their properties, which would be worse, for they are as numerous as they are useful.

In the first place, sage is digestive: taken as an infusion in place of coffee (2 or 3 fresh or dried leaves to a cup of boiling water; leave, covered, to infuse for five minutes), it stimulates sluggish stomach activity and aids the digestion of large heavy meals. One can also – this is a hint I was given, along with the first head of sage for my garden, by a chemist friend of mine – chew a leaf or two before eating those foods which one enjoys but which do not always agree with one (sardines in oil, for example), whereupon the feast will cause no unpleasant after-effects.

This remarkable action explains why, in southern countries, it is customary to cover joints of pork and veal with sage leaves while roasting (this gives them a delicious taste and makes them easier to digest); it also explains the place held by sage as a seasoning: it prevents putrefaction by combating the dreaded toxin cadaverine. However, as Robert Landry so nicely expresses it, 'in the grand opera of cooking, sage represents an easily-offended and capricious *prima donna*. It likes to have the stage almost to itself ...' So, *cordons-bleus*, do not make the mistake of combining it with other aromatic herbs such as parsley or chervil which would spoil the purity of its culinary note!

It is also apéritif and tonic; it stimulates the vago-motor nervous system, activates the circulation, sustains the heart, and is therefore particularly recommended to convalescents, persons suffering from overstrain or depression, women subject to irregular menstruation or undergoing the menopause, either in infusion (2 or 3 cupfuls per day in the same amounts as above), or as a 'sage wine', more practical and pleasing to the palate: macerate 80 to 100 grammes of sage leaves (preferably fresh) in 1 litre of good white wine for eight to ten days;

sweeten with honey to taste; press and strain through a fine cloth; one sherryglassful before lunch and dinner. This wine is also recommended for chronic bronchitis, night-sweats and vertigo.

The decoction of sage (15 grammes of leaves to 1 litre of water; boil for five minutes at least and leave to infuse for the same length of time) is an exceptionally effective remedy used as a repeated gargle (hot) for sore throats and angina; used as a mouthwash it will cure all kinds of mouth ulcers and inflammation (aphtha, sore gums, dental abscesses), so much so that the ancients used to say: 'Sage will restore speech to those who have lost it.' A stronger decoction (100 grammes to 1 litre of water) applied on compresses will cure eczema, scabbing, spots, and cicatrize badly-healing sores; mixed with rum, in equal proportions, and used as a daily friction, it arrests falling hair and combats dandruff.

You can also make use of sage unguent (pound 5 good handfuls of fresh leaves in a mortar; mix together with 500 grammes of unsalted lard or fresh butter and boil over a low heat until the moisture from the plant has evaporated; press and strain while still hot through a fine cloth; store in a tightly-sealed earthenware or glass pot); applied morning and evening, massaging well into the skin, it fortifies the nerves, restores suppleness to the joints, and is recommended for rheumatism, gout, sciatica and muscular pains.

Lastly, let me add that: (1) sage leaves dried and smoked like tobacco, bring relief to asthma sufferers; (2) a pinch of sage leaves infused (for five minutes) in a cup of boiling milk will prevent an incipient cold from developing; (3) an infusion of sage (cold) is prescribed for infantile diarrhoea; (4) sage leaves burnt on hot embers or boiled in an open saucepan (as for eucalyptus) disinfect rooms which have harboured serious illness; (5) mulled wine with sage can be used to advantage as a substitute for mulled wine with cinnamon.

Considering that it has so many virtues in addition to its subtle aroma, one can understand why the Chinese have long been astonished that Europeans should want the tea from their country when they possess sage in their own, and in the days of commercial barter they went so far as to give two chests of their tea in exchange for one of ours.

SANICLE
Sanicula europaea.   Wood sanicle, Pool root, Butterwort

It was once held to be a panacea, as its name bears witness, being derived from the Latin *sanus*: healthy; then it fell into neglect, because, finding that it did not have the virtues that had been attributed to it, people also overlooked the benefits of those it does in fact possess.

Let me first of all describe it to you: it is a small umbelliferous plant very common in woods, hedges, moist and shady places; its leaves, glossy green above, rather paler on the under surface, have long petioles (leaf-stalks); they are divided deeply into three or five lobes, irregularly serrate at their extremity; its small flowers, white or slightly reddish in colour, are arranged in umbels at the summit of a slender stalk rarely more than 40 to 50 centimetres in height.

The parts used are the flowering tips and especially the leaves, picked when the plant comes into flower (May July) and dried in the shade; rich in tannin, resin and essential oil, their action is tonic, antiseptic, anti-inflammatory, stomachic, astringent and haemostatic.

In the country, the fresh leaves are used by both animals and man; by cows, who have just calved, to promote expulsion of the afterbirth or placenta; by the farming community as a remedy for haemorrhages, the spitting of blood, and other blood troubles, chronic dysentery and diarrhoea. After crushing a handful of sanicle in the hand, it is left to infuse overnight in a glass of cold white wine; in the morning the mixture is strained through a cloth, squeezing to extract as much as possible, and drunk before breakfast.

But most of the time it is the decoction of dried plant which is used: internally (40 to 50 grammes to 1 litre of water; cold-soak for a few minutes, bring gently to the boil; continue to boil for two minutes and infuse for ten to fifteen minutes; 3 or 4 cupfuls per day, between meals) it is recommended for diarrhoea, dysentery, stomach ulcers, passive haemorrhages, leucorrhoea, haemorrhoids, varicose veins and other circulatory complaints; externally (100 grammes to a litre of water) as a lotion and on compresses, it is used in the treatment of sores, contusions, ecchymosis, varicose ulcers, scabbing; also, as a gargle and mouthwash, for ulcerous conditions of the mucous membranes, aphtha, inflammation of the gums and throat.

SAVORY

Satureia hortensis. Garden or summer savory
Satureia montana. Mountain or winter savory

Whether you sow it each year in your kitchen garden or take advantage of your holidays to gather it on the moors in Provence where it grows as a wild perennial, this little aromatic herb, which in scent and appearance is similar to thyme, should have a place in your home.

Added to salads, sauces, marinades, vegetables (especially haricot beans, as indicated by its German name *Bohnenkraut*: bean-herb), it lends them a delicious aroma and above all renders them easily digestible. By regarding it simply as an aromatic herb, we seem to have overlooked the fact that it possesses remarkable therapeutic properties which act particularly on the stomach and the bowels, and for which it was formerly deservedly renowned as a medicinal plant.

That it was held in high repute is evidenced by the fact that most treatises make no reference to the aphrodisiac virtues originally attributed to it (and clearly indicated by its name, which derives from the Latin *satyrus*), but praise only its exceptionally beneficial action on the digestive apparatus, which earned it the name of 'poor folks' sauce'. This action is due to the fact that it stimulates the stomach, calms spasms and regularizes intestinal contractions, inhibits fermentation of intestinal contents (it is antiseptic) and favours the expulsion of gases.

It is therefore recommended in infusion (50 grammes to 1 litre of boiling water; leave to infuse for five to ten minutes; 3 cupfuls per day, after meals) for poor digestion, stomach pains, chronic diarrhoea, distension and flatulence (it has also been employed as a vermifuge: one cupful, highly concentrated, taken in the morning on an empty stomach).

SHEPHERD'S PURSE

Thlaspi bursa pastoris. Shepherd's sprout, Mother's heart (Poor man's) Permacety, Toywort, Pickpurse, Pickpocket, Casewort, St James's wort

Things are still the same as when a writer in the time of Louis XV commented: 'Old walls and tumbledown cottages are covered with this plant, which multiplies marvellously.' This cruciferous plant is to be found everywhere, and if you have never noticed it, it is because it possesses hardly any remarkable features, although it flowers from spring through into autumn.

Its stems rarely grow to a height of more than 50 centimetres; its hairy, greyish-green leaves are varied in shape: long and deeply cut at the basal rosette, becoming smaller and entire on the upper part of the stems; its tiny flowers, with four dirty-white petals, are borne in terminal clusters, those at the summit being still in flower while the lower ones are already succeeded by almost fully-ripened seeds; its seed-vessels (capsules), each on a stalk about 2 centimetres long, give the plant its name, their flat triangular shape resembling in form the pouch formerly worn by shepherds on their belts.

It should preferably be used fresh, for drying causes it to lose a part of its properties; but if picked and dried at the moment it comes into flower, it will nevertheless give excellent results. It acts on circulatory disturbances, inflammation of the mucosae, temperature.

For excessive menstrual discharge, metrorrhagia, haemorrhages, spitting of blood, haemoptysis in general: one handful of fresh plant to a litre of water in decoction, reducing by a third; one cupful every two hours (in most cases the haemorrhage is arrested after the first cupful).

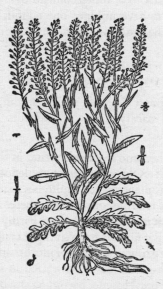

To regularize menstruation and reduce menstrual pain (at puberty and menopause): macerate 180 grammes of fresh plant cut in small pieces in a litre of wine (red or white) for eight days; press and strain; one tablespoonful every hour. Alternatively: cold-soak 50 grammes of dried plant (or 25 grammes of shepherd's purse and 25 grammes of mugwort) in a litre of water for two hours; then boil for one minute and leave to stand for a quarter of an hour; 3 or 4 cupfuls a day during the ten days preceding the expected date of menstruation. (*Thlaspi bursa pectoris* is the homoeopathic prescription for women who suffer from excessive menstrual discharge and is also considered to promote uterine drainage).

To arrest nasal haemorrhage; insert into the nostril a wad of cotton wool soaked in the decoction or the fresh juice of the plant.

For external wounds and contusions: wash the affected part with the decoction; the wound will start to heal within twelve or fourteen hours after treatment.

For disturbances of circulation (varicose veins, haemorrhoids, arteriosclerosis, hypertension) and inflammation of the mucosae (respiratory, digestive and urinary): a three-week course of treatment, either of 2 cupfuls per day of decoction, or of 2 or 3 tablespoonfuls per day of wine; repeat if necessary after suspending treatment for two weeks.

For intermittent fevers: at the first signs of shivering, keep the patient warm in bed and apply to his wrists poultices of fresh plant pounded together with plantain leaves, a spoonful of vinegar and a large pinch of salt; leave in place for twenty-four hours and renew if the fever returns.

Shepherd's purse is also an excellent tonic and spring depurative (decoction of 30 to 50 grammes of fresh plant to a litre of water, to be drunk a cupful at a time over two days); lastly, if mixed with spinach (which some people find indigestible), it will make it easier to digest.

SLOE
Prunus spinosa. Blackthorn

This spiny shrub – of which hedges mostly consisted before they were largely swept away by industrial agriculture – might well be called 'the regulator of the stomach' since, by a happy scheme of nature, its flowers loosen the bowels and its fruits bind them.

The Abbé Kneipp sang the praises of the former: 'The flowers of the blackthorn', he wrote, 'make the most harmless laxative and should be to the forefront of every family medicine chest. Think how many times you know you would feel the benefit from or even need a purge! The state of your stomach or your bowels or your general state of health tells you so. These are the times one has to hunt around for a mild medicament – and yet one could so easily have it to hand! So collect these blackthorn flowers, boil them for a minute, and drink a cupful of the infusion each day for three days. It acts very gently, without in any way upsetting your system; and yet it will purge you thoroughly. I recommend it also as a stomachic, depurative, and to fortify the stomach.'

This infusion is made in the amounts of 2 or 3 grammes of dried flowers to a cupful (100 cubic centimetres) of water and should be taken first thing in the morning on an empty stomach. It is also prescribed as a diuretic and depurative in the treatment of complaints of the urinary tract (cystitis, gravel), dropsy, rheumatism, gout, obesity, diabetes.

The small bluish-black fruits or sloes, from which a delicate liqueur and spirit are made, but which are so acid to the taste before the frost has tempered their sharpness, are highly astringent. Picked before fully ripe and dried, they are employed in decoction (50 grammes to a litre of water or red wine; boil for five minutes; leave to infuse for ten to fifteen minutes; to be drunk in one day, a cupful at a time) as a remedy for diarrhoea and dysentery.

SOAPWORT
Saponaria officinalis. Soaproot, Bouncing Betty/Beth/Bet, Fuller's herb

As its names so clearly indicate, it is a plant which cleanses. It cleanses everything: linen with which it is boiled in place of soap, woollen materials before dyeing, fabrics with delicate colours, and the human body when there is distension with an accumulation of toxins which seek a way out through the skin. (*Saponaria* is the homoeopathic remedy prescribed for its detersive action in the treatment of all skin complaints, and Arab doctors similarly prescribed it for scabbing, ulcers and leprosy.)

It is one of the most commonly used medicinal plants; its stems, from 30 to 70 centimetres in height, are hard and cylindrical; they bear opposite leaves, delicate green in colour, printed

with pronounced longitudinal ribs; its delicate pink flowers are grouped in small terminal clusters; they have five petals and a subtle fragrance.

Stems and leaves may be employed, but the root is generally preferred (it is a yellowish-white creeping rhizome, much branched, of the thickness of a finger), collected in spring or autumn, dried in the sun and cut in small pieces.

It is prepared by decoction (40 to 50 grammes to 1 litre of water; boil for five minutes and strain immediately; it must not be allowed to macerate because of possible side-effects – tremor, partial paralysis of the tongue, dryness of the mouth; 2 or 3 cupfuls per day, half an hour before meals, and recommended for skin diseases (scabbing, acne, pimples, urticaria, etc.), rheumatism, gout, gravel, liver disorders (jaundice in particular), lymphatic or bronchial fluid accumulation (bronchitis), oedema, obesity, as well as to eliminate toxins following an infectious disease.

The Swiss herbalist Jos. Triponez notes a further usage which might prove helpful: when, after eating a large meal, a person's stomach, bowels or liver are upset, when his face is red, suffused and swollen, a cupful of simple decoction of root (5 grammes to 100 cubic centimetres; boil for five minutes and drink hot, without leaving to infuse) will prove 'an effective, simple and swift remedy'.

The same decoction, used as a gargle, is prescribed for angina, particularly Vincent's angina, and as a lotion or on compresses for cutaneous eruptions.

SORREL
Rumex acetosa.   Sorrel dock

Cultivated or wild, it has the same taste and the same constituents, but also the same disadvantage: the oxalic acid it contains can lead, if it is taken too often, to gravel, in other words the formation of small stones of calcium oxalate.

So it is to be avoided if you are subject to biliary or renal colic, or if you have a tendency to rheumatism or gout, or if you suffer from gastralgia (stomach pains), asthma and pulmonary complaints (just as you should also avoid spinach, which is similarly rich in oxalates).

Otherwise sorrel can be useful both as a laxative and depurative (it was formerly prescribed as a preventive against plague). Its leaves in infusion (20 to 30 grammes to a litre of boiling water; leave to infuse for ten minutes; 3 cupfuls per day) or its root in decoction (30 to 40 grammes to a litre of water; boil for three or four minutes; leave to infuse for five minutes; 3 cupfuls per day) are prescribed for furunculosis, scabbing, eczema, acne, as well as for intermittent fevers (one glassful (100 cubic centimetres) of sorrel juice, taken at the start of an expected attack, will abort it or reduce its intensity).

Externally, cooked sorrel, reduced to a pulp and applied as a poultice, will bring boils and abscesses more rapidly to a head. The decoction, used as a lotion and on compresses, is used in the treatment of scabbing.

The housewife can use sorrel for various cleaning operations: jars that have contained oil (chopped sorrel stalks in a little water, shake vigorously, rinse and repeat until all traces of oil have disappeared); wicker and bamboo furniture and silver-ware (rub with a cloth soaked in the water in which sorrel has been cooked); ink stains on white cloth (rub with freshly-picked sorrel, soap and rinse, repeating if necessary – this procedure is preferable to the sorrel salt sold commercially, which often leaves a yellow stain).

In mountain regions, especially around Alpine chalets, is found a variety of sorrel (*Rumex alpinus*) known as Monk's rhubarb because of its large heart-shaped leaves. Its root – or rather its rhizome – is used as a purgative in place of buckthorn alder (1 or 2 grammes of powdered dried rhizome, taken in honey or a little water); its fresh crushed leaves are applied as a poultice on badly-healing sores and wounds.

SPEEDWELL
Veronica officinalis.   Veronica, Ground-well, Bird's eye, Cat's eye, Fluelin (Wales)

Looking at this charming little plant, so pure and unobtrusive with its sky-blue flowers, it is hard to credit that it has been the object of bitter quarrels that were intended to be strictly scientific or gastronomic but which smacked of nationalism.

Because it was the Germans who championed the speedwell and published several treatises devoted solely to singing its praises, the French reacted with such comments as: 'Praised by P. Hoffmann as a substitute for China tea, this plant may have pleased German palates despite its pungent taste, but in France we find it lacks that aromatic taste, that special fragrance which characterizes the foreign plant.'

Speedwell is obviously no panacea, and it is doubtful whether alone it has ever succeeded in curing pulmonary tuberculosis as several writers east of the Rhine have claimed. However, it is deserving of our attention for the valuable medicinal qualities it does possess.

It is a common wild plant, growing in hedgerows, on the edges of woodland, in clearings and meadows. Its slender, slightly hairy stems creep over the ground; only the flowering stems are erect; its leaves are opposite, ovate, slightly hairy, with serrate edges; its flowers, grouped in elongated clusters, often two on the same stem, are small, very pale purplish-blue, and a calyx with four unequal lobes in the shape of a cross.

The part used is the flowering plant (it flowers from June to August), picked and dried in the shade and employed in a mild decoction (40 to 50 grammes to a litre of cold water; steep and then heat gently; boil for only a few seconds; leave to infuse for ten to fifteen minutes; 3 cupfuls per day, between meals or half an hour before) for its diuretic and vulnerary properties, its soothing, expectorant and tonic action on the mucosae: bronchitis, fluid accumulations in the respiratory tract, whooping-cough, tracheitis, digestive atony, aerophagia, indigestion, gastro-enteritis, gravel, gout, rheumatism, liver complaints.

ST JOHN'S WORT
Hypericum perforatum

'St John's Wort was once called the "fairy herb" because of its efficacity. Nowadays we have entirely forgotten it and the services it can render.' So wrote the Abbé Kneipp in 1891, and the observation is even more true today.

Yet St John's wort has been a kind of panacea. Because it exhales when crushed an odour of incense and because incense is 'the perfume reserved for God', it was credited with protective powers against harm from evil spirits and witchcraft; in many countries it was customary to hang a branch of it over the door of the house on Saint John's day, and it was given to the possessed to drink or to inhale, which earned it the name of *Euga daemonum* or 'flight of the demons'.

It was incorporated in countless mixtures, balms and unguents used as a treatment for gout, rheumatism, burns, and above all as a dressing for the wounds which were common in those times when swords were so frequently out of their scabbards – Ambroise Paré always used it and treatises called it the 'valuable remedy for deep wounds and those which go through the body'.

With its susceptibility to fashion and the marvels of chemistry, medicine has virtually rejected so commonplace a medication (St John's wort grows wild everywhere, on grassy slopes, at waysides, in copses); but, fortunately, it has been retained by homoeopathy and popular tradition.

As a homoeopathic remedy, '*Hypericum*', Doctor André Thibault writes, 'is to the nerves what *Arnica* is to the muscles. It is therefore prescribed for contusions and nerve injuries. Strongly advocated for sciatica. Also acts on all wounds from sharp instruments.' In popular medicine it is one of the most useful plants in both internal and external use for curing the majority of the ills commonly called 'minor ailments'.

The height of the St John's wort varies from 40 to 80 centimetres; its stems are angular, woody and much-branched towards the top; its leaves, ovate, veined and in opposite pairs, seem to be perforated with a number of hole-like dots which are actually small transparent gland-pockets full of an essential oil that is also found on the flowers; its flowers are golden-yellow, small, graceful, grouped in umbels; they have five petals and numerous stamens; when pressed between the fingers, they let out a purplish-red liquid 'almost as strongly coloured as bilberry juice, and with the same characteristic odour', as one herbal describes.

It is most generally employed as a balm which, because it can be made in advance, has the advantage of being immediately to hand. There are various methods of preparation, of which these are the least complicated: either macerate 500 grammes of fresh flowers in a litre of olive oil for six or eight weeks in the

sun, shaking frequently, and then strain; or macerate 500 grammes of fresh flowers in a mixture of a litre of olive oil and half a litre of white wine for three days, then boil together in a *bain-marie* until the wine has evaporated; strain; store in a tightly-stoppered jar.

This balm, of a fine dark red colour, is prescribed for use on compresses for abrasions, badly healing wounds and sores, varicose ulcers, contusions, sprains, skin irritations, and burns which it immediately soothes. Used as a friction (previously slightly warmed) it relieves rheumatism, gout, sciatica and lumbago. It can also be used internally (6 to 8 drops on a lump of sugar) in cases of colic, stomach cramps and pains.

But generally for these latter complaints which are often chronic, the infusion is preferred (30 to 50 grammes of dried flowering tips or flowers to a litre of water; bring gently to the boil and leave to infuse for five to ten minutes; 3 cupfuls per day, before or between meals), and it is also recommended for the following: bronchial catarrh, asthma, acidity, gastritis, enteritis, cystitis, dropsy, enuresis (bedwetting), congestion of the liver, impaired gall-bladder function, irregular menstruation, metritis, ovarian inflammation.

You can, if you prefer, in place of the infusion use St John's wort wine (macerate for a minimum of two weeks 30 to 50 grammes of flowering tips, fresh or dried, in a litre of good wine; press and strain through a fine cloth; one wineglassful before the two main meals of the day). This wine is apéritif, tonic and has a beneficial effect on the female reproductive organs.

STRAWBERRY
Fragaria vesca

Here is what Matthiolus said about the strawberry four centuries ago: 'It seemed good to me to receive this joyous and profitable plant into the bourgeoisie of my garden and to speak of it as follows: the leaves and the root cause to urinate and greatly serve the spleen; the decoction of the root, taken as a drink, helpeth inflammations of the liver and cleanses the kidneys and the bladder; the juice of strawberries cureth blotches on the face.'

Time, and then science (by analysis of the chemical components of the different parts of the plant), have confirmed these medicinal qualities of the strawberry – wild or cultivated, the former seemingly the more active – which we shall now consider in detail.

Strawberries, with their high iron content, are recommended to persons suffering from anaemia. They are similarly rich in salicylic acid, which acts favourably upon the liver, the kidneys and the joints, and are therefore recommended also for persons with liver complaints, or persons suffering from autointoxication, rheumatism or gout. The famous botanist Linné called them a 'blessing of the gods' after he was cured of gout by eating almost nothing but large quantities of strawberries morning and evening; as for Fontenelle – who lived to be a hundred – he attributed his longevity to eating a great amount of strawberries (we now know that they act beneficially on the blood pressure: an intravenous injection of an extract of strawberry has been shown to bring about an immediate lowering of the blood pressure).

They are advocated (a month's course of treatment, 300 to 500 grammes daily) for chronic gastro-enteritis; they combat constipation; their seeds (or achenes) – which are not attacked by the gastric juices – exercise an irritant action on the bowel and stimulate bowel contraction.

Externally, strawberries are used as a beauty treatment to tone the skin, combat wrinkles and freckles and clear the complexion: last thing at night, smear the face with a few crushed strawberries; allow to dry; leave on the face overnight and in the morning rinse off with lukewarm water or, better still, chervil water. Strawberries also constitute an excellent preventive remedy for chilblains, which will not recur in the winter if during the summer the parts concerned have been rubbed with crushed strawberries, and poultices of pulped strawberries applied overnight.

The dried leaves can be used to make a herbal tea highly recommended by the Abbé Kneipp as a health drink for children. 'The mother', he wrote, 'takes about as many strawberries as she can pick up with three or four fingers; on to these she pours about a quarter litre of boiling water, then covers and leaves to stand. After fifteen minutes she decants the infusion thus obtaining a pure strawberry tea. Into this she stirs some hot milk and a little sugar, and in this way has made a good health drink.'

The fresh leaves in decoction (one handful to a litre of water; boil for four or five minutes) are prescribed for chronic diarrhoea, and an American doctor in the nineteenth century, Doctor Blackburn, left us a tried and tested prescription for dysentery: place 375 grammes of green wild strawberry leaves in a litre and 15 centilitres of good spirits; boil until the liquid has reduced to 55 centilitres; strain; administer the potion in the amount of one tablespoonful every three hours until the symptoms have disappeared (8 to 10 spoonfuls generally suffice to cure the condition).

Lastly, the roots in decoction (25 to 30 grammes to a litre of water; boil for at least ten minutes; may be drunk freely) are employed as a remedy for intestinal disorders (enteritis with diarrhoea, dysentery, internal haemorrhages), and are also prescribed for inflammatory conditions of the kidneys and bladder (cystitis, calculi) and the liver (jaundice), arthritis, bronchitis, dropsy, gout (it should be mentioned that they redden the stools and give a pink colour to the urine).

Externally, the decoction of leaves or roots (30 to 50 grammes to a litre of water; boil for about ten minutes) is utilized, on account of its astringent properties, as a gargle for angina, and as tepid douches for leucorrhoea.

T

TANSY
Tanacetum vulgare

It belongs to the same family – the Compositae – as worm-wood,[1] and similarly exhales a strong aromatic odour, possesses more or less the same properties and has virtually the same uses, accompanied by the same warning regarding duration of treatment and dosage to be observed to avoid undesirable effects (vertigo, cramp).

It grows by the roadsides, on the edges of woodland, in fields and slightly moist waste places. It is also cultivated as an orna-mental garden plant, and in Anglo-Saxon countries as an aromatic herb (in England tansy pudding traditionally marked the end of Lent).

Its stems, which often grow to a height of over 1 metre, bear alternate feathery leaves, broad and finely divided and toothed, of a handsome green with a slightly woolly under-surface; its golden-yellow flower-heads, about 1 centimetre in diameter, are grouped in decorative almost flat umbels. They flower from June to August, the period during which the flowering tips and the leaves are picked and dried in the shade (the seeds are also active but less commonly used).

For centuries the tansy has been known above all as a vermi-fuge – ascaris and oxyuris (the Germans call it 'Worm wort'). Treatment is over the course of several days, and consists either of drinking before breakfast and before one other meal an infusion of leaves or flowering tips (5 grammes to a cupful (100 cubic centimetres) of boiling water; leave to infuse for five minutes), or of administering an enema (15 to 30 grammes in

1. See page 317.

infusion to 1 litre of boiling salt water; leave to infuse for twenty minutes).

The fresh leaves, pounded and applied as a poultice to the tummy, are often sufficient to cause children to expel worms. Fresh or dried, they are also held to keep away fleas and bed-bugs if sprinkled between the sheet and the mattress, and to keep dogs free from fleas if mixed with the straw in the dog-kennel.

The tansy is also known for its tonic and stimulant action on the digestive organs, as well as for its antiseptic and diuretic effects. It is therefore recommended for anaemia, chlorosis,

dyspepsia, rheumatism, gout, either in infusion (5 grammes to a cup; 2 or 3 cupfuls per day before meals), or as a wine (macerate 50 to 80 grammes of plant in a litre of good wine for eight days; press and strain; one wineglassful after meals, midday and evening.

TARRAGON
Artemisia dranunculus

'This plant which is grown in kitchen-gardens is more commonly used in cooking or in salads than in medicine.' So observed the writer of a medical treatise two centuries ago, and the observation is just as true today.

Yet this first-cousin of the mugwort can render other services than the culinary functions we usually ask of it (tarragon vinegar, tarragon chicken, tartare, Hollandaise, Béarnaise and Ravigote sauces, etc.). When it was introduced into Europe by the Moorish conquerors of Spain (it was originally a native of Siberia or Tartary), many virtues were attributed to it, but it eventually retained only those which make it such a valuable seasoning: it is apéritif, digestive, stomachic and stimulant.

It is therefore recommended for poor digestion, intestinal distension, nausea, colic with wind, flatulence, aerophagia, rheumatic and neuralgic pain, in infusion (25 to 30 grammes of plant to a litre of water; leave to infuse for ten minutes; one cupful after meals or during the day). Its use, either fresh and finely chopped like parsley or chervil, or dried and powdered, sprinkled on meats and vegetables, is recommended by Professor Binet 'to dyspeptics and patients on a salt-free diet' for, its stimulant action on the digestive organs not being accompanied by irritant effects, 'it can to a certain extent replace pepper, vinegar and salt'.

You can also make an excellent digestive (one small glassful after meals) by adding 30 to 40 grammes of fresh leaves, a stick of vanilla and 300 grammes of sugar to a litre of alcohol (45 or 50°C); leave to macerate for one month (shaking occasionally); strain.

There are two versions regarding the origin of its name: according to the first, it derives from the Arabic word *tharkhoum*; according to the second, equally plausible, version, it owes its name to the form of its root, which coils back upon itself like a dragon.

TEA
Thea sinensis

There is nothing new about including tea among our medicinal plants. It was originally introduced to us as such in the seventeenth century, and just because it has now ceased to be a rare commodity, we would be wrong to overlook its virtues and fail to make use of it when need arises.

Its praises have been sung by many, as for example in this passage from a medical work published more than a century after its introduction into France:

Most modern writers highly praise the rare qualities of tea, which they regard as a universal remedy ... An infusion of tea, taken with discretion, is capable of destroying harmful yeasts of the upper tract, and dissolving any viscous material in the stomach which may contaminate and cause deterioration of the chyle ... Tea is no less good for maladies of the brain and the chest than for those of the lower abdomen; for it soothes migraine, stimulates mental activity, dispels vapours, giddiness and drowsiness; restores the memory, clears the mind and prevents apoplexy, paralysis and catarrh. It is also useful to asthmatics, and to those suffering from tuberculosis and other lung conditions, taken with milk. In a word, it maintains the fluidity of the blood on which good health depends.

Of course, we no longer make such extravagant claims; nevertheless, because of its theine, the counterpart of caffein, and its high percentage of tannin, tea can render service as a cardiac tonic and remedy for diarrhoea.

So, if you are suffering from an upset stomach and have nothing better to hand, you can try this tested popular remedy: every five minutes drink one or two mouthfuls of a strong infusion of tea – preferably Ceylon tea (leave to infuse for a quarter of an hour or even boil for a few minutes) to which you have added a coffeespoonful of rum per cup, which reinforces its effect.

THYME

Thymus vulgaris.   Common thyme, Garden thyme
Thymus serpyllum.   Wild thyme, Mother of thyme,
Brotherwort

The slight differences that do exist between these two could doubtless be debated for hours by specialists in gastronomy or chemistry (their constituents not being absolutely identical, nor are their gastronomic and therapeutic virtues); but the differences are indeed so very slight that I shall leave them to the aforementioned specialists and refer simply to thyme – in other words, you can use either garden thyme or wild thyme medicinally for the same conditions and in the same doses, just as you can use either the one or the other in the kitchen.

Legend has it that thyme was born of the tears of the beautiful Helen. It grows wild in Mediterranean countries, and has been known since ancient times: the Egyptians and the Etruscans incorporated it in the preparations used for embalming their dead; the Greeks used to burn it on the altars of their gods, and also used it in their cooking; so did the Romans; whilst their women used it as a toilet water and unguent to care for their beauty.

We know now that it is a powerful antiseptic, the 'enemy of toxin' Trousseau used to call it (recent experiments have confirmed that bacilli cannot withstand the action of thyme essence for more than thirty-five to forty minutes), that it is a stimulant of the respiratory, digestive and circulatory functions, that it exerts a tonic action on the nerve centres, that it is vermifuge, antispasmodic, diuretic, etc. – in short, that it is a kind of panacea.

It is therefore prescribed for an impressive series of complaints, in the form of an infusion (20 to 30 grammes of flowering tips – fresh or dried – to 1 litre of boiling water; leave to infuse for five to ten minutes; or else one or two sprigs per cup (100 cubic centimetres); 3 or 4 cupfuls per day, after or between meals): extremely poor digestion, flatulence, distention, lack of appetite, cardiac weakness, anaemia, physical and mental exhaustion, angor, neurasthenia, fits of coughing, bronchial complaints (asthma, bronchitis), influenza, chills, insomnia, liver or menstrual disorders, infections of the urinary tract.

For whooping cough and bouts of fitful coughing: a handful of plant (fresh or dried) to 1 litre of water; boil until reduced to half the volume and sweeten with honey; one spoonful every two hours or at the start of an attack.

For ascaris and oxyuris: on three consecutive days, drink the following infusion first thing in the morning, half an hour before breakfast: one tablespoonful of fresh or dried plant cut into tiny pieces to 150 cubic centimetres of boiling water; leave to infuse for ten minutes.

Externally, the infusion (stronger, if necessary) is prescribed as a gargle for sore throats and angina; as a lotion and on compresses for suppurating wounds and sores and ulcers, and to relieve pains in the joints.

The decoction (500 grammes of plant in a cloth sachet to 4 litres of water; boil for a few minutes and leave to infuse for ten minutes), added to the bath water, stimulates the circulation and the skin; it is recommended for sickly children, convalescents, rheumatic subjects and persons afflicted with skin diseases.

The same decoction as for whooping cough – only without sugar of course! – used as a daily friction and hair lotion, is an excellent tonic for the scalp and will prevent or arrest loss of hair.

The leaves of thyme, dried and powdered and taken like snuff, will clear the respiratory tract and arrest nasal haemorrhage.

V

VALERIAN
Valeriana officinalis.   Setwall, All-heal

The mention of valerian is invariably greeted with such phrases as 'the most perfect of herbal sedatives', 'the one plant to prescribe for nervous subjects', 'the oldest method of treating nervous disorders'.

Commonly found beside rivers and streams, in moist meadows, woods and copses, on grassy slopes in lowland and mountain areas, it is a decorative plant with fluted, slightly downy stems that grow to a height of up to 1·50 metres, its opposite, deeply divided leaves, lanceolate and toothed, its small pink – very occasionally white – flowers, grouped in dense terminal inflorescences resembling umbels (in bloom from June to August).

The only part of the plant that is used is the root, which is actually a rhizome 2 to 3 centimetres long, yellowish on the outside, whitish on the inside, with numerous rootlets measuring from 10 to 20 centimetres. It is gathered in September to October and dried in the shade; however it is known that drying deprives it of a part of its active principles, which is why it is often prepared as a tincture; it has a characteristic odour, unpleasant to us, but so appreciated by cats that it sends them into frenzied transports of delight.

Pliny cited it as the remedy for nervous spasms and several writers of the seventeenth and eighteenth centuries considered it the specific for epilepsy. Today it is advocated as a sedative for the disturbances of nervous origin frequently encountered in women: vapours, spasms, vertigo, migraines, palpitations, precordial angor, breathlessness, nervous contractions of the stomach, excessive nervousness, nervous attacks, insomnia, etc.; on account of its anti-spasmodic action, it is also prescribed for hysteria, convulsions in children, St Vitus's dance, menstrual pains, stomach and intestinal cramps.

The dried root is prepared by cold maceration (10 grammes to 100 centimetres of water; macerate for twelve hours), to be taken in this amount two or three times a day, a quarter of an hour before meals or, depending on the condition, only once a day, in the evening, an hour before retiring. (To disguise its odour, other herbs may be added for their fragrance: woodruff, vervain, balm.)

It may also be employed as a powder (1 or 2 grammes in a spoonful of soup, water or honey, two or three times a day), or as a tincture (200 grammes of fresh root chopped in pieces to a litre of alcohol (45°); macerate for eight days; press and strain through a cloth) which is taken in the amount of 20 to 30 drops, two or three times a day, in half-a-glass of slightly sweetened water or in an infusion (chamomile, vervain, balm).

VERVAIN

Verbena officinalis.   Verbena, Holy herb, Juno's tears

Vervain was for long the foremost magic herb, so much so that at the end of the sixteenth century Matthiolus wrote:

'Sorcerers lose their senses at the mention of this herb. For they say that those who are rubbed with it will obtain all they ask, and that it will cure fevers and cause a person to love another and, in short, that it cures all illnesses and more besides.'

The Romans had dedicated it to Venus (they called it *Veneris herba*: herb of Venus or *Veneris vena*: luck of Venus) for they believed it to have the property of reigniting the fires of a dying love; they offered lucky nosegays of vervain at the new year, they steeped it in the water with which banqueting rooms were sprinkled so that the guests would be the merrier. The Druids, before offering sacrifices, would wash their altars with an infusion of vervain flowers. Among the Teutons, the priestesses wore crowns of vervain.

Later it entered into the preparation of most philtres (especially love-philtres), was used to foretell the future, to cast spells or to lift them (for example, the huntsman, who thought he was missing his game because someone had cast a spell on his gun, would rub his weapon with vervain), to protect houses against wicked spirits (a branch would be hung on the door) and even today, in various regions, it is said that a child who wears a sprig of vervain on his person will be 'well-behaved, lively, good-humoured and a lover of knowledge'.

'Vervaine is an opener of obstructions, clenseth and healeth . . . all the inward paines and torments of the body . . . it is held also to be no lesse effectuall against all poyson, and the venome of dangerous beasts and serpents, as also against bewitched drinkes or the like' (Parkinson).

The vervain associated with all these marvels is, of course, the indigenous variety which has always grown in Europe, for there is another variety, generally better-known, a native of South America – probably Chile – which was only acclimatized and then cultivated here after the epoch of the great seafaring discoverers of the New World.

Whatever certain writers may say, it is the wild vervain offered freely by nature which possesses the most pronounced virtues – and it is in fact the wild variety which is 'officinal' whilst its sister from the New World is known by botanists as *Verbena triphylla* (because its leaves are grouped in threes on the stem) and *Verbena citriodora* (because it exhales a scent of lemons).

Wild vervain is to be found by roadsides and in ditches, on the edges of woodland and in sandy meadows. It rarely grows to a height of more than 40 to 60 centimetres; its main stems are quadrangular; its opposite leaves are arranged in pairs, and graceful, being deeply divided in unequal lobes, the terminal one being much larger; its flowers are small, pale mauve, with a calyx with five lobes, arranged in quite long spikes at the summit of the stalks; it is slightly aromatic when crushed.

The other vervain, on the contrary, attracts attention by its strong odour, and is therefore employed both in perfumery and to mask the unpleasant taste of certain infusions. Cultivated in Mediterranean regions, it is a real shrub which often grows to the height of a man; its leaves are lance-shaped and its flowers – small, purplish pink, in terminal spikes – are in fact the only feature it shares in common with its sister.

Just as they differ in outward appearance, so do the two vervains differ in composition. Analysis has shown that the wild vervain is by far and away the richer of the two; it contains in particular a bitter glucoside, verbenaline, which acts on the liver and is considered tonic, digestive, antineuralgic and febrifuge. When possible it should therefore be employed in preference to the other.

Internally vervain is taken as a mild decoction: 50 grammes of dried plant (flowering tips and leaves dried in the shade as rapidly as possible to conserve their colours) to a litre of water; cold-soak for ten to fifteen minutes; heat and boil only for a few seconds; leave to infuse for ten minutes; 3 or 4 cupfuls per day.

It is prescribed for disorders of the liver (particularly jaundice), spleen (congestion) and kidneys (it is an excellent diuretic), for poor digestions, diarrhoea, flatulence, gravel, general debility, feverish complaints (its action has been compared with that of quinine), painful and irregular menstruation, especially when accompanied by migraine.

Externally, the same decoction (if necessary made a little stronger by increasing the amount of plant) is applied on compresses to cleanse and promote healing of wounds and ulcers, to relieve the pain from a sprain, ecchymosis and facial neuralgia, it is prescribed as a gargle for sore throats, as a mouthwash for inflammation of the gums and bad breath; bathed on the forehead and temples, it soothes headaches.

A concentrated decoction (a sachet of 200 grammes to 2 litres of water) added to the bath water is refreshing and restorative. Poultices of vervain (two large handfuls of crushed fresh plant, or dried plant cold-soaked for ten minutes, then boiled for a few seconds in the minimum amount of wine vinegar), applied as hot as possible, are commonly used in the country as a remedy for lumbago and painful stitches in the side.

VIOLET
Viola odorata.   Blue violet, Sweet violet

We can use every part of this plant which is so unobtrusive that it has long been the very emblem of modesty.

The flowers – which enter into the classic composition of the 'pectoral flowers' – are prescribed for colds, bronchitis, whooping cough and irritations of the respiratory tract, either in a mild decoction (5 to 10 grammes of dried flowers to 1 litre of water; cold-soak for a few minutes, bring to the boil and leave to infuse for ten minutes; 3 or 4 cupfuls per day, between meals), or as a syrup or violet honey (pour 1 litre of boiling water on to 150 to 200 grammes of fresh petals in a glass or china receptacle, and leave covered to macerate for ten to twelve hours; press and strain through a cloth; leave to decant or filter through a filter-paper; to the liquid thus obtained add twice its weight in sugar or honey; thicken in a *bain-marie*, skimming carefully (especially if using honey), until it acquires the consistency of syrup, and store in a stoppered jar; 3 or 4 coffeespoonfuls per day, between meals – this preparation is not only expectorant and sedative for coughs, but also mildly laxative, and therefore recommended for constipation, especially in children).

The decoction is also used for headaches and 'great overheatings of the head' (Kneipp *dixit*), together with compresses soaked in the same decoction and applied to the forehead – a usage which goes back to ancient times and the Salernitan school which declared: 'To dispel drunkenness and repel migraine. The violet is sovereign: From heavy head it takes the pain, And from feverish cold delivers the brain.'

The fresh leaves, crushed and applied as a poultice, have been advocated for benign tumours and cracked nipples. Boiled for five minutes in vinegar (one handful to half a litre) they give a decoction that is recommended for use on compresses in attacks of gout.

The decoction of root (10 to 300 grammes of water; boil until reduced to 100 grammes) is emetic and can be used in place of ipecacuanha.

W

WALNUT
Juglans regia

In 1810 Bodart wrote: 'If the walnut grew only in the New World, we would hasten to include it among the most useful medicinal plants; but because it grows freely in our own countries, we would still disregard its different properties were they not called to our attention by illustrious practitioners . . .'[1]

In 1961, in his *Leçons de biologie dans un parc*, after summarizing the virtues of the walnut and in particular the remarkable antibiotic action of its fresh leaves in the treatment of anthrax (cured in three weeks) recorded in numerous cases and twice (1857 and 1880) announced at the Academy of Medicine, Professor Binet wrote: 'It is a curious fact that no works on bacteriology, plant chemistry, medical matters, chemotherapy or antibiotics contain any reference to it at all. The walnut leaf has fallen into oblivion. Why?'

I shall not presume to answer this question, considering it was asked by a member of the Institute, and Dean of the Faculty of Medicine of Paris at the time. My sole aim in juxtaposing the two texts, which are separated by a century and a half, is to show how hard it is for a popular remedy, however proven, to be accepted by official medical science.

A native of Persia and subsequently cultivated in Greece, Italy and then France, the walnut has long been used as a home remedy. Over the centuries it has been advocated for such diverse disorders as smallpox, hysterical fainting fits, flatulent colic, tapeworm: it was said to 'revive the milk in nursing mothers' and 'help restore those who had exhausted themselves with women'. Parkinson, quoting from a scroll found in

1. *Cours de botanique médicale comparée.*

the treasury of Mithridates, King of Pontus, in Mithridates' own writing, recommends 'two dry Wallnuts, and as many good Figges, and twenty leaves of Rue or Herbegrace, bruised and beaten together with two or three cornes of salt, which taken every morning fasting preserveth from danger of poyson or infection that day it is taken'. However, it is ultimately prescribed only for those conditions which related to its essential properties: it is tonic, restorative, depurative, disinfectant; it combats inflammation of the mucosae and lowers the blood-sugar level.

The leaves, picked before mid-July and dried rapidly in the shade at a maximum temperature of 35°C, are used, both internally and externally, in decoction. The amounts are variable (20 to 30 grammes of plant to a litre of water for internal use, 50 to 60 grammes for external use), but the method of preparation is the same: macerate the leaves in cold water for at least two hours; bring gently to the boil; boil for two minutes and leave to infuse for fifteen minutes.

For skin complaints (eczema, scabbing, pruritis), anaemia, glandular disturbances, scrofula, rheumatism, gout, pulmonary complaints, disorders of the digestive tracts (digestive atony, gastro-enteritis, nausea of hepato-biliary origin, jaundice), disorders of the female reproductive organs, excessive perspiration of hands and feet, night sweats, diabetes: drink 2 or 3 cupfuls of decoction per day, between or during meals.

Externally, the stronger decoction is used in hand- and foot-baths (five to ten minutes) for chilblains, reddened hands and also excessive perspiration of hands and feet (for the latter condition, follow with an alcohol (90°) rub); as a lotion or on compresses for skin complaints, eyelid irritation, ophthalmia, styes, blisters, varicose ulcers; as a douche for leucorrhoea and metritis.

It is also used for bathing domestic animals to repel flies and horse-flies, and for keeping moths away from cupboards (fresh walnut leaves, mixed with the litter in a kennel, will also keep dogs free of fleas). If used morning and evening to moisten the eyelashes and eyebrows, it will foster their growth. (Pliny said long ago that, 'the shell, being burnt, pulverized and incorporat with oile or wine, serveth to annoint the heads of young babes for to make the haire grow thicke: and in that manner it is used to bring the haire againe of elder folke, when through some infirmitie it is shed').

Two preparations can if necessary substitute for the decoction – they are also tonic, depurative and digestive – and even make an excellent apéritif: either walnut wine (macerate 200 grammes of fresh-chopped leaves in a litre of good white wine for four or five days; sweeten to taste and strain), or walnut cordial (macerate 500 grammes of green nut rind – shuck – cut in pieces in a litre of spirits or alcohol (45°) for three months; strain and stir into 3 litres of wine, sweetening to taste); one sherry-glassful before meals, once or twice a day.

WATERCRESS
Nasturtium officinale

In France we say that a bald man has no *'cresson sur le caillou'*,[1] – an expression which perhaps derives from the fact that this cruciferous plant has for centuries been known as an excellent hair tonic.

The Salernitan school of medicine, the leading light of science in the Middle Ages, recommended rubbing the juice of watercress into the scalp to strengthen and thicken the hair, and one of the most common popular prescriptions for promoting hair growth is still to rub the scalp with a lotion composed of a mixture of 100 grammes of watercress juice with 100 grammes of alcohol (90°) and 10 grammes of geranium essence. The Salernitan doctors similarly advocated the use of watercress juice in the treatment of skin complaints, a treatment which has survived as a beauty treatment for freckles and for clearing the complexion (mix 60 grammes of watercress juice with 30

1. Has no 'cress on his head'. (*Translator's note.*)

grammes of honey; strain through a cloth; dab on the face with a wad of cotton wool morning and evening).

But these are only the least of its virtues. Hippocrates held it to be stimulant and expectorant, Dioscorides believed it to be aphrodisiac, Ambroise Paré considered it the specific for scabies in children; others, less famous, have used it in the treatment of skin diseases, diabetes, scurvy and weak chests.

Taken internally, either as a salad, as a garnish or a soup, or as a juice (80 to 120 grammes of juice – extracted by crushing the watercress or putting it through the liquidizer – either alone or mixed with an equal quantity of milk or cold clear soup, taken first thing in the morning on an empty stomach), it is prescribed for its depurative (it is one of the best natural depuratives), apéritif, diuretic, stomachic, remineralizing, hypoglycaemic action in the treatment of lack of appetite, anaemia (it contains iron, copper, calcium, potassium and is particularly rich in iodine), nervous debility, lymphatism, bronchial catarrh, chronic bronchitis, dropsy, disorders of the urinary tract, biliary complaints, diabetes (it lowers the blood-sugar level).

Chewed raw, it strengthens the gums and prevents them from bleeding; it is also effective against aphtha.

Externally, poultices of watercress (500 grammes of pulp pounded together with 30 grammes of cooking salt, to be renewed every twelve hours) have an excellent healing and detersive action on atonic ulcers, glandular or strumous tumours, lymphatic or oedematous swellings, hygroma.

I must add three important warnings:

1. Wild watercress may be contaminated by a deadly parasite, the liver-fluke (found especially in the livers of sheep) present in animal droppings; it is consequently wiser to eat only watercress that has been grown in watercress-beds.
2. Watercress must always be employed fresh and raw; cooking and drying destroy a part of its active principles, which are at their best in May and June.
3. In certain subjects the consumption of too much watercress

can sometimes lead to bladder troubles (cystitis or strangury) as already noted by Aristophanes.

WHEAT
Triticum sativus

Now that bread is no longer a sustenance (many doctors advise against it) and wheat, cultivated with the help of chemical fertilizers, is no longer the 'mother's milk' of adults, it is hard to credit that they have played a not insignificant role in classic or family medicine.

Yet this is what a medical treatise of the eighteenth century has to say: 'Everyone is aware of the common usage of wheat, which provides us with a food as useful as it is pleasant; it provides flour and the bread that is made from it, the husk of the crushed seed which we call bran and the starch which are daily employed in medicine.'

Our grandmothers incorporated wheat, in one form or another, in their good home remedies. So why not follow their example? – always providing you use proper wheat, biologically grown, that has not been treated with fertilizers or weed-killers, which you can buy in health food stores.

For infantile gastro-enteritis and convalescence following serious illness, cereal broth is an excellent means of nourishment. It is made by grinding equal parts of wheat, oats and barley in a mill and then boiling 4 tablespoonfuls of this mixture in a litre and a half of water until reduced to a litre. It is then strained and sweetened to taste.

For persistent colds and coughs, you will be surprised at the emollient and demulcent effect of 'bran tea', made by boiling a good tablespoonful of bran in a litre of water; skim, leave to stand for a few minutes, strain, and add a large spoonful of honey. Drink hot, a small cupful at a time, during the day.

The *mica panis* of the ancient pharmacopoeia is a poultice made with the soft part of a loaf (the crumb, not the crust), some milk, and one or two egg yolks, and is prescribed to soothe inflammation or bring boils, anthrax and whitlows to a head.

Bread, dried in the oven, reduced to powder and boiled in water with butter and salt, constitutes the 'toast-water' which is one of the best drinks to take in cases of pleurisy and pneumonia (it is still, happily, possible to obtain bread made from good wheat, good flour, and baked as it used to be).

Lastly, for prostate disorders, the following recipe has always brought excellent results whenever I have prescribed it, especially when the patient is suffering from acute urine retention: put 250 grammes of wheat in a litre of cold water; cover; bring gently to the boil and simmer for twenty minutes; remove from the heat; pour into a china receptacle (a soup tureen, for example), cover and leave to macerate until the following day; strain. During an attack: one large glassful on an empty stomach for three days; as a maintenance treatment: twice a year, for three weeks, one small wineglassful before breakfast.

WOOD BETONY
Betonica officinalis.   Bishopswort

The wood betony is a striking example of therapeutic snobbery: considered for centuries as a panacea, it was later completely abandoned because it was said to possess no virtues at all. In fact these attitudes are equally foolish – as are all extremes – for whilst it is obviously not, as the Latin writer Lucius Apulius claimed, the 'infallible remedy' for forty-six serious or incurable diseases (including rabies and paralysis), it can nevertheless help to relieve a few of our minor ills.

From ancient times right up to the nineteenth century, writers were forever singing its praises. Dioscorides and Galen extolled its extraordinary properties. Antonius Musa, physician to the emperor Augustus, devoted a treatise to it, in which he

declared that wood betony is to be advocated equally for difficult confinements and the injuries resulting from road accidents
(chariots, of course!), adding that it 'preserves the souls and
bodies of men and even those who go abroad at night from all
dangers and from witchcraft also'. In the Middle Ages it was
prescribed for gout, sciatica, rheumatism, stomach, kidney and
liver pains, brain disorders, and it was said to be 'good for
those who are short of breath and always panting'. Then came
the time when medicine rejected it entirely; we read that 'it is
no longer used except by practical jokers: a pinch of its powder
provokes as many sneezes as the merits once attributed to it in
the past . . .'

This was not the opinion of our grandmothers nor of the
authors of 'home doctors' who wrote that 'wood betony tea
should have a place in every home'. This tea is made from the
leaves and flowering tips of the plant, which has the following
features: stem from 30 to 60 centimetres in height, angular,
slightly hairy; slightly serrate opposite leaves which exhale an
aromatic odour (it is said that those who gather betony sometimes get dizzy, as if intoxicated); purplish flowers arranged in
terminal spikes (they resemble the flowers of the white dead-
nettle which belongs to the same family of the Labiatae). Wood
betony is a common plant of shady places, woods, copses,
meadows.

The decoction (20 to 25 grammes of dried and chopped plant
to half a litre of water; boil for two or three minutes; leave to
stand for ten minutes; 4 or 5 small coffeecupfuls per day) is employed in the treatment of inflammatory and congestive conditions (throat irritation, asthma, catarrhal disorders of the
digestive and urinary tracts), for hepatic and biliary insufficiency, weakness of the bladder, gout and rheumatic pains,
nervous states and nervous migraine. In the form of extended
vapour treatment (at least half an hour, twice a day) it is a
sovereign remedy for bronchial catarrh and 'clogging' of the
respiratory tract.

Externally, the fresh leaves (steeped for a few minutes in

boiling red wine), applied directly to purulent wounds and ulcers, are vulnerary and decongestant. You can also use compresses soaked in a decoction of 100 grammes of dried leaves boiled for four or five minutes in a litre of red wine.

The powdered dried leaves – which provoke sneezing – clear the head in colds or influenza and arrest hiccoughs (the dried leaves are used as *ersatz* snuff in some parts of Europe).

In Italy they have a saying which seems, once again, to bear out the wisdom of the common people: when they want to describe a person of rare qualities, they say 'she is even more virtuous than the betony'.

WOODRUFF
Asperula odorata.   Sweet woodruff, Woodroof, Waldmeister tea

Growing to a height of 15 to 50 centimetres, with dark green lanceolate leaves borne in whorls at intervals on the quadrangular stem and small white delicately scented flowers grouped in terminal clusters, the woodruff blooms in late spring in woods and moist shady places, forming, as one botanist poetically described it, 'miniature milky ways'.

With the exception of lavender, no other dried herb exhales such a pleasant perfume as that of the woodruff, which evokes the odour of vanilla, new-mown hay and honey. It owes this fragrance to the presence, in its leaves and stems, of coumarin, an odorous principle also found in tonka beans and which is employed in perfumery and to lend aroma to certain tobaccos such as the Amsterdamer (it should be mentioned that today coumarin, like so many other things, is made synthetically).

However, do not be surprised if you cannot smell this very distinctive odour when you crush freshly-picked woodruff leaves between your fingers: the odorous principle develops with drying, and is consequently only perceptible and at its strongest when the plant is dried. It is this characteristic which inspired an English writer to observe: 'The woodruff, like the fortune of a wealthy person, gives most pleasure to others when it is dead . . .'

Hung in garlands or branches from the beams in the house, 'it is the pleasure of winter' and 'during the heat of summer, it tempers the air and cools the room' – such was the opinion of our grandmothers, who also used to hang a bunch in their cupboards to scent the linen and protect their clothes from moths. But they laid in a plentiful supply of it chiefly for its medicinal properties: it is antispasmodic, hypnotic, anaesthetic, antiseptic, astringent, diuretic, tonic, digestive, depurative.

Its fresh leaves, applied to the forehead, are anti-neuralgic; they relieve the throbbing and stabbing pains that follow a blow or a bang on the head.

The whole dried plant, in a mild decoction (30 to 40 grammes to a litre of water, boil for a few minutes), is used lukewarm as a lotion in the treatment of scabbing, and, warm, as douches in the treatment of gynaecological complaints and on poultices for enlargement of the liver.

The infusion (5 to 100 grammes of water, three or four times a day) is recommended 'to women of all ages, who suffer from menstrual pains, disturbances of menopause, painful uterine cramps and pruritis'. It is also advocated for liver disorders (jaundice), kidney and bladder stones (renal colic), dropsy (it clarifies and increases the volume of urine), poor digestion. King Stanislas of Poland used to say that he owed his good health (he died at the age of eighty-nine) to taking woodruff infusion each morning.

However, it is chiefly remarkable for its action upon the nerves: it calms, soothes, relaxes – exactly like the tranquillizers in which people indulge so freely today, but with the advantage that it causes no side-effects and is in no way toxic. Infusion of woodruff may therefore be given safely to all those who are troubled with disturbances of the sympathetic nervous system – including children and old persons – or who suffer from insomnia, vertigo, angor, neuralgia and excessive nervous tension. One or two cupfuls in the course of the day and particularly one on retiring, will restore sleep and calm the nerves in a natural way, without any harmful effects.

Woodruff also has its gastronomic uses: in Saxon and Nordic countries it is used in the manufacture of sausages, and in Belgium, Germany and various regions of France (Burgundy, Alsace, Lorraine) a wine known as '*vin de mai*' is made by macerating woodruff flowers (60 grammes to the litre) in a good sweetened wine (60 grammes of sugar to the litre) for a week. This wine – which becomes slightly fizzy after bottling – not only has a very pleasant aromatic taste but is also an excellent tonic. 'It refreshes the heart and restores the damaged liver,' says one sixteenth-century writer. (It is advisable to take the precaution of sealing the bottles in the same way as champagne bottles, to make sure that the corks stay in place.)

WORMWOOD

Artemisia absinthium.   Bitter artemisia, Absinth, Old woman, Ajenjo

It is hard to imagine, when one comes across it growing wild by the wayside or in the dry and stony waste places it prefers, that this plant could, at the start of the century, have been at the root of a social scourge more deadly than the spreading use of drugs today. Nonetheless, until its manufacture was prohibited, in March 1915, the liqueur made from its essence wrought considerable havoc in all classes of society (its consumption in France increased from 6,713 hectolitres in 1873 to 360,000 in 1911).

'Excessive drinking of absinthe', said Doctor Cazin,[1] 'leads eventually to more pronounced and more permanent deterioration of the brain, a deeper degradation than that caused by ordinary alcoholism ... Stupor, hebetude, appalling

1. *Traité pratique et raisonné des plantes medicinales indigènes et acclimatées*, Asselin & Houzeau.

hallucinations, rapid deterioration of the mind, seem to be the characteristic effects of this substance: absinthism is twice as bad as alcoholism . . .'

But whilst absinthe taken in large amounts and a highly concentrated form becomes a poison that is rightly illegal, it is still nevertheless a valuable medicinal plant that you can employ without danger.

You can recognize it by its height (from 0·50 metres to a metre and more), by its whitish-grey leaves covered with fine silky hairs, the lower leaves pinnately dissected, the upper leaves less cut-away; by its small, yellow, nearly globular flower-heads arranged like pompons in a pretty terminal cluster; and above all by the strong aromatic odour it exhales when crushed between the fingers.

Its virtues have been known since ancient times. Galen advocates it as a powerful tonic, Avicenna as a remarkable stimulant to the appetite. The Salernitan school recommends it as a preventive against seasickness, adding that it 'soothes the stomach and the nerves', expels worms, mitigates the effects of any poison that might have been drunk and, mixed with ox-gall is a miraculous treatment for buzzing in the ears. Matthiolus recommends it for dropsy and, throughout the centuries, many have advocated it as a febrifuge, a diuretic, an aid to digestion, a vermifuge and emmenagogue, in other words having the power to promote menstrual discharge. It eliminates gases from the stomach and is recommended for bad breath caused by stomach disorders. It can equally well be employed as an eye lotion for diseases of the eye (used as an eye wash morning and evening) and also to clean atonic wounds. For dropsy, the infusion is prepared with boiling white wine (30 grammes of plant to half a litre); one tablespoonful morning and evening.

WINE Macerate 30 grammes of plant in 60 grammes of alcohol (60°) for twenty-four hours; add a litre of white wine and leave to macerate for a further ten days; strain, pressing well, and filter. One liqueur glass taken before the two main meals is diuretic; taken after meals it aids the digestion. It also acts as tonic, vermifuge and emmenagogue.

BEER Macerate 30 grammes of plant in a litre of beer for four days; for ascarides (thread-worms) and oxyuris (pin-worms) one sherryglassful to be taken on an empty stomach half an hour before breakfast every morning for three or four days.

POULTICES A handful of wormwood leaves (preferably fresh) crushed in milk with a clove of garlic, to be applied on the abdomen for ascarides and oxyuris, either in addition to the wine or the beer or not.

It should be pointed out however, that wormwood – which forms an ingredient of the drink known as Vermouth (the German name for it, incidentally, is *Wermut*, which also means 'bitterness') – should never be used for too long (eight to ten days at the most) because on the one hand its therapeutic effects would become nil, and on the other hand it might give rise to an irritation of the gastric mucosa and affect the nervous system.

Y

YARROW

Achillea millefolium.   Milfoil, Thousand-leaf, Nosebleed, Sanguinary

Its synonyms and its scientific name reflect its uses, its appearance and its legend: the yarrow cures wounds; its leaves are deeply cut into many segments 'like the wispy feathers of young birds' as Matthiolus described them; and it was fiery Achilles who is said to have been the first to make use of them to heal his companions' wounds.

It grows abundantly in both lowland and mountain areas; you can find it at roadsides, on banks and waste places, in sunny meadows (it is an excellent fodder). Its erect hairy stems attain a height of 30 to 50 centimetres. They bear alternate somewhat downy leaves, their many segments in themselves much dissected, lending them a lacy appearance, and umbels of small white or pink flowers with yellow centres. The parts used are the leaves – which have a slight aromatic odour – and the flowering tips, picked during the flowering season (June to September) and dried in the shade.

It is considered as a specific for disorders of the circulation and the mucosae. It is, of course, known for its vulnerary action upon sores and wounds (cuts, injuries, varicose ulcers), both cleansing and promoting healing: either the fresh pounded leaves applied as a poultice, or a decoction employed as a lotion or on compresses (40 to 60 grammes of plant to a litre of water; boil for two or three minutes; leave to infuse for ten minutes). But it is in internal use, for its anti-haemorrhagic, antispasmodic fortifying and decongestant properties, that it renders its greatest services (it is a homoeopathic remedy prescribed for haemoptysis, haemorrhage following tooth extraction or confinement).

A mild decoction (30 to 50 grammes of plant to a litre of cold water; bring to boiling point; leave to infuse for ten minutes; 2 or 3 cupfuls per day) is recommended for stomach cramps, painful uterine contractions, metrorrhagia, poor circulation, varicose veins, menopausal disturbances, impaired liver function of nervous origin, enteritis, diarrhoea.

It has two remarkable therapeutic properties, tested and endorsed by Doctor Cazin: (1) it significantly reduces excessive haemorrhoidal bleeding which sometimes leads to anaemia (4 or 5 glassfuls per day): (2) it restores menstrual flow when its suppression is of emotional origin or due to a sudden chill, without risk of causing any mishap should it be a case of unsuspected pregnancy (1 or 2 cupfuls first thing in the morning on an empty stomach, if necessary for three or four consecutive days).

Lastly, repeated applications of the decoction as a skin lotion will improve the complexion and remove pimples or scabbing.

Glossary of Medical Terms

Antiseptic   Preventing putrefaction
Antispasmodic   Preventing or curing spasms
Aperient   Producing a natural movement of the bowels
Aphrodisiac   Exciting the sexual organs
Aromatic   Having an aroma
Astringent   Binding. Causing contraction of the tissues
Carminative   Easing gripping pains and expelling flatulence
Cholagogue   Producing a flow of bile
Decongestant.   Relieving lung congestion
Demulcent   Applied to drugs which soothe and protect the aliment-
   ary canal
Depurative   A purifying agent
Detergent   Cleansing
Digestive   Aiding digestion
Disinfectant   Killing harmful micro-organisms
Diuretic   Promoting urine flow
Emmenagogue   Applied to drugs which have the power of exciting
   menstrual discharge
Emollient   Having a softening and soothing effect
Expectorant   Promoting expectoration and removing secretions
   from the bronchial tubes
Febrifuge   Reducing fever
Haemostatic   Drugs used to control bleeding
Hypnotic   Producing sleep
Laxative   A gentle bowel stimulant
Liquefacient   Promoting less viscid flow of mucous
Pectoral   Drugs used internally for affections of the chest and lungs
Rubefacient   Applied to counter-irritants. Substances which produce
   blisters or inflammation
Sedative   Drugs which calm nervous excitement

Sternutatory   Producing sneezing by irritation of the mucous
   membrane
Stimulant   Energy producing
Stomachic   Applied to drugs given for disorders of the stomach
Sudorific   Producing copious perspiration
Taenicide   Applied to drugs used to expel tape-worm
Tonic   Substances which give tone to the body, producing a feeling
   of well-being
Vermifuge   Substances which expel worms from the body
Vulnerary   Used in healing wounds

Weights and Measures

LIQUID MEASURES
Metric

1 litre = 10 decilitres (dl) = 100 centilitres (cl) = 1000 millilitres (ml)

Approx. equivalents

British	Metric	Metric	British
1 quart	1·1 litre	1 litre	35 fl oz.
1 pint	6 dl	½ litre (5 dl)	18 fl oz.
½ pint	3 dl	¼ litre (2·5 dl)	9 fl oz.
¼ pint (1 gill)	1·5 dl	1 dl	3½ fl oz.
1 tablespoon	15 ml		
1 dessertspoon	10 ml		
1 teaspoon	5 ml		

SOLID MEASURES
Metric

1000 grammes = 1 kilogramme

Approx. equivalents

British	Metric	Metric	British
1 lb (16 oz.)	400 grammes	1 kilo (1000g)	2 lb 3 oz.
½ lb (8 oz.)	200 g	½ kilo (500g)	1 lb 2 oz.
¼ lb (4 oz.)	100 g	¼ kilo (250g)	9 oz.
1 oz	25 g	100 g	3½ oz.

Index of Botanical and Common Names

Index of Remedies

335

339

Mucus membranes (*contd.*)
  horehound, 150
  ivy, ground, 163
  liquorice, 192
  marigold, 203
  oak, 226
  rose (buccal), 273
  purple loosestrife (gastro)
  sanicle, 282
  see also Throat infections
Myocardial infarct
  apple, 32

Nasal catarrh
  basil, 46
  bryony, 64
  chervil, 85
  coltsfoot, 90
  couchgrass, 95
  fig, 120
  honeysuckle, 148
  marjoram, 206
  poppy, 255
Nausea
  gentian, 130, 131
  tarragon, 298
  walnut, 309
Nephritis
  blackcurrant, 57
  broom, 62
  elder, 109
  hart's tongue, 136
  heath, 142
  leek, 178
  peach, 242
  pellitory-on-the-wall, 243
  plantain, 251
  poplar, 254
  rest-harrow, 269

Nervous complaints
  angelica, 32
  balm, 43
  hop, 149
  valerian, 302–3
  woodruff, 316
Nervous complaints: stomach
  balm, 43
  marjoram, 206
  passion flower, 240
  primula, 260
Neuralgia
  cabbage, 69
  chamomile, German, 82
  crane's bill, 97
  ivy, common, 161
  lemon, 182
  melilot, 210
  rosemary, 275
  vervain, 305
  woodruff, 316
Neurasthenia
  thyme, 301
Neuritis
  ivy, common, 161
  pain relievers:
    male fern, 198
    tarragon, 298
    vervain, 305
Night vision
  bilberry, 47
Night sweating
  sage, 280
  walnut, 309
Nose bleeding, *see* Haemorrhage,
  nasal

Obesity
  ash, 37

More about Penguins and Pelicans

Books on Biology and Natural History
published by Penguin Books